Patrons and Protégées

*THE DOUGLASS SERIES
ON WOMEN'S LIVES AND
THE MEANING OF GENDER*

Patrons and Protégées

GENDER, FRIENDSHIP, AND WRITING IN NINETEENTH-CENTURY AMERICA

Edited by
SHIRLEY MARCHALONIS

Rutgers University Press
New Brunswick and London

Library of Congress Cataloging-in-Publication Data

Patrons and protégées.

  (The Douglass series on women's lives and the
meaning of gender)
  Includes bibliographies and index.
    1. American literature—Women authors—History
and criticism.   2. Authors and patrons—United States—
History—19th century.   3. American literature—
19th century—History and criticism.   4. Women authors,
American—19th century—Relations with men.   5. Authors,
American—19th century—Biography.   6. Women and
literature—United States.   7. Sex role—United States—
History—19th century.   8. Influence (Literary,
artistic, etc.)
I. Marchalonis, Shirley.   II. Series.
PS147.P38   1988   810'.9'9287   87-42735
ISBN 0-8135-1270-0

British Cataloging-in-Publication information available

To
ELAINE SHOWALTER

Contents

Acknowledgments

The idea for this collection of essays grew in stages, each a little broader than its predecessor. I first became interested in the patron-protégée relationship while writing a biography of Lucy Larcom; it seemed then that a book about Whittier's protégées would be almost a cross-section of the careers of women writers.

Leslie Mitchner, Senior Editor of Rutgers University Press, widened the concept to focus on all the "mentorial" associations that were so common in the nineteenth-century American literary world. She has been a steady source of information and encouragement.

At the time the collection was first discussed, I was fortunate enough to be a participant in Elaine Showalter's National Endowment for the Humanities Summer Seminar on American women writers, "Women's Writing and Women's Culture" (Rutgers, 1984). Several of the seminar members were working on subjects whose lives fell into the category examined here. I am grateful to Cheryl B. Torsney, Mary De Jong, Dorothy Berkson, and Joanne Karpinski for rich and supportive discussions as well as for their contributions to this volume. Other scholars, hearing of the project, submitted essays that continued to widen the idea, so that this volume is truly one of exploration and discovery.

While this is not a seminar book, it owes an enormous debt to the National Endowment for the Humanities, and above all to Elaine Showalter for providing an exciting and rewarding intellectual experience that generated many ideas besides this one.

We are all grateful to the libraries that gave permission to quote from their holdings; specific acknowledgments will be found in the notes.

Introduction

From one point of view, the nineteenth-century American literary world was a social phenomenon dominated by relationships and interconnectedness. A shared sense of purpose is partly responsible: the necessity for writers to find and identify themselves as American voices. Adapting newness and bigness, pride in their own brief but dramatic past, and a growing sense of self to their European heritage led toward definition and identity, no matter how individual each path might have been.

On a less grand scale, literary America was a small world of the eastern seacoast with three publishing centers: Boston, New York, and Philadelphia. Writers knew one another on both personal and professional terms, and they influenced one another's work. The nineteenth-century is, in fact, the last great age of patronage—patronage in a unique form, not centered in wealthy families, as it had been in England, or in the universities, as it would become in the twentieth century, but existing within a group, a network of writers, an establishment that supported itself, that inspected and judged new writers, and that perpetuated itself by letting in suitable members.[1]

The title of this collection of essays, *Patrons and Protégées*, identifies the starting point for an examination of one form of sponsorship that literary historians, biographers, and critics have turned into a stereotype: the important male author and the aspiring lady writer, he using his talent and intelligence to create literature, she a "sweet singer"—an empty vessel through which the winds, or perhaps breezes, of inspiration might blow. There are enough of these literary friendships throughout the century to be significant, and, when they are not ignored, they have generally been simplified in one of two ways: either he was the mentor who taught her to write and used his influence to have her work published, or else she was in love with him.

In either case, critical interpretation has made her the inferior being, and few scholars have taken time to find out if the evidence supports the claim. Despite Hawthorne's outburst against the "scribbling women" —so often quoted as authoritative permission to ignore women writers— their contemporaries did not always share the attitudes of their later commentators; Hawthorne liked Fanny Fern's *Ruth Hall* and enjoyed Gail Hamilton's provocative essays. Women writers may or may not have been accepted as equals by their male colleagues, but evidence does not suggest that they were generally lumped together and pushed to the sidelines. The earliest *Atlantic Monthly* dinners included Harriet Beecher Stowe and Harriet Prescott; when ladies were no longer invited, it was not because they were inferior writers, but because their presence inhibited the "boys"—Stowe, who was persuaded by Francis Underwood to use her influence on publishers Phillips, Sampson to support the new magazine, prohibited the use of wine at the dinner.[2]

The critics have misled us. Assumptions once made have been accepted and passed on without verification, perhaps because women's writing has not seemed important enough for the application of scholarly principles, or, worse, because the critic needs the standardized role in order to support a thesis. Leon Edel's suggestion that Constance Fenimore Woolson committed suicide because of her unrequited love for Henry James dramatizes James, not Woolson; the picture of Margaret Fuller pursuing Ralph Waldo Emerson, or John Greenleaf Whittier helping Lucy Larcom and a host of others while he skillfully evaded their marriage plans, works the same way.

In contrast, supportive friendships between men, like that of Hawthorne and Melville, have been treated with respect, approval, and the assumption of equality;[3] when half of the friendship is a woman, it is assumed and perpetuated as fact that she was a hanger-on: less bright, less talented, a protégée, a lovesick lady. Men emerge from such analyses as strong and dedicated, women as trivial and silly. The fact that many of these women were highly regarded writers, or even that they had identities of their own and did not exist simply as reflectors of the men with whom they are associated, is generally ignored. It seems to be a truth universally acknowledged by most male scholars that a single woman, whether in possession of a good fortune or not, must be in want of a husband or a father.[4]

Feminist scholarship in recent years has called attention to women writers; their lives are being restored and their work reprinted. To all but the most fearful and entrenched, the growing scholarship on women writers offers an enlargement of knowledge and a wider understanding of time, place, social and intellectual climate, and values that, among other things, help us understand how the great and near-great functioned.

One of the things that becomes clear as this world opens up is that women writers often did need help, or felt they did; the conditions of their society, the standards set for women, especially before the Civil War, made stepping out of womanly reticence a bold and daring act.[5] Social forces throughout the century told women to be silent, invisible, and above all, noncompetitive.

Yet in spite of cultural constraints, women wrote. Often they wrote behind pen names, and they sought help, particularly in the business of selling their work.[6] (So did Jane Austen.) Even when they wrote best-selling novels, their work has been lost under the male-engendered concept of American literature that Nina Baym has identified as melodramas of beset manhood.[7] Although after the Civil War the constraints on women lessened and fewer writers sought the protection of anonymity or disguise, some still looked for mentors or preceptors, as if the approval of an established figure gave them permission to use their talents. It is not as surprising that women sought male patrons as it is that the results have been so unimaginatively accepted or neglected. The situation should raise a host of questions: How real or how political were these mentorial relationships? Were they perhaps a romantic convention acted out? How did they function? Was there a pattern? Was the help given inspirational or practical? Did the influence ever work the other way, from woman to man? What did it mean to be a protégée? What were the gains and losses for both? Since implicit in the concept of mentorship is the fact that the pupil must break away, what happened then? And did mentorship encourage individuality, or did it draw writers into the establishment?

Finding a so-called woman's voice is complicated by social and cultural forces. Certainly the work of most women novelists of the period is identifiable, for women followed a basic precept: Write about what you know. What they knew in a world where male and female roles were supposed to be separate circles, overlapping only in the home, were the conventions of womanly behavior and the structure of home and family, with the problems, complexities, and interpersonal relationships that resulted. They knew as well religious belief and their increasing importance as its upholders. The age-old pattern of the tale, the initiation structure in which a hero moves through tests and ordeals to responsibility and resolution, was presented in the terms of their lives: the tests and ordeals came from their world and were essentially internal. The woman hero did not pit herself against the wilderness, unless it might be the wilderness of human behavior. The work of women writers was informed by the reality of their lives, and their subjects determined by the role society imposed on them. And it reflected life. The manless villages that Sarah Orne Jewett and Mary E. Wilkins Freeman wrote about were empty because young men went to the war, to cities, and to the west, driven by adventure and economic necessity; dying ladies abound (and not just in the work of women) because the conditions of childbearing and the prevalence of tuberculosis killed them.[8]

For women poets the circumstances were somewhat different. This "higher" and more respectable form of literature was familiar and better defined: Poetry must not only please, it must instruct as well, giving the reader a religious, moral, ethical, or in some way inspirational direction. All poets, male and female, understood the definition. Their poetic area was defined by an establishment that had educated popular taste.

It was, for some reason, more acceptable for women to write poetry than fiction, possibly because few of either sex made money from poetry[9] and possibly because of the "sweet singer" label. No matter how many drafts and revisions they made or how long they agonized over the right word, a great many women poets hid behind that protective image; they could not be thought "unwomanly," that terrible indictment, if they were simply agents for higher forces.[10] It might be added that the comparative acceptability of women as poets created a mass of newspaper verse characterized by rhyme, excessive sentimentality, and a fondness for children's deathbeds: Little Nell and Little Eva in ballad meter and fourteeners. Both male and female poets saw these effusions as bad writing, although the sentiments were to be respected, for the message of a poem mattered more than its form.

In fact, it was a sentimental age, and women were both allowed and expected to be sentimental. When they showed intellect, like Margaret Fuller, they became threatening; when they made money they could be damned for their scribbling. They might be singers as long as they sang acceptable songs; a "woman's voice" was male defined.

The years toward the end of the century saw a tension between the directions of the old established hierarchy—Emerson, Longfellow, Lowell, Hawthorne, Holmes, and Whittier, who still dominated popular taste—and newer writers like Howells, Twain, and James. The definition of what literature was, set by the giants, prevailed both critically and in popular taste. Editors, themselves connected to the inner circle, upheld the importance of the vanishing greats, creating a problem for the newer men: "At the same time he sought to spread a taste for the great figures of continental realism, Howells, without apparently feeling the slightest strain, made the proper obeisance to a body of literature which, theoretically, he could not possibly have accepted."[11]

If younger men hesitated to challenge the establishment, how much less likely were most women writers to attempt a distinctive voice and how much more likely were they to seek male approval. American individualism then, and even more in the eyes of later critics, was a male prerogative; under these conditions it is not surprising that women had to stay within the establishment or pay the consequences. No wonder that Howells found Charlotte Perkins Gilman frightening, or that Thomas Wentworth Higginson was bewildered by Emily Dickinson's poems.

Clearly, it cannot be easy to find a woman's voice, and where mentorial relationships existed, they probably worked against the recognition of individuality and gender-marked writing. If patronage was the kind of apostolic sucession that it seems to have been, then it is logical to assume that it inhibited; however, the essays presented here suggest no simple answer, since interrelationships between people do not, except on the most superficial level, follow a pattern or conform to a label.

The original intent of this volume was to explore these taken-for-granted presentations, to find the truth, and finally to present these findings as an entry into the world of nineteenth-century American letters. Knowing the conditions under which women lived and wrote raised expectations: those romantic, paternalistic friendships existed, but would be less simplistic and patterned than the conventionalized readings. What became apparent, however, was that the image in both its forms—the inferior writer and the lovesick lady—was incomplete or untrue.

Lucy Larcom and John Greenleaf Whittier come closest to the accepted pattern, although the dynamics of their long friendship are far more complicated than the common, oversimplified versions. Other pairings, long taken for granted, fell apart with close study of the evidence. In the cases of Margaret Fuller and Ralph Waldo Emerson, Fanny Fern and Walt Whitman, Frances Sargent Osgood and Edgar Allan Poe, and Constance Fenimore Woolson and Henry James, instead of the mindless followers or the annoying, sentimental, or lovesick ladies, there are realities sometimes startlingly different from the standard interpretations. Even the often-examined preceptor association of Emily Dickinson and Thomas Wentworth Higginson can be looked at in a way that presents something more valuable than the usual sneer at Higginson for not recognizing the genius with which he was confronted.

Once the stereotype began to disintegrate, its pieces led in some un-expected directions. According to one scholar, not represented here, Elizabeth Palmer Peabody had long talks on Saturdays with her "men-tor," William Ellery Channing, and then often heard her own ideas in Channing's Sunday morning sermons.[12] Might women, even from their postures as adjuncts or followers, be mentors? Annie Adams Fields is given credit for her charm and her ability as a hostess; it is sel-dom noticed that she influenced the choices of her powerful publisher-husband. If the mentorial convention was so acceptable, what about the ones that failed? With everything in favor of a patron-protégée relation-ship between Charlotte Perkins Gilman and William Dean Howells, none developed, for reasons that perhaps say as much about Howells as about Gilman. And what happened in the curious and little-known asso-ciation between Henry Wadsworth Longfellow and Sherwood Bonner, the rather exotic Southern writer whose name Bostonians virtually erased from history?

This collection of essays is only a sampling. Each study looks at a life and an association; collectively they not only illuminate time, place, and people, but indicate the disservice done by affixing labels and then presenting them as truth. There are many other pairings, either real or unthinkingly accepted, that need to be examined with the evidence and without the narrow vision inherited from the past.

It is important to remember that nineteenth-century biography had, in keeping with the moral and artistic standards of the time, an exemplary purpose. Longfellow, a poet of his age, put it in verse: "Lives of great men all remind us / We can make our lives sublime." There was no point in telling the life of an eminent man or woman unless that life offered a message in keeping with the beliefs and aims of the time. Just as Lincoln was painted without warts, so the great were presented as flawless, or perhaps with youthful flaws that had to be and were over-come before true greatness could be achieved.

In an essay that deserves to be better known, especially by those writ-ing biography or literary history, Marchette Chute identifies the force that prevents what she calls "Getting at the Truth" as desire.[13] There is the desire of the source to see the event or person as it wishes, and the very human desire of the writer to make the evidence fit his emotional involvement with his thesis. Such desire has shaped our pictures of the past and still remains a danger.

The task of the literary historian or the biographer is always to find and present the truth—to cut through error and distortion to show what really was. If absolute truth is not possible—and in dealing with human beings it seldom is—then the scholar must prize objectivity; she is at least obliged to raise questions about the assumptions that rest on insecure or insufficient evidence or on the demands of a thesis. We have tried in this volume to reexamine stereotyped mentorial relationships between male and female writers that have been accepted without much question, believing that many of these accounts are one-sided, that perpetuating inaccuracies is bad scholarship, and, finally, that an understanding of the real situation, or even the possibility of a different interpretation, broadens our knowledge of the writers, the writing, and the critics of nineteenth-century American literature.

Notes

1. This "hierarchy," as it is called by Leonard Lutwack, "The New England Hierarchy," *New England Quarterly* 28 (1955):164–185, consisted of Hawthorne, Emerson, Longfellow, Lowell, Holmes, and Whittier, with lesser figures like Howells, Stedman, Aldrich, and others, many of whom were editors. Lutwack points out that even after the deaths of its members their importance remained as strong as ever.

2. M. A. DeWolfe Howe, *"The Atlantic Monthly" and Its Makers* (Boston: Atlantic Monthly Press, 1919).

3. There are, of course, critics who like to interpret this friendship as homosexual, but that is not the issue here.

4. My apologies to Jane Austen.

5. Barbara Welter, "The Cult of True Womanhood, 1820–1860," *American Quarterly* 18 (1966):151–174. This essay is so important and so well known by now that I assume everyone is familiar with the standards of purity, piety, domesticity, and submissiveness that dominated women's lives.

6. See Mary Kelley, *Private Woman, Public Stage* (New York: Oxford University Press, 1984).

7. Nina Baym, "Melodramas of Beset Manhood: How Theories of American Fiction Exclude Women Authors," *American Quarterly* 33 (1981): 123–139.

8. René Dubos and Jean Dubos, *The White Plague: Tuberculosis, Man and Society* (Boston: Little, Brown, 1952). The authors estimate that 50 percent of the world's population had some form of tuberculosis.

9. There were exceptions; Whittier made a small fortune from *Snow-bound*, and after that his name on a volume guaranteed its sales.

10. While the term was generally restricted to women, both Whittier and Holmes called themselves "singers." See letter from Whittier to Holmes, 17 December 1879, in John B. Pickard, ed., *The Letters of John Greenleaf Whittier*, 3 vols. (Cambridge: Harvard University Press, 1975), 3:413–414.

11. Lutwack, "Hierarchy," 174.

12. From Margaret Neussendorfer, in conversation. I am sorry that other commitments prevented her from writing about Peabody and Channing for this collection. I would like to take this opportunity to thank Lisa Pater Faranda, Cheryl Oreovicz, and Mary De Jong for their help and suggestions with this Introduction.

13. Marchette Chute, "Getting at the Truth," *Saturday Review* 36 (19 September 1953):11–12, 43–44.

Patrons and Protégées

DOROTHY BERKSON

"Born and Bred in Different Nations": Margaret Fuller and Ralph Waldo Emerson

A MAJOR REASSESSMENT OF MARGARET FULLER'S LIFE and career has begun in the last few years, led by such scholars as Paula Blanchard and Bell Gale Chevigny, who have attempted to dispel the myth that Fuller was merely a "handmaiden"[1] to the male transcendentalists. The work of Blanchard and Chevigny has been aided by the 1983 publication by Robert N. Hudspeth of Fuller's letters—we now have the complete version of her extant letters through 1844, and it is possible to read her words without the selective editing and dense commentary of Emerson, William H. Channing, and J. F. Clarke, who edited her papers after her death and published them in 1852 as the *Memoirs of Margaret Fuller Ossoli*. The "Margaret Myth," as it came to be known, grew out of the version of Fuller's character and work that Emerson and his coeditors chose to present in the *Memoirs*, and it has persisted with remarkable tenacity during the more than one hundred thirty years since her death. The Margaret Fuller of this myth is an eccentric, physically ugly, brilliant but erratic and highly emotional woman who could barely write coherently, but who exercised a mesmeric charm over her friends. She lived in the shadow of the male transcendentalists, especially Emerson, who served as her mentor and intellectual guide and who rejected her emotional advances toward him. The fact that she wrote *Woman in the Nineteenth Century*, the most brilliant feminist tract since Wollstonecraft's *Vindication of the Rights of Women*, merely confirmed the view that Fuller was an anomaly, an emotionally starved bluestocking, who sought unsuccessfully to compete with men when she was not trying to ensnare them in embarrassing emotional relationships.

Fuller's relationship with Emerson lies at the center of any effort to reexamine her work and reassess her reputation. They met in 1836 when she was twenty-six years old and he was thirty-three. It was a critical transitional moment in both of their lives and the beginning of an intensely creative period for both of them. Emerson had recently resigned his post as pastor of the Second Church in Boston because of doctrinal disagreements and because he did not have the disposition for the ministry. He had in the past two years lost his first wife, Ellen, and two of his brothers, Edward and Charles. He had just married his second wife, Lidian Jackson, and moved to Concord where he was to live for the rest of his life. In 1836 Emerson published *Nature*, his first son, Waldo, was born, and within the year he would deliver "The American Scholar" address at Harvard. At thirty-three, Emerson was at the beginning of his long career.[2]

Fuller, too, was at the beginning of her much shorter career, although, unlike Emerson's, the shape and direction of that career would never be clear and straightforward. Her father, a major influence on her education and intellectual development, had died the previous year, leaving her in great conflict over her future. She was forced to assume much of the financial and practical responsibility for her mother and younger siblings, including the responsibility of preparing her brothers for the formal education she as a woman had been denied, and she had to cancel a long-dreamed-of trip to Europe. She was looking for a way to support herself and her family. Her father, a martinet and rigorously practical man, nonetheless had left his financial affairs in disarray and his family at the mercy of his older brother, who assumed the role of executor of his brother's estate, and meted out in equal portions advice and disapproval but not much cash. Uncle Abraham, as one might expect, thoroughly disapproved of his niece's intellectual ambitions.

Fuller's intellectual and literary ambitions made the problem of finding suitable employment, severely limited under any circumstances for women in the nineteenth century, even more difficult. She had been planning for several years to write a biography of Goethe; she was among the first in America to read and appreciate his genius, and it was largely due to her influence that Emerson and other American intellectuals were introduced to the writings of the German romantic. She had met and become close friends with Harriet Martineau in 1835 and at Martineau's urging had planned a trip to Europe where she was to complete her research on Goethe. A year after the death of her father, Fuller was looking for a home, a means of livelihood, a career as a woman of letters, and active engagement in the world. None of those would come so easily to her as they did to Emerson. Still, within a year of meeting him, she had her first paying job as Bronson Alcott's assistant in his

Temple School in Boston, and within three years she had published her translation of *Eckermann's Conversations with Goethe* and had become a major figure in the Transcendental Club. All this activity culminated in her editorship of the *Dial* between 1840 and 1842.

Fuller was, at this crucial moment in her life, one of the best-read people in America. Under her father's tutelage, she had read by the age of eight Vergil, Plutarch, Cicero, Ovid, and Shakespeare and had discovered on her own Smollett, Fielding, Molière, Cervantes, Goldsmith, and Cowper. During her sixteenth year she was reading simultaneously Madame de Staël, Epictetus, Milton, Racine, and Castilian ballads.[3] During the same year she decided to read systematically the Italian poets: Dante, Petrarch, Tasso, Berni, Ariosto, Alfieri, and Manzoni. She was able to read in several languages and at one point undertook to tutor Emerson in German so that he could read, as she had, Goethe in the original. She also began to read the English writers with whom she shared significant intellectual affinities: Wordsworth, Coleridge, Lamb, Browne, and Carlyle (whom she later met). During the time her family lived in Cambridge (1825–1833), Fuller met a number of Harvard students who were to become lifelong friends, among them William Henry Channing, James Freeman Clarke, and George Davis. It was always a sore point with her that she was barred from the formal education received by her male friends at Harvard, but she read voraciously, following in many cases their course of study. It was during this time that she and Clarke began reading Goethe together. By the time she met Emerson she had also read Alfieri and Schiller and had read extensively in European history. Emerson is reported to have said that Fuller's reading during these years rivaled Gibbon's.[4]

Fuller and Emerson's friendship, large as it was in the mutual influence they had on one another, was actually short in duration. After meeting through friends in 1836, they formed a close and intense personal and intellectual relationship that had lasted for seven years when Fuller left New England permanently. Although they continued to correspond with each other until her death in 1850, the friendship never regained the intensity it had had during those seven years. Most of the myths about Fuller arise from this period and are based primarily on the accounts of her personality and accomplishments put together by Emerson and his fellow editors in the *Memoirs*. Now that carefully edited and complete versions of her letters and some of her journals are available, it is clear that many of those myths need reexamining.

One of the myths that arises from Emerson's interpretation of their relationship in the *Memoirs* is that Fuller was intellectually dependent on him and that he served as her mentor. He describes the beginning of their friendship this way: "When she came to Concord, she was already rich in friends, rich in experiences rich in culture. . . . I was seven years her senior, and had the habit of idle reading in old English books, and though not much versed, yet quite enough to give me the right to lead her."[5] It is a statement filled with curious contradictions. In Emerson's memory, Fuller was already full of accomplishments when he met her, yet "though not much versed," he felt that he had "the right to lead her." Like many other statements in the *Memoirs,* this one is not supported by the evidence of their letters to one another. Certainly Fuller saw Emerson as the most eminent intellectual figure on her horizon, but there is no hint in either of their letters that they did not meet as intellectual equals. Their letters are full of fascinating debates and disagreements about writers and philosophy. Emerson, for instance, was convinced that Bronson Alcott was the greatest genius of the Concord circle, while Fuller found Alcott's ideas vague and elliptical, unanchored in any sense of reality or the concrete, a judgment with which most critics agree. They also disagreed about the "genius" of Ellery Channing; once again, friendship and intellectual empathy led Emerson to overvalue Channing, while Fuller was the keener judge of Channing's limited talent, even though he was a valued friend and became her brother-in-law. During their respective periods editing the *Dial,* these disagreements sharpened and led to some illuminating discussions on the theory and policy of editing.

The most misunderstood debate between Fuller and Emerson, however, focused on the subject of friendship itself. The debate was conducted in conversations and letters over several years, although it reached its most intense point during several months in 1840. Untangling the complexities of the issues involved in this debate is the key to understanding the relationship between these two strong personalities and their philosophical differences about the nature of relationships, their definitions of individualism, and the characteristic modes of thought through which they arrived at and defended their ideas. A great deal has already been written about this debate; before turning to its intellectual substance, it is necessary to clear away some of the debris left by previous discussions that have focused on the possibility of a one-sided or mutual sexual or romantic attraction between Fuller and Emerson and on the issue of who initiated the discussion.

Carl F. Strauch's 1968 essay, "Hatred's Swift Repulsions: Emerson, Margaret Fuller, and Others," set the terms and the tone for the discussion. Strauch's thesis is that the debate was precipitated by Fuller who "challenged [Emerson] on the score of his friendship because hers had by degrees grown into love."[6] According to Strauch, the entire debate was sparked by Fuller's desperate attempts to entice Emerson into a more intimate and at one point even into a sexual relationship that he found himself in the "embarrassing" position of having to "repel."[7] Her charges that Emerson was cold, unfeeling, and incapable of intimacy were nothing more, according to Strauch, than the disappointed and frustrated responses of a love- and sex-starved spinster who indelicately had fallen in love with her mentor. Gay Wilson Allen in his 1981 biography of Emerson follows Strauch's lead, arguing that Emerson "soon discovered that [Fuller] desired a stronger emotional relationship . . . than the Concord recluse could give," referring to Fuller at one point as the "emotionally starved Margaret Fuller."[8] The only evidence either scholar can provide that she made sexual advances to Emerson comes from one journal entry that Emerson made in October 1840, in which he does not even refer to Fuller by name, but says,

> You would have me love you. What shall I love? Your body? The supposition disgusts you. What you have thought & said? Well, whilst you were thinking & saying them, but not now. I see no possibility of loving any thing but what now is, & is becoming; your courage, your enterprize, your budding affection, your opening thought, your prayer, I can love,— but what else?[9]

There seems to be a logical inconsistency in the assumption that Fuller (or whomever the entry refers to) made sexual advances to Emerson if "the supposition disgust[ed]" her. It is entirely possible that during the course of their many conversations about love and friendship the question of sexual relations did arise in the generalized context in which much of this discussion took place. This does not automatically mean that either Emerson or Fuller had erotic designs on the other.

The treatment of this relationship at the hands of feminist scholars unfortunately has not added much light. Two scholars, Marie Olesen Urbanski and Margaret Vanderhaar Allen, have challenged Strauch's conclusions, but only to argue that the sexual attraction was mutual and that Emerson did as much to perpetuate a romantic or erotic tone as did Fuller.[10] Paula Blanchard in her excellent biography of Fuller challenges that view of the relationship, but unfortunately does not examine the complex series of letters about friendship.

In addition to the lack of real evidence for making such a case, there are substantive reasons for doubting that the debate on friendship disguised an erotic or romantic attraction. Granted, the language of the debate is often highly charged emotionally and is full of what twentieth-century readers would regard as exaggerated language and metaphors. In one letter, for instance, Emerson hails Fuller as "O divine mermaid or fisher of men, to whom all gods have given the witch-hazel-wand, or caduceus, or spirit-discerner which detects an Immortal under every disguise in every lurking place . . . do say . . . that I am yours & yours shall be, let me dally how long soever in this or that other temporary relation."[11] This kind of hyperbole was typical of the language of romantic friendship, and Fuller and Emerson often used even more fanciful and highly charged language in their letters to other friends. At times the language seems deliberately exaggerated as if to parody the conventions of romantic friendship. In one letter to Emerson, Fuller signs herself, "Your affectionate Magdalen," adding the postscript, "I have changed my name for tonight because Cary says this is such a Magdalen letter."[12]

Perhaps the most important reason to doubt that these were disguised love letters is that they were not private letters. Three friends of Fuller and Emerson—Carolyn Sturgis, Samuel G. Ward, and Anna Barker—were involved in this discussion of friendship, and the five exchanged letters and frequently referred to such exchanges in their letters to one another. The "Cary" mentioned in the letter quoted above, for example, is Carolyn Sturgis who read and commented on this particular letter before it was sent. In other letters Emerson asks Fuller to send him letters written by one of the other three. While it is impossible to dismiss the possibility that Fuller or Emerson or both were disguising a sexual attraction in these letters, one can only say that if their language constitutes the proof, then Fuller and Emerson must have been involved in a most unusual five-way erotic relationship that included the other members of their circle. Several letters Emerson wrote to Carolyn Sturgis come much closer to statements of erotic attraction than anything he ever wrote to Fuller. In one letter to Sturgis, he says, "But I dare not engage my peace so far as to make you necessary to me as I can easily see any establishment of habitual intercourse would do, when the first news I may hear is that you have found in some heaven foreign to me your mate, & my beautiful castle is exploded to shivers."[13]

One factor that may have contributed to some of the highly charged language of the letters during this period is that the friendship between Anna Barker and Sam Ward did turn into a romance, and they were married on 19 October 1840, right in the midst of the most intense flurry of letters. Most commentators have focused on Fuller's reaction to this marriage, since she and Ward had been intimate friends for a number of years, and there does seem to be some evidence that that relationship had romantic overtones at one time. The letters, however, suggest that Emerson had as much if not more of a reaction than did Fuller to the marriage of these two friends. Anna Barker was by all accounts an extremely beautiful and magnetic woman. Emerson described Barker's effect in a letter to Carolyn Sturgis in September 1840:

> Anna's miracle, next to the *amount* of her life, seems to be the intimacy of her approach to us. The moment she fastens her eyes on you, her unique gentleness unbars all doors, and with such easy and frolic sway she advances & advances & advances on you, with that one look, that no brother or sister or father or mother of life-long acquaintance ever seemed to arrive quite so near as this now first seen maiden. It is almost incredible to me, when I spoke with her the other night—that I have never seen this child but three times, or four, is it? I should think I have lived with her in the houses of eternity—[14]

Emerson's use, three times, of the word "advances" suggests a powerful but ambivalent reaction to Barker's magnetism and the sense of intimacy she created. The same exalted but ambivalent tone pervades a letter he wrote to Barker and Ward a few days later, a month before their marriage:

> When I dream by myself of my road, it sometimes shows itself lone rough & odious—possibly abhorred by the beautiful & happy & that I can only assure myself of your sympathy late late in the evening when we shall meet again far far from Here. And then I say, Do these lovers—(every hair of whose heads may the dear God keep from harm!) truly know me that they challenge me thus early by the thrilling name of Brother?—But perhaps I shall never deserve so high a call as the post of solitude & reproach. And I will not mistrust your fitness for every sweet & solemn emergency of your own blended fate. May the Infinite Goodness bind us all! Farewell, my brother, my sister![15]

Interestingly, as Emerson's language and emotions become more highly charged, his meaning becomes more elliptical, making passages such as this one difficult to interpret. This sounds very much like a farewell letter, yet Emerson continued to correspond with Barker and Ward for years, and after Fuller's death in 1850, he tried to talk Ward into editing her memoirs. What *is* clear in this letter is that Emerson responded with powerful but ambivalent emotions to this marriage and that he felt that something significant in his relationship with these friends was either ending or changing fundamentally. While Fuller's response to the marriage was also highly charged, this is not so surprising, since she had once apparently thought of Ward as a lover, and since Anna Barker was one of a number of women with whom Fuller had had (and continued in Anna's case to have) intense relationships of the sort Carroll Smith-Rosenberg has documented.[16] The point is twofold: first, that the language of nineteenth-century friendship was frequently charged with emotion and words that seem suspect to post-Freudian twentieth-century readers. Given the realities of nineteenth-century attitudes about sexuality, it is always possible that this language did conceal, perhaps even from the writers, erotic feelings. In the case of Emerson and Fuller, however, this language was not exclusive to their letters to one another—any speculation about possible sublimated erotic feelings must extend to their relationships with a number of other people. The second point, however, is that in examining their correspondence, critics have tended to focus almost exclusively on Fuller's intense emotionalism during this period and have ignored the equally intense emotional tone of Emerson's letters. This selective reading extends to other aspects of their correspondence and in every case has created a picture of Fuller as the neurotic aggressor in the relationship and of Emerson as the cool, detached defender of his privacy and even of his honor.

Certainly in discussing the way that the debate on friendship unfolded, the critics have seen Fuller as the initiator of the debate, drawing Emerson into a discussion in which he did not want to participate and which he tried to end. The letters, however, suggest that it was probably Emerson who initiated the discussion and that he used Fuller and his other friends as sounding boards for the essay, "Friendship," which he was writing during one of the heaviest exchanges of letters on this topic between August and October 1840. A number of critics, Strauch among them, have noted that Emerson used much of the material in these letters in the essay. It was characteristic for Emerson to use a number of sources, usually his journals, for his essays, culling his own words, selecting sentences or paragraphs, and inserting them, often with little revision, into the essays. Using letters to his friends was not so characteristic, but as Strauch and others have pointed out, entire sections of his letters, particularly those to Fuller and Sturgis, appeared not just in "Friendship," but also in the essays, "Love" and "Self Reliance." What these critics have not noted is that Emerson was talking about the essay,

"Friendship," as early as January 1840, before the debate reached its peak, and that the first mention of this topic comes from Emerson, not Fuller, in a letter written on 7 June, 1840, in which he discusses his growing friendship for Carolyn Sturgis, saying, "We are beginning to be acquainted and by the century after next shall be the best of friends. Beings so majestic cannot surely take less time to establish a relation."[17] On 16 August of the same year in a letter to Carolyn Sturgis, he uses a similar phrase saying, "You & I should only be friends on imperial terms."[18] It is in this letter, eight months after he has told Ward that he is planning an essay on friendship, that for the first time there is any suggestion that Fuller or any of the others have criticized his attitude toward or practice of friendship. He says, "But that which set me on this writing was the talk with Margaret F last Friday who taxed me on both your parts with a certain inhospitality of soul inasmuch as you were both willing to be my friends in the full & sacred sense & I remained apart critical, & after many interviews still a stranger."[19] In a letter to Fuller on 24 October of the same year, Emerson calls off the discussion, squarely placing the responsibility for having begun the discussion on her shoulders, saying, "I ought never to have suffered you to lead me into any conversation or writing on our relation, a topic from which with all persons my Genius ever sternly warns me away."[20] Given the number and intensity of the letters Emerson wrote on this subject, not just to Fuller but to Sturgis, Ward, and Barker, one must question his objectivity and motives here. Clearly he was tired of the topic and he was beginning to hear things from the others about his practice and theory of friendship that could not have been pleasant.

After Emerson terminated the discussion on friendship in October 1840, the topic disappeared from their correspondence for several months, but in the following March, Emerson, not Fuller, reopened the topic, asking Fuller as a friend to "protect" him from friendship. He brought the subject up again in letters in July and August 1841. Finally, in October 1841, while Fuller was visiting the Emersons in Concord, she wrote a long letter to him, which critics have interpreted as *her* effort to reopen the topic. She did not need to reopen it; Emerson had already done that. In this, as in almost every aspect of their relationship, the force of the "Margaret Myth" has been so strong that critics have seen what they expected to see, aided in great part by Emerson's own misleading words.

Because the debate on friendship has so often been seen as an emotional battle between Fuller and Emerson, little serious attention has been paid to the intellectual and philosophical issues raised in the letters. Indeed no one has suggested that Fuller had an intellectual or philosophical position worth discussing, although everyone has discussed her practice of friendship. As far as most critics are concerned, Emerson, speaking as the apostle of American individualism and self-reliance, was simply restating with complete consistency his own creed. In fact, the positions on both sides are complex and represent two opposing modes of thought about issues of individualism, responsibility, and intimacy, and the appropriate response to weakness and evil in human nature.

In a letter to Fuller written in March 1841, Emerson defines in paradoxical language the role a friend should play:

> You, instead of wondering at my cloistered & unfriendly manners should defend me if possible from friendship from ambition, from my own weakness which would lead me to variety, which is the dissipation of thought. . . . Our friendship should be one incompatible with the vicious order of existing society, and should adjourn its fulness of communion into pure eternity.[21]

Or, in an earlier letter written in October 1838, in words that are nearly replicated in the essay on friendship, he tells Fuller,

> We are armed all over with these subtle antagonisms which as soon as we meet begin to play, & translate all poetry into such stale prose! It seems to me that almost all people *descend* somewhat into society. All association must be a compromise; and, what is worst, the very flower & aroma of the flower of each of the beautiful natures disappears as they approach each other. What a perpetual disappointment is actual society even of the virtuous and gifted.[22]

If, on the one hand, friendship is "weakness" and "dissipation of thought" for Emerson, or, on the other, "a perpetual disappointment," "a descent," or a "compromise," why does he bother with it all—why does he not simply retreat into the "Stylite seclusion" he speaks of in another letter?[23]

In fact, Emerson did not retreat into seclusion; he surrounded himself with friends all of his life, enticing Alcott, Hawthorne, Ellery Channing, and Fuller herself to Concord to form an ideal "domestical" community as he described it to Fuller in one letter. Thoreau lived with the Emersons several times, once for a year. In the letter he wrote describing the ideal "domestical" community, Emerson said to Fuller, who was then in Rome,

> Shall we not yet—you, you, also,—as we used to talk, build up a reasonable society in that naked unatmospheric land, and effectually serve one another? In some sense I certainly do not grow old,—perhaps tis the worse for me—but, I believe, all the persons who have been important to my—imagination—shall I say? personal-imagination (is there no such thing in just psychology?) retain all their importance for me. I am their victim, & ready to be their victim, to the same extent as heretofore.[24]

This statement brings together all of Emerson's ambivalence about friendship. There is the double use of the word "victim" in the last sentence, which expresses Emerson's fear of intimacy even when he is, as he is here, the clear initiator, yet there is also the touching yearning for a community of friends and his unequivocal statement that there are people who have been and continue to be important to his "imagination." The last word is central to an understanding of his definition of friendship and the grounds on which Fuller took issue with it. For Emerson the function of the friend is primarily to provide stimulation for the imagination and the intellect and to bring out the best in the other. It is a narrow but exalted role he sees the friend playing. In the essay, "Love," he defines *love* as "the deification of persons,"[25] and in "Friendship," he says, "Worship [your friend's] superiorities; wish him not less by a thought, but hoard and tell them all."[26] In worshiping this superiority in the friend the individual draws on the wisdom, imagination, intelligence, but most of all the inspiration of the friend to feed the self. Again, in "Friendship," Emerson says, "Love is only the reflection of a man's own worthiness from other men," and friendship "must not surmise or provide for infirmity. It treats its object as a god, that may deify both."[27] What is significant here is not just that the friend should inspire and ennoble, but that "infirmity" must be ignored. There is no place in Emerson's system for weakness or unhappiness in the friend. This is friendship on "imperial terms" as he described it to Carolyn Sturgis in a letter quoted earlier, the meeting of "celestial bodies" who must show one another only the best parts of themselves.[28]

It was precisely this narrow and overly exalted definition of friendship to which Margaret Fuller objected, and she clearly saw it as an impediment to the kind of friendship she believed in philosophically and practiced personally. Her own philosophy of friendship was never developed in an essay as was Emerson's, but it is eloquently stated in a number of letters to him and other friends. One difficulty in reconstructing the debate on friendship is that many of the letters Fuller wrote to Emerson on this subject were either lost or destroyed after her death. Fortunately some of the letters she wrote to other friends have survived. Especially valuable are her letters to William H. Channing, whose views on friendship she explicitly compares to Emerson's. One letter to Channing is worth quoting at length, for it is the fullest and most revealing statement of her philosophy of friendship:

> The more I think of it, the more deeply do I feel the imperfection of your view of friendship which is the same Waldo E. takes. . . . It is very noble but not enough for our manifold nature. Our friends should be our incentives to Right, but not only our guiding but our prophetic stars. To love by sight is much, to love by faith is more; both are the entire love without which heart, mind, and soul cannot be alike satisfied. We love and ought to love one another not merely for the absolute worth of each but on account of a mutual fitness of temporary character. We are not merely one another's priests or gods, but ministering angels, exercising in the past the same function as the Great Soul in the whole of seeing the perfect through the imperfect nay, making it come there. Why am I to love my friend the less for any obstruction in his life? is not the very time for me to love most tenderly when I must see his life in despite of seeming; when he *shows it* me I can only admire; I do not *give* myself; I am *taken captive.*[29]

For Fuller, the friend's role is active, not passive. The friend does not simply stand waiting to receive bolts of celestial wisdom and inspiration. As she said of Emerson in her journal, "His creed is, show thyself, let them take as much as they can. . . . His friendship is only strong preference and he weighs and balances, buys and sells you and himself all the time."[30] In Emerson's variety of friendship both parties must always prove their worth. There is no room for weakness, unhappiness, comfort or compassion.

In the letter to Channing quoted above, Fuller goes on to say, "Do not, I implore you, whether from pride or affection, wish to exile me from the dark hour. The manly mind might love best in the triumphant hour, but the woman could no more stay from the foot of the cross, than from the Transfiguration."[31] She objected to Emerson's philosophy because it includes no provision for anything but perfection—not only is there no psychological or emotional response to the friend who is in pain or who has failed, there is a philosophical denial that there should be. For her, the twin metaphors of the Transfiguration and the cross captured what Carol Gilligan has called "an ideal of care."[32] She believed that friendship had to encompass both the poles of beatitude and of suffering.

Another related aspect of her concept of friendship is revealed in a letter written to Emerson in October 1841, in which she says, "You go upon the idea that we must love most the most beauteous, but this is not so." She goes on to explain that as she begins to see "changes" in her friends or as they do not live up to their fullest potential, she feels "a deeper tenderness and even a higher hope than did these forms in the greatest perfection they ever attained."[33] For Fuller the practice of friendship was, as many of her contemporaries have described it, an active seeking out of the potential in others, encouraging them to express their highest natures. Unlike Emerson, however, who wanted only to gaze upon the finished perfection, Fuller was excited by the potential. In many ways, her view is more romantic than Emerson's for it is more formative and generative, finding promise in the process of discovery rather than in the finished, perfect object or condition. More romantic and holistic, it encompasses the possibility of failure to achieve perfection and the suffering and anguish that may accompany defeat. She goes on to say in the same letter, "I seem to myself to say all when I say that the chivalric idea of love through disease, dungeons and death, mutilation on the battle field, and the odious changes effected by the enchanter's hate answers my idea far better than the stoical appreciation of the object beloved for what it positively presents."[34]

This philosophical divergence between the ideals of "perfection" and "care" corresponds closely to Fuller and Emerson's disagreement about the nature of evil and the individual's response to it. Emerson did not believe in the existence of evil anymore than he believed in the possibility of failure. His insistence that evil is only the absence of goodness has been noted by virtually everyone who has written about him. Emerson and Fuller engaged in a public debate on one occasion when he and several other men attended one of her conversations for women in Boston. On this occasion Emerson argued that one should ignore evil, saying, "Good was always present to the soul;—and was all the true soul took note of. It was a duty not to look [at evil]." Fuller responded, according to a member of the group who kept a record of the conversation, that "she believed evil to be a good in the grand scheme of things. . . . In one word she would not accept the world . . . did she not believe evil

working in it for good! Man had gained more than he lost by his fall."
Emerson answered that "to imagine it possible to fall was to *begin* to
fall."[35]

While Fuller's statement is couched in the language of Calvinism and
might seem to suggest that dark view of human nature, other statements
she made suggest a slightly different interpretation. In a letter to a friend
in 1838, she says, "I have lived to know that the secret of all things is
pain and that Nature travaileth most painfully with her noblest product."[36] For Fuller, whose life was at times unbearably painful and full
of uncertainty, struggle, and loss, this is a philosophy of acceptance
and growth through pain that is consistent with her statements about
friendship and her desire to "no more stay from the foot of the cross,
than from the Transfiguration," while Emerson's philosophy of deliberately ignoring pain and evil is consistent with his determination to look
upon only the most elevated aspects of his friends' minds and accomplishments. While the doctrine of self-reliance calls out the best in each
individual, it does not allow for anything but the best. As the debate on
friendship demonstrates, this can be a cruel philosophy. For Emerson, a
friend's suffering was something one must simply ignore since it did not
inspire celestial thoughts. As a number of his critics and biographers
have suggested, this rather stoic and even blind refusal to acknowledge
the negative aspects of life may have been his defense against the pain
and tragedies of his own life raised to the level of philosophy. It cost
him a great deal personally, as he acknowledged at various times. When
his favorite son, Waldo, died in 1842, he wrote to Carolyn Sturgis:

> Alas! I chiefly grieve that I cannot grieve, that this fact takes no
> more deep hold than other facts, is as dreamlike as they; a lam-
> bent flame that will not burn playing on the surface on my river.
> Must every experience—those that promised to be dearest &
> most penetrative,—only kiss my cheek like the wind & pass
> away?[37]

Emerson's inability to feel deeply or to express his emotions openly
made it impossible for him to achieve real intimacy in any of his relationships, a failure that at times caused his wife and friends great pain.
During Fuller's 1842 visit to the Emersons, Lidian Emerson asked her
to walk one day and poured out all of her pain about her husband's coldness. Fuller noted in the journal she kept of this visit that she feared
Lidian "will always have these pains, because she has always a lurking
hope that Waldo's character will alter, and that he will be capable of an

intimate union; now I feel convinced that it will never be more perfect between them two."[38] Within a month of Waldo's death, Emerson left on an extended lecture tour, leaving Lidian prostrate with grief. Lidian's judgment of her husband's philosophy and its effect on others is revealed in a bitter satire of transcendentalism that she wrote sometime during the 1840s. In one portion of it, she says,

> Loathe and shun the sick. They are in bad taste, and may untune us for writing the poem floating through our mind. . . .
>
> Despise the unintellectual, and make them feel that you do by not noticing their remark and question lest they presume to intrude into your conversation. . . .
>
> It is mean and weak to seek for sympathy; it is mean and weak to give it. . . . Never wish to be loved. Who are you to expect that? Besides, the great never value being loved.[39]

It is a statement that forcibly brings one to a halt to consider what marriage to Emerson felt like to Lidian. It is a painful condemnation of what she perceived to be his contempt for her and suggests the ways he may have used his philosophy to justify his coldness.

There are many indications in his letters, however, that Emerson was aware of the way he affected others. During his frequent long absences from home on lecture tours, he often wrote to Lidian apologizing for not writing more "personal" letters, saying that he was too busy. Ironically, these letters are often long and full of the trivial details of his days. In one sad letter written in 1848 while he was in England, however, he stops making excuses and says,

> Ah you still ask me for that unwritten letter always due, it seems, always unwritten, from year to year, by me to you, dear Lidian,—I fear too more widely true than you mean,—always due & unwritten by me to every sister & brother of the human race. I have only to say that I also bemoan myself daily for the same cause—that I cannot write this letter, that I have not stamina & constitution enough to mind the two functions of seraph & cherub, oh no, let me not use such great words,—rather say that a photometer cannot be a stove. It must content you for the time, that I truly acknowledge a poverty of nature, & have really no proud defence at all to set up, but ill-health, puniness, and Stygian limitation.[40]

This is another of Emerson's letters full of ambivalence. He acknowledges his "poverty of nature," yet reiterates his conviction that the two "functions," presumably of intellect and emotion, are incompatible, then excuses himself on the grounds of "ill-health and puniness," a remarkable admission that intimacy required enormous feats of strength and endurance beyond his capacity.

In fact, many of his utterances reveal that intimacy and emotion are not only beyond his strength, but that they threaten him. This fear is expressed in a number of striking images of violence and pain in his writing. In a letter to Fuller cited earlier, Emerson reveals this anxiety by saying, "You, instead of wondering at my cloistered & unfriendly manners should *defend* me if possible from friendship from ambition, from my own *weakness*" (emphasis added). In another letter he uses a violently masochistic image, saying, "They say in heaven that I am a very awkward lover of my friends. . . . My love reacts on me like *the recoiling gun: it is pain*" (emphasis added).[41] In the essay, "Friendship," this anxiety is couched in language that also hints at violence. He says, "Why insist on *rash* personal relations with your friend? Why go to his house, or know his mother and brother and sisters? Why be visited by him at your own? Are these things material to our convenant? Leave this *touching and clawing*. Let him be to me a spirit" (emphasis added).[42] The violence of these images seems to reflect a fear of entrapment or betrayal and a sense of self so fragile that it fears annihilation.[43] That his own ego and sense of identity are what is threatened by intimacy is clear later in the essay when he says, "Though I prize my friends, I cannot afford to talk with them and study their visions, *lest I lose my own*" (emphasis added).[44] One is again reminded of Emerson's letter to Carolyn Sturgis in which he fears she may find "in some heaven foreign to me your mate, & my beautiful castle is exploded to shivers." For Emerson, the fear of losing his identity or of being rejected by someone was so powerful that he not only locked himself away in Stylite solitude all of his life, but he developed a philosophy to justify that withdrawal which, not too surprisingly, has become the creed of masculine America.

If Emerson was terrified by intimacy, Fuller craved it all of her life, and her letters are full of the pain of not finding it. In one letter to Channing, she asks, "Can no soul know me wholly? shall I never know the deep delight of gratitude to any but the All-Knowing?"[45] Fuller frequently went through periods of deep depression, suffering terrible headaches and periods of physical prostration. Her biographers have speculated about the causes of these physical disorders, but it seems likely that they were in some way connected with those periods of disil-

lusionment and emptiness which she so eloquently describes in her letters.[46] In two early letters, Fuller describes the sense of emptiness and
loss brought about by the end of an intense friendship with George
Davis:

> It is painful to lose a friend whose knowledge and converse min-
> gled so intimately with the growth of my mind,—an early friend
> to whom I was all truth and frankness, seeking nothing but equal
> truth and frankness in return. But this evil may be borne; the hard,
> the lasting evil was to learn to distrust my own heart and lose all
> faith in my power of knowing others.[47]

In a letter written several months later, she says, "I feel quite lost; it
is so long since I have talked myself. To see so many acquaintances,
to talk so many words, and never tell my mind completely on any
subject—to say so many things which do not seem called out, makes
me feel strangely vague and moveable."[48] Her description of herself
here as feeling "strangely vague and moveable" suggests that she felt
unanchored, as if her identity were slipping away, in the absence of intimate relationships.

What is striking is that Fuller took what could have been (and is for
many women) a crippling defect and turned it into a strong philosophy
of mutuality, compassion, and connection. She turned conversation into
an art and used the form of conversation to help draw out the intellectual
as well as the personal potential in her friends. It is significant that she
found herself most intellectually as well as personally alive, not when
she was writing (a solitary act—the act preferred, not surprisingly, by
Emerson), but when she was talking to people. In a letter in 1833, she
says, "Nobody can be more sensible than myself that the pen is a much
less agreeable instrument for communication than the voice, but all
our wishes will not bring back the dear talking times of Greece and
Rome."[49] She looked back in other letters to the "talking times of
Greece and Rome" as the golden age of conversation and community.

Fuller began her famous conversations for women in Boston in 1839
in an effort to recreate that golden age of conversation and to provide an
opportunity for women who lacked intellectual opportunities to develop
their potential. In a letter to Sophia Ripley, she says that the goals of the
proposed conversations are

> to pass in review the departments of thought and knowledge and
> endeavor to place them in due relation to one another in our

minds. To systematize thought and give a precision in which our sex are so deficient, chiefly, I think because they have so few inducements to test and classify what they receive. To ascertain what pursuits are best suited to us in our time and state of society, and how we may make best use of our means for building up the life of thought upon the life of action.[50]

If the goal is to develop the intellectual capacity of women, a radical idea for its time, Fuller's methods were even more radical, for she did not believe that the way to achieve this was through lecturing or solitary reading. She had apparently been told that some women wished to attend the conversations, but preferred to listen rather than talk. She tells Sophia Ripley in the same letter,

> I do not wish anyone to join who does not intend, *if possible,* to take an active part. No one will be forced, but those who do not talk will not derive the same advantages with those who openly state their impressions and consent to learn by blundering as is the destiny of Man here below. And general silence or side talks would paralyze me. I should feel coarse and misplaced if I were to be haranguing too much. In former instances I have been able to make it easy and even pleasant to twenty-five out of thirty to bear their part, to question, to define, to state and examine their opinion. If I could not do as much now I should consider myself unsuccessful and should withdraw.[51]

It is noteworthy that Fuller once again focuses on the generative principle of developing the intellectual potential in others by encouraging them to "blunder," "to define, to state and examine their opinion." It is the process as much as the product that interests her.

In her essay, "A Feminist Critique of the Liberal Arts," Elizabeth Minnich defines the masculine mode of "rhetoric" as the "product of a speaker who stands before an audience," and the "feminine" mode of conversation as an "exchange between people that actively involves both,"[52] and suggests that the feminine mode will bring us closer to the old Socratic ideal of learning, the ideal of the "talking times of Greece and Rome," which Fuller sought to recreate in her conversations. It is worth noting that on the one occasion that Emerson attended one of Fuller's conversations, it was reported that rather than engaging in conversation, he delivered a lecture.

The fact that Fuller genuinely wanted to hear what other people had to say while Emerson wanted to hear his own philosophy repeated back to him or wanted to persuade people to his own point of view is also consistent with Minnich's analysis, for she goes on to develop the distinction between conversation and rhetoric in this way: "Conversation is the art of those who hold us together, *in enjoyment of our differences. . . .* Rhetoric is the art of those who move us together, *overcoming our differences*" (emphasis added).[53]

This particular difference in Fuller's and Emerson's modes of thinking is nowhere more evident than in the way they conducted themselves during their stints as editors of the *Dial*. During the two years Fuller edited the *Dial* she included as many different perspectives and kinds of writing as she could. Emerson, who took over the editorship when she resigned in 1842 for financial reasons, took the position that the *Dial* should reflect only the views of the tight circle of people who made up the Transcendental Club. Fuller and Emerson had disagreed over her policy while she was the editor, and when Emerson took over, she wrote him a letter taking him to task for his narrowness, saying,

> I think you will sometimes reject pieces that I should not. For you have always had in view to make a good periodical and represent your own tastes, while I have had in view to let all kinds of people have freedom to say their say, for better, for worse.[54]

When Emerson lived up to Fuller's prediction, rejecting among other things in 1843 a French piece she had translated and submitted, she wrote him another letter reiterating their differences in even stronger terms:

> When I had care of the Dial, I put in what those connected with me liked, even when it did not well please myself, on this principle that I considered a magazine was meant to suit more than one class of minds. . . . I thought it less important that everything in it should be excellent, than that it should represent with some fidelity the state of mind among us as the name of Dial said was its intent. . . . You go on a different principle; you would have everything in it good according to your taste, which is in my opinion, though admirable as far as it goes, far too narrow in its range.[55]

It is remarkable in Fuller's and Emerson's letters how often she explains or paraphrases his ideas back to him in an effort to arrive at some understanding and how infrequently he does the same. In fact, in letter after letter, Emerson complains that he cannot understand what she is saying. In one letter he says to her: "There is a difference in our constitution. *We use a different rhetoric[.] It seems as if we had been born & bred in different nations.* You say you understand me wholly. You cannot communicate yourself to me. I hear the words sometimes but remain a stranger to your state of mind" (emphasis added).[56] In another letter he says, "I . . . do constantly aver that you & I are not inhabitants of one thought of the Divine Mind, but of two thoughts, that we meet & treat like foreign states, one maritime, one inland, whose trade & laws are essentially unlike."[57] Just as Emerson could not or chose not to acknowledge the existence of evil, of ideas incompatible with his own, he is unable or unwilling to hear what Fuller is saying to him.[58]

Emerson's failure to "hear" Fuller, no matter how often or in how many ways she explains herself, conforms to the pattern anthropologist Edwin Ardener describes in his articles, "Belief and the Problem of Women" and "The Problem Revisited," where he explains why the experiences of women traditionally have been ignored or misinterpreted by anthropologists. Ardener's explanation is that women live in a "muted" culture where they speak but are not heard, because the values and patterns of their experience do not translate into the patterns of male experience or rhetoric.[59]

Fuller's voice is "muted" in Ardener's definition of that word. She speaks but Emerson cannot hear her. One can imagine the frustration she must have felt as she tried again and again to explain her position to Emerson only to receive the response, "I hear the words sometimes but remain a stranger to your state of mind." It is significant, I think, that he wrote this in the letter in which he told her that he did not wish to continue their discussion of friendship. It is also significant, as both Gilligan and Ardener point out, that women, because they are dependent both on relationships and on the goodwill of men who hold power, must be able to listen and understand what men say. The result all too frequently is that women internalize the message that they make no sense, that they express themselves badly, that their ideas are illogical. Much of Fuller's insecurity about herself as a writer may have come from just such a sense that she could not make herself heard. Emerson's metaphor that he and she met like "foreign states" and were "born & bred in different nations" is not far from the mark. What he did not understand was that one of them was bilingual and the other was not. As Elaine Showalter has pointed out, women must live in two cultures, their own and the male culture, and understand them both to survive; men need only understand their own.[60]

While the modes of thinking and the patterns of intimacy and individuation that Gilligan describes seem to shape Fuller's and Emerson's patterns of response, both struggled throughout their lives toward the opposite poles. As Gilligan points out, it is not that men never achieve intimacy nor that women never achieve individuation, rather they often must struggle to achieve those states. Emerson's letters are a testimony to his struggle against his tendencies toward isolation and solipsism. Although he tells Fuller that he "remain[s] a stranger to [her] state of mind," he continued to write to her, urging her to make her home in Concord, trying to maintain the bond between them. It was Fuller who always rejected the suggestion that she come to live in Concord, sometimes for practical reasons, more often because she sensed that too close an association with Emerson was preventing her from developing her own identity and was standing in the way of the richer involvement in the world she eventually chose. In one letter to Channing, she says, "I do indeed feel [Emerson's] life stealing gradually into mine; and I sometimes think that my work would have been more simple, and my unfolding to a temporal activity more rapid and easy, if we had never met."[61] She wrote to Emerson after a visit to Concord, "I have not felt separated from you yet. — It is not yet time for me to have my dwelling near you. I get, after awhile, even *intoxicated* with your mind, and do not live enough in myself."[62]

It was not until Fuller finally did separate herself from Concord and Emerson that she was able to immerse herself in the life of action about which she and Emerson so fundamentally disagreed. After she left New England, she became a reporter on Horace Greeley's *New York Tribune* and then went to Rome in 1847 to become a partisan of the Italian revolution and the first American correspondent to cover it. There she met and fell in love with Marquis Giovanni Angelo Ossoli, had a child, and eventually married Ossoli. In this relationship Fuller apparently found the intimacy she had longed for all of her life, while her commitment to the revolution and her work for the *Tribune* satisfied her longing for active engagement in the world. One of the ultimate ironies of Fuller's and Emerson's lives is that she became a woman of action living in a male world, while he lived a quiet life of domesticity in Concord surrounded by his family and friends.

It is significant that Fuller did her best writing after she left New England and Emerson's influence. In 1844 she published *Summer on the Lakes in 1843*, completed and published *Woman in the Nineteenth Century*, and began her remarkable series of articles for Greeley on social problems, writing about such issues as prison reform and prostitution. In 1846 she published *Papers on Literature and Art*, a collection of essays that places her along with Edgar Allan Poe as one of the first critics in America to elevate artistic and literary criticism to a professional level. Friends who saw her *History of the Italian Revolution* before she sailed for America believed it was the best thing she had written. When the ship she, Ossoli, and her child were on sank off Fire Island, Fuller was at the peak of her career, and it is impossible not to wonder what she might have achieved had she lived.

Emerson's response to Fuller's death showed the ambivalence he had felt toward her during her life. He wrote in his journal, "In her I have lost my audience,"[63] suggesting that even at that moment he saw her primarily as a reflector of his own ideas. Almost immediately he began constructing the "Margaret Myth" that has dominated nearly all studies of her for over a century. He began to collect her papers and writings, even sending Thoreau to Fire Island to see if anything had survived the shipwreck. Even in this task, however, he was ambivalent. He urged the priority of his own work in writing to Clarke, Channing, and Ward, urging them to take on the task of editing her papers. Once he began to examine the papers, however, he became nervous and decided he did not want to give up control. In a letter to Ward written in September 1850, he said,

> The Margaret Manuscripts begin to come in . . . and yesterday, hints from Ellery [Channing], that the Journals contain so many allusions to people, that they can hardly be seen, or perhaps by one only, meaning me. . . . Some Journals were, it seems, included in the package made up & addressed by Margaret herself to Caroline [Sturgis] before she left America, & Caroline is to decide what is for the fire, & what for the eyes.[64]

No one knows what was lost in "the fire," but the butchering process that went into the "editing" and writing of the *Memoirs* is suggestive. Her papers were cut up and large passages blacked out. Words and sentences were changed to create the image deemed proper by Emerson and his fellow editors. Equally destructive, moreover, were the comments written by Fuller's editor friends. It is largely from the reminiscences written for the *Memoirs* that the image of Fuller as a physically ugly, overwhelming, and egotistical woman has emerged. These descriptions differ in tone and detail from what these same friends wrote to and about her while she was alive; in almost every case the descriptions written after her death are harsher.

A similar and even more disturbing discrepancy appears in Emerson's evaluation of Fuller's writing before and after her death. Emerson often wrote Fuller letters full of praise for her writing, in one letter commending the "superior tone . . . discrimination & . . . thought" that "indicate a golden pen apt for a higher service hereafter."[65] In the *Memoirs,* written nearly twenty years later, he creates the impression that she could barely write coherently, culminating in the infamous remark that "her pen was a non-conductor."[66] Can a pen be both "golden" and a "non-conductor"? What prompted Emerson to such inconsistent statements? Why would he praise her writing lavishly during her lifetime and then create the impression, which still persists today in the minds of many, that she could scarcely write? There is no satisfactory answer to this question, but a certain spirit of malice cannot be discounted. He may have felt betrayed and abandoned when she left New England and the tight circle he tried to maintain there. Certainly his remarks on friendship suggest that he felt a fear of just such abandonment. It is also possible that Fuller's relationship with Ossoli disturbed Emerson and colored his view of her. Emerson was nothing if not puritanical about sexual matters. Certainly there seems to be a tone of vindictiveness in some of the remarks and descriptions of her in the *Memoirs,* such as the passage in which he describes "her extreme plainness—a trick of incessantly opening and shutting her eyelids,—the nasal tone of her voice,—all repelled."[67]

The extreme emphasis on her physical appearance in many of the passages in the *Memoirs* is, although perhaps not consciously intended by the writers, a constant reminder that Fuller is a woman, an unwomanly woman who has stepped out of her role. For Emerson, whose views on women's roles in general were as ambivalent as his views about Margaret Fuller in particular, the very fact that she was a woman who did not conform to the prescribed roles for nineteenth-century women (the roles fulfilled by nearly every other woman he knew) no doubt explains some of his ambivalence toward her.

Gender in a more subtle and profound way, I would suggest, explains the differences in Fuller's and Emerson's philosophies and the general misunderstanding and even blindness to many of Fuller's ideas shared by Emerson and most modern critics and readers. Fuller, in spite of her transcendental and romantic grounding, clearly was at odds with some fundamental precepts of the transcendental point of view. Although she subscribed in certain ways to the transcendental emphasis on individualism and drew on it heavily in formulating her arguments for women's rights in *Woman in the Nineteenth Century,* hers was a modified version of self-reliance and individualism that recognized, as Emerson's theories did not, that human relationships are both necessary and many faceted.[68] Her vision, though not so fully and often articulated as Emerson's, is, I would argue, a larger and more complex vision than his in that it recognizes and attempts to accommodate human weakness, the existence of evil, and the potential for failure and despair. Modern psychologists like Nancy Chodorow and Carol Gilligan have argued powerfully that cultural and developmental patterns have predisposed women to more complex and less rigid and hierarchical views of relationships and moral issues. That Fuller herself recognized this is suggested by her statement to Channing that a woman could "no more stay from the foot of the cross, than from the Transfiguration."

Fuller, however, as the mother of American feminism, living in a culture that had just begun to question its own assumptions about gender, had no theoretical system to explain her brilliant intuitions. Emerson, riding the crest of eighteenth- and nineteenth-century Kantian and romantic philosophy, was perfectly positioned both to articulate his theories of individualism and to have them recognized. Fuller, even when she did brilliantly explain her ideas, as she does her theory of friendship in the letters discussed here, was doomed to be misunderstood. Marge Piercy, commenting on her own efforts to articulate her sense of what it meant to be a woman in the 1960s before the current women's movement had created a context for such ideas, has said, "I cared about women's issues before I could understand them. For so long I lacked a vocabulary." Speaking to the same issue in another place, Piercy states her sense of frustration even more strongly:

> There was nobody to write for, nobody to communicate with about matters of being female, alive, thinking, trying to make sense of one's life and times. . . . There was little satisfaction for me in the forms offered, yet there seemed no space but death or madness outside the forms.[69]

Piercy, in the 1970s, could look back on her frustration in the 1960s and understand it in the context of the theories of women's culture and of gender differences that had evolved in the last decade. Margaret Fuller had no context at all for her brilliant insights. In *Woman in the Nineteenth Century* she would begin to create that context, but in the years of her friendship and correspondence with Emerson she was just beginning to struggle with these ideas. One can only imagine her frustration, her sense of herself as an anomaly, of not being heard, of being misunderstood sometimes in the most appallingly personal ways, of having her motives questioned. It is no wonder that her letters to those from whom she most expected understanding and intellectual support so often speak of discouragement and despair. Her own brilliance reached out to other brilliant minds. Emerson was the most brilliant mind of the Concord circle, and it was natural that she should turn to him as he did to her for intellectual nourishment. Yet, Fuller, who understood Emerson while disagreeing with him, did not realize that he was incapable of understanding her "different rhetoric." More than one hundred thirty years later, theory and culture are finally catching up with Margaret Fuller. Her rhetoric no longer seems foreign, and the full complexity of her ideas is beginning to emerge.

Notes

1. Bell Gale Chevigny, *The Woman and the Myth: Margaret Fuller's Life and Writings* (Old Westbury, N.Y.: Feminist Press, 1976), 1. Chevigny's imaginative book combines biographical information, selections from Fuller's writings, and selections of material written by her contemporaries about Fuller, as well as Chevigny's analysis and interpretation of Fuller's life and works. The best standard biographies of Fuller are Paula Blanchard's excellent *Margaret Fuller: From Transcendentalism to Revolution* (New York: Delacorte Press, 1978); and Thomas Wentworth Higginson, *Margaret Fuller Ossoli* (1890; reprint, New York: Greenwood Press, 1968), still a valuable source of information about Fuller.

2. The standard biography of Emerson is Gay Wilson Allen, *Waldo Emerson: A Biography* (New York: Viking Press, 1981).

3. Blanchard, *Margaret Fuller*, 65. For an excellent discussion of Fuller's reading and intellectual interests during these years, see Blanchard's discussion, 65–72.

4. Ibid, 76–77.

5. *Memoirs of Margaret Fuller Ossoli*, ed. Ralph Waldo Emerson, William Henry Channing, and James Freeman Clarke (1852; reprint, New York, Burt Franklin, 1972), 204. Both Emerson's and Fuller's punctuation and syntax are sometimes eccentric; I have not altered the punctuation in any way.

6. Carl F. Strauch, "Hatred's Swift Repulsions: Emerson, Margaret Fuller, and Others," *Studies in Romanticism* 7(1968):70.

7. Ibid., 71.

8. Allen, *Waldo Emerson*, 352–353, 356.

9. *The Journals and Miscellaneous Notebooks of Ralph Waldo Emerson*, ed. A. W. Plumstead and Harrison Hayford, 16 vols. (Cambridge: Harvard University Press, 1969), 7:400.

10. Margaret Vanderhaar Allen, *The Achievement of Margaret Fuller* (University Park: Pennsylvania State University Press, 1979); and Marie Olesen Urbanski, "The Ambivalence of Ralph Waldo Emerson towards Margaret Fuller," *Thoreau Journal Quarterly* 10(1978):26–36.

11. *The Letters of Ralph Waldo Emerson*, ed. Ralph L. Rusk, 6 vols. (New York: Columbia University Press, 1939), 2:336 (hereafter cited as *LRWE*).

12. *The Letters of Margaret Fuller*, ed. Robert N. Hudspeth, 3 vols. (Ithaca: Cornell University Press, 1983), 2:213 (hereafter cited as *LMF*).

13. *LRWE*, 2:325.

14. Ibid., 2:333.

15. Ibid., 2:339.

16. Carroll Smith-Rosenberg, "The Female World of Love and Ritual: Relations between Women in Nineteenth-Century America," *Signs* 1 (1975):1–29.

17. *LRWE*, 2:304–305.

18. Ibid., 2:325.

19. Ibid.

20. Ibid., 2:352.

21. Ibid., 2:385.

22. Ibid., 2:168.

23. Ibid., 2:380.

24. Ibid., 3:447.

25. *The Collected Works of Ralph Waldo Emerson*, ed. Joseph Slater, Alfred R. Ferguson, and Jean Ferguson Carr (Cambridge: Harvard University Press, 1979), 2:107.

26. Ibid., 2:124.

27. Ibid., 2:125, 127.

28. *LRWE*, 2:304–305.

29. *LMF*, 2:321.

30. Quoted in ibid., 2:161.

31. Ibid., 2:214.

32. It is striking that Fuller identifies these two modes of approaching relationships, these two definitions of friendship, as masculine and feminine, for on many levels the pattern of Fuller and Emerson's relationship and their ways of thinking about friendship fit the shape of male and female patterns in relationships and modes of thinking defined by Carol Gilligan, who describes women as living in "a world of relationships and psychological truths where an awareness of the connection between people gives rise to a recognition of responsibility for one another, a perception of the need for response." While the man operates from an "ideal of perfection, against which he measures the worth of himself," the woman "counterposes an ideal of care, against which she measures the worth of her activity" (*In a Different Voice: Psychological Theory and Women's Development* [Cambridge: Harvard University Press, 1982], 30, 35).

33. *LMF*, 2:235.

34. Ibid.

35. Quoted in Chevigny, *Woman and the Myth*, 226–227.

36. *LFM*, 1:347.

37. *LRWE*, 3:9.

38. Joel Myerson, "Margaret Fuller's 1842 Journal: At Concord with the Emersons," *Harvard Library Bulletin* 21(1973):331–332.

39. Quoted in Joyce W. Warren, *The American Narcissus: Individualism and Women in Nineteenth-Century American Fiction* (New Brunswick, N.J.: Rutgers University Press, 1984), 42.

40. *LRWE*, 4:33.

41. Ibid., 2:438.

42. *Collected Works of Emerson*, 2:123.

43. Ibid., 2:126.

44. Again, one is reminded of Carol Gilligan's theories of male development patterns. Drawing upon Nancy Chodorow's theories of mothering and the effect that the primacy of the mother and the absence of the father have on the ego development of children, Gilligan explains that "since masculinity is defined through separation . . . male gender identity is threatened by intimacy. . . . Thus males tend to have problems with relationships" (*Different Voice*, 8). Even more striking is Gilligan's analysis of the prevalence of violence in males' fantasies about intimacy. Gilligan reports that when men and women are asked to respond to pictures on the Thematic Apperception Test, "as people are brought closer together in the pictures, the images of violence in the men's stories increase. . . . The danger men describe in their stories of intimacy is a danger of entrapment or betrayal, being caught in a smothering relationship or humiliated by rejection and deceit" (42). See Nancy Chodorow, "Family Structure and Feminine Personality," in *Woman, Culture, and Society,* ed. Michele Zimbalist Rosaldo and Louise Lamphere (Stanford: Stanford University Press, 1974), 43–66; and idem, *The Reproduction of Mothering: Psychoanalysis and the Sociology of Gender* (Berkeley and Los Angeles: University of California Press, 1978).

45. *LMF*, 2:171.

46. Fuller's pattern is also similar to the one Carol Gilligan describes as the pattern for female identity. Gilligan explains that for women the problem of defining an identity is the opposite of the process for men: "Femininity is defined through attachment"; therefore, "female gender identity is threatened by separation," and "females tend to have problems with individuation" (*Different Voice*, 8).

47. *LMF*, 1:175.

48. Ibid., 1:178.

49. Ibid., 1:189.

50. Ibid., 2:87.

51. Ibid., 2:88.

52. Elizabeth Minnich, "A Feminist Critique of the Liberal Arts," in *Liberal Education and the New Scholarship on Women: Issues and Constraints in Institutional Change—A Report of the Wingspread Conference* (Washington: Association of American Colleges, 1982), 29.

53. Ibid.

54. *LMF*, 2:57–58.

55. Ibid., 2:160.

56. *LRWE*, 2:353.

57. Ibid., 2:336.

58. One is reminded in Emerson's phrase, "We use a different rhetoric," of the title of Carol Gilligan's book, *In a Different Voice,* by which she refers to the different mode of thinking we define as feminine—a mode that has been ignored or devalued because it does not conform to masculine norms.

59. See Edwin Ardener, "Belief and the Problem of Women," and "The Problem Revisited," in *Perceiving Women,* ed. Shirley Ardener (London: Malaby Press, 1975), 1–17, 19–27.

60. Showalter's ideas about women's culture are articulated in her brilliant analysis of feminist theory, "Feminist Criticism in the Wilderness," in *Writing and Sexual Difference,* ed. Elizabeth Abel (Chicago: University of Chicago Press, 1982), 9–35. In the summer of 1984 I was fortunate enough to be a member of her NEH Summer Seminar, "Women's Writing and Women's Culture," at Rutgers University, in which she had the time to articulate and illustrate those ideas in more complexity and depth. I cannot overstate the immense intellectual debt I owe her. This chapter was in large part inspired and made possible by what occurred in that seminar.

61. *LMF*, 3:92.

62. Ibid., 3:96.

63. *Journals of Emerson,* 11:258.

64. *LRWE*, 4:228.

65. Ibid., 2:135.

66. *Memoirs of Fuller,* 1:294.

67. Ibid., 1:202.

68. For an excellent discussion of Fuller's concern for self-development and individualism within the context of New England transcendentalism, see J.W. Warren, *American Narcissus,* 71–84.

69. Marge Piercy, *Parti-Colored Blocks for a Quilt* (Ann Arbor: University of Michigan Press, 1982), 143, 118–119.

MARY G. DE JONG

Lines from a Partly Published Drama: The Romance of Frances Sargent Osgood and Edgar Allan Poe

SCHOLARS HAVE OFTEN PUZZLED over Edgar Allan Poe's interest in Frances Sargent Locke Osgood (1811–1850), a popular personality and magazine poet of the 1840s. For the past century, many critics
and literary historians have perceived his generally favorable reviews of
her as a problem to be analyzed in terms of his Southern gallantry or his
partiality for a pretty "lady poet" who admired him. He has been portrayed as the master, while she has generally been miniaturized as his
pupil and protégée—sometimes flirt, sometimes pathetic sentimentalist, often talentless and slightly ridiculous.[1] Two recent studies revise
that tradition by taking the relationship more seriously: one contends
that Poe and Osgood exerted mutual poetic influence, the other that they
were lovers.[2]

The exact nature and significance of their association has yet to be established, but Osgood can no longer be dismissed as a parasite or victim: she purposefully maintained an interaction with Poe that affected
both parties' writing, reputation, and personal lives. Set in the highly
competitive New York literary world, her story illustrates the gains and
losses in store for the woman poet who sought validation as the protégée
and personal favorite of a powerful male critic.

This essay undertakes to demonstrate that Poe and Osgood were mutual admirers and literary allies from early 1845 until his death in October 1849. I will not speculate about whether they were lovers; unless
new evidence is discovered, physical intimacy cannot be proved or dis-
proved. Indeed, exactly what happened between them may never be
known. Most of the contemporaries who published their impressions of

31

the Poe-Osgood relationship did so after years had passed and for their own purposes. The letters that Osgood and Poe exchanged in 1845/1846 have been lost, and the consciously literary texts that they published as tributes and messages to one another give ambiguous and contradictory signals about the nature of their personal interaction. The ambiguity may have been deliberate, intended to tease one another, the reading public, or interested parties who wished to interfere; the inconsistency probably reflects a divergence in their motives and expectations as time went on and their relationship became a topic for gossip. The nineteenth-century record, then, reflects the prejudices and interests of the persons who wrote it, and most twentieth-century interpretations treat Osgood as if she existed only in relation to Poe.

But a careful reading of the surviving poems, critical notices, letters, and reminiscences reveals that Osgood and Poe assumed starring roles as patron and protégée. Dramatizing themselves as romantic hero and heroine, they advertised their literary and personal gifts; they promoted their own and one another's careers—first in the *Broadway Journal,* later in other magazines and collections of poetry. What the careful reader must bear in mind is that every text in their published dialogue, and every other word they wrote about one another and their relationship, contains an admixture of fiction: two complex, ambitious individuals were writing their romance as they lived it, and Osgood, at least, began revising her version even before the real-life story was over.

Osgood's literary career began long before she met Poe. She had been publishing poetry since her early teens; throughout the 1840s, she edited giftbooks and contributed poetry and short fiction to many literary annuals and leading periodicals.[3] Fond of recognition and gratified by editors' ready acceptance of her work, she presented herself socially and in her autobiographical writings as a high-minded woman inspired and empowered by love. Her childlike enthusiasm evoked protectiveness and affection. Most people found her apparently artless manners, graceful slenderness, large gray eyes, thick black hair, and pale oval face attractive, if not beautiful. She enjoyed amusing and surprising her friends; her playfulness was sometimes interpreted as indiscretion, but she laughed at warnings and asserted her feminine prerogative: "I revel in my right divine, / I glory in Caprice!"[4]

Her writings, especially her first-person poems, often have the sound of an authentic voice. Talented at articulating the thoughts of other persons, real and fictive, she also drew upon her own experience. Many poems were conceived as verse letters to friends, relatives, and fellow poets. Samuel Stillman Osgood, a portrait artist whom she married in

1835, was often absent from home while he painted and made social contacts that could lead to commissions. He carried on a flirtation in 1842, and the couple began living apart some time in 1844.[5] In December 1844 she published "Yes! 'lower to the level' / Of those who laud thee now," an address to an errant husband that ends by hinting that he would be welcome back in "Love's deserted bowers."[6] The heroine of Osgood's "Florence Errington: 'An O'er True Tale'" (February 1845) is a gray-eyed, gentle, misunderstood wife who fades away upon learning that her husband has been seeing another woman.[7] Friends recognized "Fanny" in these and other poems and stories by Osgood, for she used writing to define a self and communicate with others.

She generally enjoyed her reputation as an improvisatrice. In company she dashed off clever impromptus that she never bothered to revise. Though pleased by others' admiration of her facility, she occasionally verbalized a sense that she had not done her talents justice. In "To the Spirit of Poetry" (January 1845), the speaker admits having "wrong'd" the poetic altar with "the light offerings of an idler's mind." Announcing in "Aspirations" (June 1844) that she feels "a glorious power within," she dedicates herself and her "song" to higher purposes. Osgood's preface to her 1846 collection of poems asks for "that just and true criticism, whose praise and blame are alike valuable."[8] By the mid-1840s, then, despite the Victorian sanction against women who desired fame,[9] she seems to have harbored ambitions for literary achievement. Taught by marital and other personal conflicts that love could not shield her from pain, she found satisfaction in writing poems and stories that often had featured roles for versions of herself. Because many of her writings had personal significance, applause meant acceptance and felt like affection. Publication also offered a sense of accomplishment and autonomy, no doubt enhanced by the knowledge that she was better paid than many women poets.[10]

But admiration was as necessary to her as independence, and ultimately more necessary than literary distinction. When Samuel Osgood was afield, and when he was not, she exchanged visits and letters with other men. Her extramarital attachments have been explained in terms of her childlike unconventionality, hunger for attention, and design to win back her roving husband.[11] All of these explanations have some validity. Her history and writings as well as contemporaries' observations reveal Osgood's deep-seated need for others' sympathy—or, failing that, their acknowledgment of her right to be herself. Another fact often passed over by scholars who see her only as one of Poe's hangers-on is that she attracted several admirers who were able to further her career. For example, Hiram Fuller, a close friend in 1842/1843, published a book by her, *The Snow-drop* (1842). If Alice James made a career of invalidism, and Catharine Beecher fulfilled herself by advocating self-sacrifice, Osgood made a profession of being a protégée.

Not that she was a parasite or disciple: she made the most of opportunities offered by Lydia Maria Child, Sarah J. Hale, Caroline Norton, the English dramatist Sheridan Knowles, and others. By her early thirties she was regarded as a successful *poetess*—in contemporary terms, an artless songstress whose effusions gushed forth as naturally as bird song. The critics and public generally approved of "lady poets" who seemed modest and sincere, endorsed traditional morality, and neither meddled with politics nor evinced an unfeminine desire for fame. So long as she did not attempt to step out of her sphere, the reasonably competent woman poet received the special treatment that amounts to condescension. Aware of the delimitations of the poetess, yet aspiring to be taken seriously, Osgood was ready by early 1845 for a new, more powerful patron.

She knew that Edgar Allan Poe, New York's literary lion since the publication of "The Raven" in late January 1845, had noticed her work, for some of her writings were accepted by *Graham's Magazine* while he was on its editorial staff in 1841/1842; he praised her in the lecture on American poets and poetry he delivered in New York on 28 February 1845.[12] Osgood did not attend the lecture, but she let it be known that she valued his opinion. A mutual friend introduced them in early March 1845. As she told the story in 1850, Poe sought her out to ask what she thought of "The Raven." She recalled, "He greeted me calmly, gravely, almost coldly; yet with so marked an earnestness that I could not help being deeply impressed by it. From that moment until his death we were friends."[13]

During the next year she met Poe frequently at small private parties and at literary soirees. Observers recalled her wit, enthusiasm, and "infantile act" (as one critic put it) of sitting on a low stool and turning her face upward to the person whose attention she meant to engage—in particular, Edgar Poe. Her cheeks were wet with tears when he recited "The Raven,"[14] and she found his conversation fascinating: "[F]or hours I have listened to him, entranced by strains of such pure and almost celestial eloquence as I have never read or heard elsewhere."[15]

Soon after their first meeting, Osgood initiated the exchange generally known as their literary courtship by contributing lyrics to the *Broadway Journal*, a new literary weekly Poe and two other men were editing in early 1845. "Courtship" is both apt and misleading, for it focuses on sexual difference but has been intepreted to mean that Osgood needed to woo him in order to be published. Poe already admired her when she approached the *Journal*. But he did treat her contributions differently from those of his male friends and allies William Gilmore Simms, Thomas Holley Chivers, and Fitz-Greene Halleck. Exercising his privileges as editor and writer of literary notices for the *Journal*, he encouraged Osgood (and, as we shall see, one other woman poet) to submit amatory verse and poems complimentary to himself. Intent on making a name for herself—with the benefit of his expertise and power—Osgood willingly cooperated. Since both used the magazine for self- and mutual promotion, the texts they wrote to and about each other are not simply expressions of mutual attraction; they are more accurately called the earliest published evidence of a literary alliance.

On the basis of the poems he addressed to Osgood, Poe scholars have discounted his investment in their association.[16] The *Journal*'s accepting eleven of her poems has been taken as evidence that he rewarded her for courting him. That partial truth obscures a significant dimension of their pact. Poe brought more than poems to the exchange: he declared himself her patron by naming her more than twenty times in the *Journal* between March and December 1845.[17] On 5 April, for example, in a notice of the current *Graham's Magazine*, he singled her out for "contribut[ing] the best poem she has yet written—a more exquisitely graceful thing . . . we have rarely if ever seen."[18] Furthermore, no one has yet remarked that his placement of Osgood's poems in the *Journal* deliberately links his name with hers. His motives cannot be fully known, but in light of his passion for publicity and his sense of critical authority, it is safe to say that he believed his noticing her harmed neither the *Journal* nor his reputation as a critic. It follows that he meant what he said when he called her a talented writer capable of growth. I propose that he praised her work and used her contributions to promote not only her career but also his own poetry; himself as critic, patron, and romantic "hero"; and his fledgling magazine.

As for Osgood's contributions to the *Journal*, they have been deprecated as sentimental or flirtatious and read as direct expressions of her affection for Poe.[19] Her writings and actions in the years from 1845 to 1850 demonstrate that she indeed came to care about him. But her *Journal* poems, especially those published in early 1845, cannot be taken literally as love messages for him: not all of them are amatory; not all are spoken in her own person. For Osgood, writing itself was a kind of performance, and she reveled in drama as much as Poe did. She secured

his editorial attention by portraying wistful and admiring females that
Poe might, if he wished, take as representations of herself, and by casting him as a loved one, intimate friend, genius, and guide.

To date, however, only John E. Reilly has commented on the role-
playing in Osgood's *Journal* poems. He remarks, "It is apparent that
Mrs. Osgood has *distorted* her relationship with Poe in the interest of
exploiting its melodramatic potentialities, especially the potentialities of
her own role."[20] In her *Journal* publications, and certain later writings
meant both for Poe's eyes and for public perusal, she did exactly that.
Reilly implies that her strategy was reprehensible. To my knowledge,
no critic has suggested that Poe, the other principal player, was not
entitled to portray emotions he may not have felt or to "exploit" a role
and a promotional opportunity offered by another, essentially professional writer. Her "distortion" of their relationship can be profitably
viewed as a kind of fictionalizing that, in a canonized poet, would be
admiringly explicated—as Emily Dickinson's marriage fiction has
been. The compliments Poe and Osgood paid one another in the *Broadway Journal* in 1845 define their roles as patron and protégée, artist and
admirer—not the quality or depth of their emotions, which can only be
inferred after examining what they said, wrote, and did during a relationship spanning more than four years.

By 29 March, within a month of meeting Poe, she had already submitted two pseudonymous poems to the *Journal*. His complimentary
editorial acknowledgments, recognizing both "Kate Carol" and "Violet
Vane" as pen names, invite further contributions and attempt to pique
readers' curiosity about the identity of the evidently lovelorn poetesses
who were writing for the *Journal*.[21] As he and Osgood well knew, the
public enjoyed love songs and assumed that lady poets—rich in sensi-
bility but not in imaginative power—record what their hearts would
say. (Poe himself, reviewing Elizabeth Barrett in early 1845, had stated
that "a woman and her book are identical.")[22]

Three of the five Osgood poems published in the *Journal* in April and
May 1845—"The Rivulet's Dream," "Spring," and "To Lenore"—
portray the devastating effects of unrequited or wildly passionate love. It
should not be taken for granted that these lyrics are confessional. Although personal experience was a primary source of material for
Osgood, she was a practiced writer thoroughly familiar with popular literature. Of the three tragic-love lyrics, only "Spring" is spoken in the
first person, the form Osgood generally used for personal statements,
and its heartsick "I" could be anyone that readers—including Poe—

wanted her to be. "Love's Reply," the one lyric signed with Osgood's own name, is not concerned with romantic love. But the fifth, " 'So Let It Be': To ———," seems to invite being read as a bid for Poe's personal attention. The speaker reproves a man "bound by nearer ties" for treating her coldly. Asking for a life-giving smile, she argues that "the fair, fond girl . . . at [his] side" could not begrudge an innocent "Friendship."[23] The speaker presents herself as unattached (as Osgood was not) and tormented by memories of a shared past (Osgood had known Poe for a month when " 'So Let It Be' " was published on 5 April). Clearly a fictive character, she could be any unregarded woman; the addressee might be any married man. Still, because the poem suggests a Frances-Edgar-Virginia triangle, it has always titillated readers who assume that poetesses write from the heart—and scholars who know that the Poe-Osgood friendship eventually raised a scandal. Protected by her pseudonym Violet Vane, Osgood may have playfully sent " 'So Let It Be' " to the *Journal* to compliment Poe as a faithful husband—or as the romantic lead of a private drama. There is no telling how he interpreted it, but he certainly encouraged its author to submit more amatory verse.

In April and May he noticed Osgood three times—once as "the most truly graceful, delicate, and yet impassioned of American poetesses"[24]—and acknowledged her contributions with three poems of his own. On 26 April, in the same issue with the magazine's fourth compliment for Osgood's poetry, his lyric dedicated "To F——" and signed "E" compliments the "Beloved's" serenity, while his anonymous "Impromptu: To Kate Carol" treats Kate's poems and eyes as equally brilliant.[25] On 24 May a poem addressed "To ———" and signed "M." replies to " 'So Let It Be.' " Taking seriously Violet's need for his attention, the speaker suggests that although each has "found a life-long love" with someone else, they can enjoy a "pure" "Friendship."[26] Through their literary personae the two poets, whose identities were as yet unknown to most contemporary readers, seem to have agreed to be poetic and platonic "lovers."

From this point forward, however, encouraged by Poe's reception of her poems, Osgood began to weave a web of intertextuality and to hint at less ethereal love affairs. On 31 May appeared "To Lenore," which sketches a woman delicate as a Venetian chalice, shattered by passionate love. Osgood's last *Journal* publication that spring, it alludes to the heroines of "The Raven" and Poe's own "Lenore," whose opening line is "Ah, broken is the golden bowl!" She used the signature "Clarice" to protect her identity while paying tribute to Poe as the poet of lost love. He recognized the compliment and evidently wanted others to know who had paid it: while reviewing Osgood's *Poems* in the *Journal* in December, he devoted about 10 percent of his space to quoting and assessing "To Lenore" (a poem he considered faulty)—thus subtly advertising two of his own favorite works and calling attention to his influence on his protégée.[27]

Osgood is unrepresented and unnamed in the June and July issues of the *Journal,* though her publication in monthly periodicals in the summer and fall of 1845 suggests that she was not idle. She spent part of the summer with friends in Providence, possibly so that she, or Poe, or both, could reassess their alliance. By midsummer their increasingly complex friendship was common knowledge. "Poe was enamored of her," recalled one acquaintance, "or fancied that he was, which with him was the same thing."[28] At the end of June Poe drunkenly confided to a Southern visitor that he was caught up in " 'the d——dst amour you ever knew a fellow to be in' " with the wife of a painter who was often away from home. A few days later, he firmly denied involvement in any love affair—but asked his friend not to tell Virginia and her mother, Mrs. Clemm, that he was accepting Osgood's invitation to visit her in Providence.[29]

Osgood's view of the relationship evidently changed as well, for she began to portray characters that the public could interpret as representations of herself and Poe. Rumors abounded after her story "Ida Grey" appeared in the August number of *Graham's.* Ida, like several of her fictive heroines, is fondly characterized as a childlike coquette, who was "sent into the world to be happy and beautiful—'only that and nothing more.' " Eighteen months after her husband dies, Ida is sought out by a married man whom she immediately recognizes as a soul-mate, despite his initial reserve. She writes in her journal: "We spoke but a few formal words, and then we parted—parted! ah no! we shall never part again! Our souls are one forever! . . . cold and careless as he seems, he loves me—or *will* love me! . . . I do not care to see him again in this world. It is better not, for his earthly nature is another's." The next journal entry reveals that her ideal lover has declared his passion: "How perfectly already he sees into my soul. He understands, he appreciates me as no one else does or can. . . . He bids me tell him that I love him, as proudly as if he had a right, an unquestionable, an undoubted, *a divine right* to demand my love." In a poem written shortly before retiring to a convent, Ida imagines the bliss that might have been theirs, had they but met sooner:

How had I knelt hour after hour beside thee,
  When from thy lips the rare, scholastic lore
Fell on the soul that all but deified thee,
  While at each pause, I, childlike, prayed for more.[30]

Ida's poem ends with a renunciation of improper love in favor of a heavenly union. This was Osgood's first treatment of the soul-mate theme that she would later use to explain her relationship with Poe.

Despite the veil of fiction, there are obvious similarities between Ida's affair and Osgood's own history, part of it published in her avowedly autobiographical writings. Her 1850 account of her initial meeting with Poe reads like a revision of Ida's journal, itself a version of that same encounter. Alerted by the quotation "'only that and nothing more,'" contemporaries could also have associated Ida's "rare, scholastic lore" with the "quaint and curious volume of forgotten lore" pored over by the bereaved narrator of "The Raven." Poe, not adverse to advertising his celebrated poem or himself as an intellectual and an almost irresistible lover, complimented "Ida Grey" in the *Journal* for 16 August as "a tale of passion, exceedingly well written, by Mrs. Osgood."[31]

Surely aware by late summer of the gossip about her, she nevertheless resumed contributing to the *Journal*. Osgood was no fool, but she evidently believed that a woman as popular and respected as she could do no wrong. Prepared to have her lyrics read as personal statements, she signed her own name to all six of her poems published in the *Journal* during the last four months of 1845. Two of those poems clearly indicated that Poe was her subject or addressee. Poe himself placed other Osgood lyrics not thus marked so that they, too, would be perceived as compliments for him.

By 12 July he had become the *Journal*'s literary editor; as of 25 October, sole editor and proprietor. In the last five months of 1845 he printed nine poems bearing on his relationship with Osgood and the interference of other people. The physical placement of poems now becomes significant. Within three weeks of his gaining control of the magazine, each issue began with a poem, frequently a selection that promoted Poe or one of his friends. The first woman poet to occupy the position of honor was Osgood. On 30 August, directly under the masthead containing Poe's name, and above his own "William Wilson," appeared her signed poem "Slander," which develops the idea that a cruel "whisper" has broken the heart of "that guileless girl so pure and true."[32] This victim could be anyone, or Virginia Poe, or Frances Osgood as wronged wife and maligned platonic lover. Many years later, an acquaintance recalled that Osgood's "supposed intrigue [with Poe] became the town talk, at least among literary people," and that the gossip made Poe's mother-in-law suspicious of her.[33]

Unwilling to end the exchange of compliments, Osgood proceeded as if there could be no legitimate objection to their association. "Echo-Song," which Poe printed over her name on the front page of the 6 September *Journal,* was hardly calculated to silence wagging tongues. The speaker teasingly claims intimate knowledge of

> . . . a noble heart that beats
> For one it loves how "wildly well!"
> *I* only know for *whom* it beats;
> But I must never tell!
> ....
> I know a voice that falters low,
> Whene'er one little name 't would say;
> Full well that little name I know,
> But that I'll ne'er betray![34]

Again, "I" could be anyone, as could the owner and the beloved of that "noble heart." Printed over a pseudonym or in another magazine, "Echo-Song" would have occasioned little comment. But interpretation has always been shaped by the poem's placement in the *Journal* and its quotation from "Israfel," which Poe had reprinted on 26 July. Poet and editor conspired to tease readers into wondering whether the "low" voice was Poe's (contemporaries so described it) and the "little name" was "Fanny."

One week later, as if in response to "Echo-Song," Poe printed an ambiguous stanza affirming that the addressee is lovable, but suggesting that she offers to do something out of character:

> Thou wouldst be loved?—then let thy heart
> From its present pathway part not!
> Being everything which now thou art,
> Be nothing which thou art not!

The quatrain is unsigned, but its title, "To F——," appears one-quarter inch below the signature to one of his own tales.[35] Osgood's identity was made even clearer when he included the eight-line version of "Thou wouldst be loved?" in *The Raven and Other Poems* (published 19 November 1845) under the title "To F——s S. O——d."[36]

She may have received the stanza as a veiled request for discretion, for no new work of hers appeared in Poe's *Journal* for the next eleven weeks, and the magazine published no more of her amatory lyrics. In the meanwhile, Poe mentioned or complimented her eight times, once as "the most graceful of American poetesses,"[37] and reprinted two of her poems from other periodicals. During the same interval, however, he also began to notice the writings of translator, talewriter, and poet Elizabeth F. Ellet (1818–1877). She is mentioned or complimented eight times between 20 September and 1 November, six of these times in the same notice with Osgood. The two women had been aware of one another as writers since both contributed to Sarah J. Hale's *Ladies' Magazine* in the 1830s; they were personally acquainted in the 1840s when Ellet joined the same New York literary circle frequented by Osgood and Poe. Eventually, Osgood would say that Ellet had contrived to meet Poe;[38] he would assert that he had scornfully rejected Ellet's love;[39] both recognized her as a purveyor of gossip about their association. In late 1845 Poe was promoting two widely published women who had sought his attention. Osgood could hardly have failed to notice that the *Journal*'s lead poems for 4 October and 1 November were written by Ellet, a woman accomplished in more genres than she was.

Poe continued to act as Osgood's patron, however, announcing her forthcoming *Poems* and *The Flower Alphabet* in August, September, and November.[40] He also took more than one opportunity that fall to emphasize her interest in him, meanwhile portraying their relationship— more specifically, himself—as innocent. On 22 November, directly under a tale signed "Edgar A. Poe," he printed Osgood's signed poem "To———," which began, "Oh! they never can know that heart of thine, / Who dare accuse *thee* of flirtation!" The text suggests a female addressee: line 7 refers to "your beauty and grace." When Poe quoted this poem in his "Literati" sketch of Osgood (September 1846), he restored—or affixed—the title "To Sarah," thus dissociating it from the "courtship" sequence at a time when scandal was buzzing around his ears. But its *Journal* placement, just below his name in the first column, prompted readers to interpret it as a message for him. Perhaps he was indeed the intended addressee: Osgood delighted in complimenting friends, and she was not the only contemporary to comment on his "beautiful" head and graceful manners. But most readers would not interpret this text as an exoneration of Poe if he had not invited them to do so. At the bottom of the second column of the same page is a sonnet by William Gilmore Simms, one of his literary allies, that would have fit neatly into the space occupied by Osgood's twelve-line "Oh! they never can know that heart of thine."[41] Indeed, in every issue with a signed poem by Osgood, there is at least one other poem of comparable length; of the seven signed Osgood lyrics, five border on a tale signed by Poe or introduced as his. Her poems were not just printed in the *Journal*—they were placed.

A sonnet by Ellet leads off the 29 November issue, followed by one of Poe's tales. Again, directly below his signature is a signed Osgood poem titled "To———." Her epigraph—"In Heaven a spirit doth dwell, / Whose heart-strings are a lute"—and reference to "Heaven's poet, Israfel" clearly identify the addressee of these lines: "I cannot tell *the world* how thrills my heart / To every touch that flies thy lyre along."[42] She eulogized his artistry in order to reaffirm their alliance, now that Ellet had stepped forward. Perhaps she was imprudent, but she did not ask to have her "honor" impugned: if the poem were not signed "Frances S. Osgood," it would be taken for a fan letter, not a love note. As if with deliberate irony, Poe this time placed his work—his literary self—between Ellet's and Osgood's contributions. Both writers were paying court to him, acknowledging his power, supplying copy, and helping to sell magazines. By placing Osgood's compliment directly under his signature, he purposely emphasized that his name belonged in the blank in her title.

Ellet—characterized as "ambition incarnate"[43]—had been watching Osgood's performance and decided to emerge from the wings. Her "Co-quette's Song," beginning "Ah yes—gentle sir—I will own / I ne'er saw perfection till now" stands at the head of the 13 December issue.[44] Next comes "The Oblong Box," signed by Poe, then Osgood's "A Ship-wreck," a protest against his replacing her as the leading woman poet of the *Broadway Journal:*

> I launched a bark on Fate's deep tide—
> A frail and fluttering toy,
> But freighted with a thousand dreams
> Of beauty and of joy.
> ....
> And you, who should its pilot be—
> To whom in fear it flies—
> Forsake it, on a treacherous sea,
> To seek a prouder prize.[45]

The addressee might be anyone—but the "you" of stanza three appears only two inches under Poe's printed name, as if he wanted the poem read as a compliment to his power as critic and editor, his influence as patron. That "Shipwreck" was meant for him is likely. Osgood had portrayed her poetry-writing self as a bark in "Aspirations," and other writings support the identification of this "pilot" as her current patron. She braved the dangers of amplified whispers to remind him publicly of the arrangement that was to link their names for mutual enhancement. By contemporary standards, she was already a successful writer, but her depiction of him as her career guide was not mere fiction. He praised her work in his public lectures, he encouraged her to develop her talents, and the *Broadway Journal* under his direction noticed and printed her writings more than thirty times. No wonder she regarded her understudy, Ellet—who now had four lead poems to her own two, and had been gossiping about her and Poe—as a threat.

Osgood's "To 'The Lady Geraldine,' " on the first page of the 20 December *Journal*, rebukes Ellet for feigning friendship and then slandering her.[46] Ellet's rejoinder, which opens the 27 December issue, righteously exhorts her to value the suffering that will "keep [her] safe for heaven."[47] Their mutual accusations and competition for position in the *Journal* abruptly halted when Poe's control of the magazine ended with the 27 December issue, but their hostility persisted. Largely because of Ellet's efforts to displace Osgood, within the next few months each woman faced, in her own way, the consequences of having her name linked with Poe's.

During the year of Osgood's personal association with him, she called on the Poes at home, sometimes at Virginia's "pressing invitation." Periodically absent from New York to avoid the city's heat and to visit relatives (or, as she told Griswold in 1850, to escape Edgar's importunities), she corresponded with him "in accordance with the earnest entreaties of his wife," who believed that Osgood had "a restraining and beneficial effect" on him. She recalled his letters as "divinely beautiful."[48] At least one of her own was sufficiently unconventional to raise fears of scandal. Their correspondence, probably destroyed by 1850, had more serious effects on their personal reputations than did their public exchange in the *Broadway Journal*.[49]

Poe shared his correspondence with his wife and mother-in-law. According to Elizabeth Oakes Smith (1806–1893), an active member of New York's literary coteries, one day when Virginia and Frances were laughing together over a fond letter Poe had received, its writer—Elizabeth F. Ellet—unexpectedly stopped by. Recognizing her own words being read aloud, "she walked into the room and snatched [the letter] from their hands. There would have been a scene with any other woman, but they were both very sweet and gentle, and there the matter ended."[50] But the matter of Poe's extramarital relationships had hardly begun: Ellet concluded that "feminine" passivity would leave intact his power over women's reputations.

In early 1846, during another visit to Virginia Poe, Ellet saw a letter to Edgar whose contents she construed as damaging to the writer, Osgood. Assuming the duty of protecting Osgood's name, Ellet somehow persuaded her (pregnant with Fanny Fay, born 28 June 1846) that she must retrieve her correspondence.[51] Literary hostess Anne C. Lynch and Margaret Fuller were dispatched to ask for Osgood's letters. Poe handed them over, but, enraged at female interference, blurted out that Ellet had better think about her own incriminating letters. According to him, immediately upon the departure of the Osgood deputation he was ashamed of his unchivalrous outburst; he collected Ellet's letters and "with [his] own hands left them at the door."[52] Now bent on vengeance as well as vindication, Ellet commissioned her brother, William Lummis, to challenge Poe either to return her letters (which she claimed had never existed) or to retract the slander. Poe having replied that he could do neither, Lummis advised the poet to arm himself. His attempt to borrow a pistol from a journalist developed into a quarrel that led to a newspaper war, and eventually to Poe's suing the *New York Evening Mirror* for libel.[53] Virginia was tormented in her last year by anonymous letters alleging that her husband and Osgood were adulterers. Convinced that Ellet was responsible, Poe later told another woman whose esteem he valued that "the *only* thing for which [he] found it impossible to forgive Mrs. O. was her reception of Mrs. E." and that "on her death-bed [Virginia] declared that Mrs. E. had been her murderer."[54] The valentine poem Virginia sent her husband on 14 February 1846 expressed her wish to share a cottage with him, "Removed from the world with its sin and care / And the tattling of many tongues."[55]

He had composed a valentine of his own. Recklessly, or perversely, or to tell Osgood that he still cared about her and her reputation, he sent a poem to Anne Lynch's Saint Valentine's Day party for 1846. It begins:

> For her these lines are penned, whose luminous eyes,
> Bright and expressive as the stars of Leda,
> Shall find her own sweet name that, nestling, lies
> Upon this page, enwrapped from every reader.

Poe teased readers to guess whose name is concealed in the verse: "A musical name oft uttered in the hearing / Of poets, by poets—for the name is a poet's too." A week later, this puzzle poem appeared in the *Evening Mirror,* and in March 1849 Poe published it in two magazines to which Osgood contributed. One of them printed a key: "Frances Sargent Osgood" is spelled out by the first letter of the first line, the second of the second line, the third letter of the third line, and so on. Rufus W. Griswold (1815–1857) included "For her these lines are penned" in the second volume (January 1850) of his edition of Poe's works, along with instructions for deciphering it.[56] Griswold had become Osgood's close friend and patron by early 1849, so she must, at some point, have learned that the valentine was for her.

But, unnerved at last by unwelcome publicity, she stopped meeting Poe early in 1846. Samuel Osgood, who had returned to their New York lodgings by mid-February, demanded that Ellet write an apology for gossiping about his wife and Poe. To ward off a libel suit, Ellet did so, nevertheless attempting to lay the blame elsewhere:

> The letter shown me by Mrs Poe *must have* been a forgery, and any man capable of offering to show notes he never possessed, would not, I think, hesitate at such a crime. Had you seen the fearful paragraphs which Mrs Poe first repeated and afterwards pointed out—which haunted me night and day like a terrifying spectre—you would not wonder I regarded you as I did. . . . [Neither] of us [has] anything to apprehend from the verbal calumnies of a wretch so steeped in infamy as he is now.[57]

Poe was indeed in disgrace, and he had to deal with it while Virginia was obviously nearing death.

Even after their personal association ended, however, he and Osgood spoke well of one another and showed interest in each other's work, reputation, and welfare. They *were* friends, and, by then, the personal reputation of each was partly dependent on the "good name" of the other. In "The Literati of New York" (September 1846) he portrayed her not only as a promising writer but also a wife and mother, even mentioning her daughters Ellen and May (but not Fanny Fay). Still taking credit as her patron, he noted that some of her poems had first appeared in the *Broadway Journal.*[58] Still willing to be known as his friend and admirer, she continued using poetry to communicate, to idealize spiritual love, and to interpret herself.

With "Ida's Farewell" (June 1846), she began to leave a public record of what her bond with Poe had meant to her. The speaker painfully envisions life without her beloved:

No more thy pen of fire shall pour to charm me,
The poet-passion of thy fervent vow!

We part for ever! Proud shall be the story
Of hearts that hid affection fond as ours.

She consoles herself that through honoring "hallow'd duty" on earth they will be united in Paradise, "where love will be no wrong": the soul mate's "rare, gorgeous fantasies" will raise up "rich palaces mid wondrous scenes," while her "tender, timid" words call forth "a fair bower."[59] In just sixty-four lines Osgood complimented Poe's genius, evoked images of his fantastic castles, affirmed and claimed credit for her own fidelity as wife and friend, and served notice that she and Poe had honorably parted. Such published fantasies of pure sympathy also served other purposes: conveying to Poe that she still admired and cared for him, thus "keeping" him as friend and patron—but at virtuous arm's length.

She was concerned about the damage her personal reputation had suffered. Poetess Kate Carol, narrator of "Glimpses of a Soul" (February 1847), explains her reserve in literary society by saying that she is her best self only among people "who seem to love [her]." And, speaking for Osgood, Kate claims that her amatory lyrics are purely fanciful: "I am forever singing to myself impromptu love-songs, from imaginary damsels to imaginary youths."[60] Osgood's works indeed are not all and only autobiographical, yet this very sketch is typical of her self-dramatization. No longer naive enough to suppose that she could publish her fantasies, live by idiosyncratic standards, and still keep everyone's respect and affection, she sought to rebuild a social identity and reaffirm her right to be herself.

"Life in New York: A Sketch of a Literary Soiree" (March 1847) is another attempt to reinstate herself—on her own terms. The narrator describes the " 'grotesque and arabesque' " and the stately personages attending a salon; she dwells on one "capricious" but attractive woman who defends in herself what others call coquetry: "V——" (for Violet?) is searching an imperfect world for the ideal love her soul requires.[61] Osgood had been writing sympathetically about coquettes for years, and would continue to do so, but the subject took on new meaning after she had been scorched by scandal. Her deliberate allusion to *Tales of the Grotesque and Arabesque* is not just a compliment to Poe. It also expresses an impulse to declare that if he was her master, that did not mean she was his mistress.

Some time after Virginia died on 30 January 1847, Poe called on Osgood and, according to her brother-in-law, tried to persuade her to elope with him.[62] Upon her refusal they parted, never to see each other again. The Osgoods reconciled by mid-1847, but Frances did not stop writing poems that Poe could interpret as expressions of her regard for him. She may even have determined to divert his and the public's attention from the other literary women he was seeing in his last years.

In Providence with Poe in July 1845, she had offered to introduce him to Sarah Helen Power Whitman (1803–1878); she and Lynch forwarded to him the complimentary poem Helen Whitman addressed to him at Lynch's Saint Valentine's Day party in 1848. Upon seeing Whitman's "Oh! thou grim and ancient Raven" in the *Home Journal,* she wrote the Providence poet inquiring whether Poe had visited her and warning her—perhaps playfully—of his eloquence.[63] Having heard of the Whitman-Poe engagement, she called on Poe's fiancée in November 1848, revealing her "mingled joy & sorrow" at the news. Whitman later recalled Osgood's highly emotional declarations of "unchanged & unchanging interest in him & his best welfare." Osgood asked many questions about the poems and letters he had sent Whitman and "seemed almost incredulous" when told of his ten-page letters: "She said his letters to her were all very brief, were in fact mere notes filled with expressions of devoted friendship & admiration, but very brief." Whitman also remembered telling Poe "all that Mrs. Osgood had said in his praise"[64] and acceding to her request to pass along to him "many things which she said to me during that interview although I knew well that the tendency of these communications would be to increase her influence over him & consequently to weaken my own."[65]

If Whitman's observations and memory were accurate, Osgood's surprise that Poe would write longer letters to a Rhode Island widow whom he wished to marry than he had written to herself—a wife and mother whom he saw frequently in New York—shows her resistance to the idea that he could form new alliances. Her treatment of Whitman suggests not only a conscious determination to convey that she was not Poe's mistress, but also a partly conscious purpose to remain and be acknowledged as the woman uniquely important in his life.

Her "Lines from an Unpublished Drama" (January 1849) begins, " 'A friend,' Are you a friend? No, by my soul!" The speaker demands acknowledgment of her (or his) absolute loyalty, despite appearances to the contrary, and declaims:

> If *I* be not more than *all* worlds to you,
> I will not stoop to *less!* I will have all—
> Your proudest, purest, noblest, loftiest love—
> Your perfect trust—your soul of soul—or nothing!
> ....
> Speak! do we part? or are we *one* for ever?[66]

Presented as a dramatic monologue, this poem might be addressed, as the title suggests, to a fellow fictive character. It can be taken for an address to or by Osgood's husband. But some of its phrases recall "Ida Grey," "'So Let It Be,'" and "Ida's Farewell." Because of these echoes, or because Osgood was reproducing an actual conversation or letter, Poe took the poem personally. In late 1848 he told Whitman that he had seen a manuscript poem addressed to him and soon to be published in the *Metropolitan Magazine*.[67] The Whitman-Poe engagement was broken in late December, and by mid-January 1849 he could assure his new friend Nancy ("Annie") Richmond, "From this day forth I shun the pestilential society of *literary women*. They are a heartless, unnatural, venomous, dishonorable *set,* with no guiding principle but inordinate self-esteem. Mrs. [Osgood] is the *only* exception I know."[68] In June he sent Mrs. Richmond some poems, including "lines to me (or rather about me) by Mrs. O——in which she *imagines me writing to her*."[69] Whether he considered himself the speaker or the addressee of Osgood's "Lines" to a soul-mate, it is clear that he perceived the monologue as part of a drama in which he had a leading role—and that Osgood's poem affected his other relationships.

Meanwhile, Ellet—by then at war with Osgood's new patron, Griswold—had resumed her gossip.[70] Osgood responded with "To a Slandered Poetess" (March 1849), which exhorts the addressee, a version of herself, to dismiss slander as a base expression of "pigmies'" envy: "You must have *stooped* your haughty heart, / Oh, willful, wayward child!—to feel it."[71] Evident once again is Osgood's penchant for role playing: she sometime spoke as herself, sometimes to herself, sometimes in the voice of a "supposed person," as Emily Dickinson characterized her own literary persona. In scorning her detractors she was, of course, justifying herself—and, more subtly, exonerating Poe as well as any other man whose name was linked with hers. She had good reason to believe that someone in the small literary world would call Poe's attention to her second poem about mean-minded Slander (this time personified as female). He probably saw it, for it appears in the same issue of *Sartain's Union Magazine* as his valentine for her.

His comments on Osgood in the April and August 1849 issues of the

Southern Literary Messenger are open letters, if not replies, to the "slandered poetess" who wrote "Lines from an Unpublished Drama." In his "Marginalia" for April he attempted to define her "grace" and called her *"the first of American poetesses,"* adding, "Yet we must judge her less by what she has done than by what she shows ability to do."[72] Ignoring Whitman's conciliatory "Lines" in the June *Messenger,* he reiterated in the August issue his confidence in Osgood's potential but predicted that she would never reach it: "mere fame" did not interest her—a naturally graceful singer, not a disciplined artist. The implied criticism is softened by his statements that there was already too much "uncongenial ambition and pretence" among writers and that she had recently shown greater depth. For the third time in his four reviews of Osgood, he remarked that in failing to collect her poems, she was careless of her literary reputation; for the third time, he ambiguously excused her amateurism while indicating that she might be an artist if she cared to be.[73]

Poe approved of her aspirations and wanted her to validate his favorable estimate of her potential. He enjoyed his power to shape literary reputations. Exercising his critical prerogatives to correct public taste and discover new talent, he denigrated popular favorites Henry Wadsworth Longfellow and Lydia Huntley Sigourney as unoriginal and encouraged far less famous poets as promising: Anne C. Lynch, Thomas Holley Chivers, Susan Archer Talley, Philip Pendelton Cooke, and Mary E. Hewitt. While courting Whitman, he offered to make her a literary "queen," his consort in "the sole unquestionable aristocracy— that of intellect."[74] Urged by poverty and obligations incurred by his mother-in-law, he even puffed the affluent Sarah Anna Lewis, whose poems he despised.[75] By turns generous and arrogant, according to the demands of his ego and critical conscience, he promoted, castigated, and condescended to American poets in the name of developing an estimable national literature.

Cultivating a reputation as an analytical, independent critic, he made enemies. But his patronage and constructive criticism were sought after—not just by unknowns but also by rising stars and established writers, many of them women. Male patrons had considerable power in the 1840s, for there were many women who "sang" but few who wrote reviews (Margaret Fuller, the only one taken seriously as a critic, paid little attention to American women's poetry, and Sarah J. Hale was a high priestess of noble womanhood, not literature); it was far more prestigious to publish in literary and intellectual magazines than in periodicals specifically for "the ladies"; reputations resting solely on magazine verse were ephemeral; publishers were not eager to invest in books of poetry by unknowns; and, because "ladies" were not supposed to understand the business of authorship, for a woman poet to put herself forward was not only improper but virtually impossible. Poe's four-year critical fidelity to Osgood heightened her celebrity, though not exactly to her liking, for she intended to link their names in ways favorable to both, if possible—but certainly to herself.

The flickering flame of Osgood's literary ambition may have been rekindled by Poe's qualified expression of confidence in her potential, for she evidently saw both of his notices of her published in the last year of his life. In a letter of 23 April 1849, she mentioned an item about her work in "the 'Southern Literary Magazine,'" probably the *Messenger*.[76] In an undated letter to her sister May, written shortly after learning that her "friend"—"The Author of the Raven"—had died on 7 October 1849, she recalled, "Half an hour before I heard of his death I was reading with much emotion a later critique of his upon my poems—a most kind & beautiful one."[77] This stirring critique must have been his review in the August *Southern Literary Messenger*. Finally convinced that she should publish another book if her name were to live, she prepared a collection of her poetry that fall, as Poe had urged her to do. Her health was failing, and she became concerned about her personal as well as her literary reputation.

Her desire to be regarded as thoroughly respectable is evident in the statements about Poe she prepared for his biographer Rufus Griswold. Shortly before her death she sketched her reminiscences of Poe, portraying him not as her patron but as "that stray child of Poetry and Passion." Conceding his reputation for irregular behavior, she blamed other women for problems they had with Poe by asserting that he invariably behaved well toward well-behaved women. During the year when he sought her "counsel and kindness," he "never spoke irreverently of any women save one, and then only in *my* defense." Having taken her cut at Ellet, she assumed a sisterly tone as she recalled the Poes' domestic life and their "charming love and confidence"—"always delightfully apparent" to Osgood, despite the "many little poetical episodes" he allowed himself. She called Virginia "the only woman whom he ever truly loved" and urged that his last ballad, "Annabel Lee," does not "illustrate a late love affair" but rather commemorates his "lost and loved and unforgotten wife."[78]

Stepping out of her accustomed roles as admirer and protégée, she had set herself a complex rhetorical task: maintaining her virtue without seeming to argue the point; counteracting rumors that affected her reputation as well as Poe's; and minimizing his "late love affairs," thereby reasserting her own uniqueness as the true friend. Her success was remarkably complete. Her personal relationship with Poe has generally been portrayed as intense but not overtly sexual, and many readers have accepted her interpretation of "Annabel Lee," disregarding various claimants' insistence that Poe wrote it for them and despite the commonsense objection that a love ballad need not refer to any particular love.[79] Whether she expected Griswold to publish verbatim her final version of the Osgood-Poe romance is unknown. She did not live to see it in print.

But a letter she wrote Griswold in 1850 reveals both her dread of being remembered as the woman who had pursued Edgar Allen Poe and her hope that Griswold—her new "pilot" as well as Poe's literary executor—would silence her critics. She mentioned letters (now lost) by Virginia and Edgar that would "fully establish [her] innocence in a court of justice." Still stung by the consequences of her romantic friendship, she asserted that both of the Poes had begged her to be affectionate with Edgar, and declared:

> I wish the simple truth to be known,—that he sought me, not I him. It is too cruel that I, the only one of those literary women who did not seek his acquaintance,—for Mrs. Ellet asked an introduction to him and followed him everywhere, Miss Lynch begged me to bring him there and called upon him at his lodgings, Mrs. Whitman besieged him with valentines and letters long before he wrote or took any notice of her, and all the others wrote poetry and letters to him,—it is too cruel that I should be singled out after his death as the only victim to suffer from the slander of his mother.[80]

Unable to let go of the idea that the public could be persuaded of her innocence, she assumed the unwonted role of victim and exaggerated Whitman's aggressiveness. There was no question of Poe's loving Lynch or Ellet, and Whitman was both a painstaking writer and an intellectual.

Griswold did not publish that letter. He had no interest in publicizing Poe's popularity with literary women, and he did not want to enhance Osgood's reputation. They became friends during the late 1840s; by early 1849, she had placed her career in his hands. Eager to demonstrate her status as an esteemed poetess, Griswold proposed an opulent illustrated collection of her poems and worked with her in selecting and

arranging them. He reported that she set little value on most of her
" 'Miscellaneous Verses' " and wanted to " 'get them out of the way' " so
that she could write " 'MY POEM,' " an extended work that " 'the public' " would not forget. She "lingered, with subdued and tearful joy,"
over great literary works—but she was not ambitious.[81] His inconsistency suggests discomfort with her attitude about her career. The dominant culture, whose values had shaped and been shaped by Griswold as
critic, editor, and anthologist, prescribed that a "true woman" does not
seek worldly renown. But Osgood's own poetic statements of aspirations, requests for constructive criticism, relationships with patrons who
could further her interests, and collection of her fugitive pieces while
she was ill argue that she was not without ambition.

She dedicated her *Poems,* published in December 1849, to Griswold.
But she placed at the end of the volume two poems inspired by her relationship with Poe: "I Know a Noble Heart That Beats" (the "Echo-
Song" of 1845) and "The Hand That Swept the Sounding Lyre" (an el-
egy whose refrain echoes the "nevermore" of his most famous work).
For the last time she asserted her right to admire him. Suppressing any
resentment he felt at playing bookends with a dead rival, Griswold promoted her collection and often visited her sickroom. After she died on
12 May 1850, he quoted her sketch of Edgar and Virginia in his widely
read Poe memoir, which secured for her an equivocal kind of immortality as Poe's sympathetic friend and admirer—supporting roles after all.

Griswold meant to have the last word on both his protégée and her
former patron. His sketch "Frances Sargent Osgood," published three
times before he died, portrays its subject as an innocent, sympathetic
person "exquisitely sensible to applause." She wrote as naturally as she
conversed, "simply in conformity to a law of her existence." He asserted that some of her emotionally charged songs are narrated by personae, whereas others—those proceeding from "the mother's heart,"
for example—are pure expressions of personal feeling. Griswold's Osgood was graceful, spontaneous, tasteful, not ambitious except to touch
others' hearts: by mid-Victorian standards, quintessentially feminine.
Unlike Poe, who encouraged her to transcend amateurism, Griswold
maintained that she had already attained immortality by virtue of her
"womanly" genius.[82]

But her fame withered with her generation. It was Griswold's idea of
her, not Poe's ideal for her, that prevailed—evidently with Osgood
herself and certainly with her public and with literary historians. Fatally
ill with consumption by age thirty-eight, she never got around to acting
on Poe's advice and her own intermittent impulse to commit herself to

art. Accustomed to applause as a natural "singer," she may have been incapable of disciplined revision and more selective publication, ambivalent about relinquishing her claim on "feminine" spontaneity. Winning immediate admiration as a charming woman and "sweet poetess" finally meant more to her than earning artistic distinction. She played the role of "lady poet" for all it was worth.

Her choice was temporarily rewarded, but, like many women, she paid for the exposure gained through her association with powerful men. She suffered from malicious gossip, some of it actually meant to discredit her patrons, and expended energy in rivalries with women who might have become her allies. Her literary talent received less attention than her feminine charm. Later generations of critics considered her personal attributes and conduct and a few of her love songs important only as evidence of Poe's predilection for delicately beautiful women. Like Ellet, Whitman, Lynch, and Lewis—other contestants for the male-conferred title of literary queen—she became known for her cameo appearance in "The Life and Loves of Edgar Allan Poe." It is no small irony that Osgood herself had written and revised part of the text for that long-playing romantic drama.

Notes

I have learned much from Professor G. A. Oman's insightful commentary on early drafts of this essay.

1. See my article, "Her Fair Fame: The Reputation of Frances Sargent Osgood, Woman Poet," in *Studies in the American Renaissance, 1987* ed. Joel Myerson (Charlottesville: University Press of Virginia, 1987).

2. Buford Jones and Kent Ljungquist, "Poe, Mrs. Osgood, and 'Annabel Lee,'" in *Studies in the American Renaissance, 1983*, ed. Joel Myerson (Charlottesville: University Press of Virginia, 1983), 275–280; John Evangelist Walsh, *Plumes in the Dust: The Love Affair of Edgar Allen Poe and Fanny Osgood* (Chicago: Nelson Hall, 1980). Walsh establishes that a liaison could have occurred but not that Poe fathered Osgood's third child, Fanny Fay.

3. J. G. Varner, "Frances Sargent Locke Osgood," in *Notable American Women, 1607–1950*, ed. Edward T. James, 3 vols. (Cambridge: Harvard University Press, 1971), 2:653–655.

4. "Caprice," *Graham's Magazine* 28 (February 1846):71. The sketch of Osgood is based on accounts by contemporaries Elizabeth Oakes Smith, 7 November 1855 journal entry, quoted in Mary Alice Wyman, *Two American Pioneers: Seba Smith and Elizabeth Oakes Smith* (New York: Columbia University Press, 1927), 123; Oakes Smith, "Autobiographic Notes," *Beadle's Monthly* 3 (January 1867):30, 33; Richard Henry Stoddard, "Mrs. Botta and Her Friends,"

Independent, 1 February 1894, 17; and Edgar Allan Poe, "Frances S. Osgood," in *Complete Works of Edgar Allan Poe,* ed. James A. Harrison, 17 vols. (New York: Thomas Y. Crowell, 1902), 15:94–105.

5. *Collected Works of Edgar Allan Poe: Poems,* ed. Thomas Ollive Mabbott, 3 vols. (Cambridge: Harvard University Press, 1969), 1:556 n. 4; Walsh, *Plumes,* 113–115.

6. *Poems* (New York: Clark, Austin, 1846), 223–224.

7. *Graham's Magazine* 26 (February 1845):54.

8. *Poems* (1846), 15; 131, 133, [5]. See also "Glimpses of a Soul—No. III," which deprecates "newspaper *puffs* and drawing room flattery" and praises "candid" criticism (*Illustrated Magazine* 3 [1847]:235).

9. Cheryl Walker, *The Nightingale's Burden: Women Poets and American Culture before 1900* (Bloomington: Indiana University Press, 1982), 34–37.

10. On remuneration of poets, see *Passages from the Correspondence and Other Papers of Rufus W. Griswold,* ed. W. M. Griswold (Cambridge, Mass.: W. M. Griswold, 1898), 134, 152.

11. Osgood as coquette and Osgood as Eve are omnipresent in Poe scholarship. The influential T. O. Mabbott saw her as a flirt who used men (*Collected Works,* 1:556–557). Walsh argues in *Plumes* that she initially turned to Poe in hopes of becoming a serious writer but that the two became lovers. Elizabeth Oakes Smith recalled her as "unjustly traduced by those who could not appreciate the purity of her heart" (journal entry for 7 November 1855), quoted in Wyman, *Two American Pioneers,* 123).

12. Arthur Hobson Quinn, *Edgar Allan Poe: A Critical Biography* (New York: D. Appleton-Century, 1941), 330, 477.

13. Quoted in Rufus Griswold, "Edgar Allan Poe," *International Magazine* 1 (October 1850):343.

14. John D. Haskell, "Poe, Literary *Soirees,* and Coffee," *Poe Studies* 8 (1975):47; [George G. Foster], *New York in Slices,* rev. ed. (New York: W. F. Burgess, 1849), 62; Thomas Dunn English, "Reminiscences of Poe," *Independent,* 29 October 1896, 1448; Oakes Smith in Wyman, *Two American Pioneers,* 122.

15. Quoted in Griswold, "Poe," 343.

16. Detailed discussions are found in Sidney P. Moss, *Poe's Literary Battles: The Critic in the Context of His Literary Milieu* (Durham, N.C.: Duke University Press, 1963), 207–217; John E. Reilly, "Mrs. Osgood and *The Broadway Journal,*" *Duquesne Review* 12 (1967):131–146; and *Collected Works,* 1:379–391, 556–560. Chiefly concerned with his motives, Poe scholars have noted that some of his contributions to the series had earlier been addressed to other women—as if composing complimentary poems demonstrates genuine involvement, whereas recycling them indicates mere gallantry (see, for example, Moss, *Poe's Literary Battles,* 209, 210, 214 n. 34).

17. He wrote all but one of the notices in which Osgood is named. His editorial contributions to the *Journal* are identified in an unpublished dissertation by William Doyle Hull (Reilly, "Mrs. Osgood," 145 n. 3).

Frances Sargent Osgood and Edgar Allan Poe 55

18. *Broadway Journal* 1 (5 April 1845):220.
19. See especially Reilly, "Mrs. Osgood"; and Frances Winwar, *The Haunted Palace: A Life of Edgar Allan Poe* (New York: Harper and Row, 1959), 275–277, 281–288.
20. Reilly, "Mrs. Osgood," 134, emphasis added.
21. *Broadway Journal*, 1:207, 215.
22. *Complete Works*, 5:1.
23. "'So Let It Be,'" *Broadway Journal*, 1:215. Other Osgood poems mentioned in this paragraph are found at 1:231, 347.
24. Ibid., 1:317.
25. Ibid., 1:269, 260, 271.
26. Ibid., 1:325; *Collected Works*, 1:379–382.
27. Ibid., 1:347; *Complete Works*, 13:24.
28. Stoddard, "Mrs. Botta," 145. He mentioned no date.
29. Thomas H. Chivers, *Chivers' Life of Poe*, ed. Richard B. Davis (New York: E. P. Dutton, 1952), 18, 59–62; Walsh, *Plumes*, 19–21, 119–120.
30. *Graham's Magazine* 27 (August 1845):83, 84, emphasis added to the quotation just above the poetry. In the October 1845 *Graham's* appeared "The Divine Right of Kings," an amatory poem paying tribute to a woman's "tyrant virtue"; signed "P.," it may be Poe's response to "Ida Grey" (and, in turn, an inspiration for Osgood's "Caprice," whose third stanza includes the sentence "I revel in my right divine"). Mabbott explains how "Divine Right" and "Stanzas," also signed "P." (*Graham's Magazine*, December, 1845), have been linked to Poe (382–385).
31. *Broadway Journal*, 2:88.
32. Ibid., 2:113.
33. English, "Reminiscences," 1448.
34. *Broadway Journal*, 2:129.
35. Ibid., 2:148. The poem had been addressed to another woman in the 1830s, a fact that has been used to support the view that he wrote to Osgood mainly out of gallantry (see n. 16 above). By late summer Poe was fighting for his editorial life (Quinn, *Poe*, 451–495) and had little time for composing new works. But any four lines would have served as filler if he were not interested in carrying on his public dialogue with "F."
36. *Collected Works*, 1:233–235.
37. *Broadway Journal*, 2:168.
38. Quoted in *Correspondence of Griswold*, 256.
39. *The Letters of Edgar Allan Poe*, ed. John Ward Ostrom, 2 vols. (1948; reprint; New York: Gordian Press, 1966), 2:393, 431.
40. *Broadway Journal*, 2:78, 143, 323.
41. Ibid., 2:307.
42. Ibid., 2:318.
43. Susan Phinney Conrad, *Perish the Thought: Intellectual Women in Romantic America, 1830–1860* (New York: Oxford University Press, 1976), 121.
44. Broadway Journal, 2:349.

45. Ibid., 2:352.

46. Ibid., 2:365.

47. Ibid., 2:381.

48. Quoted in Griswold, "Poe," 342, 343.

49. On the fate of Osgood's letters to Poe, see John Carl Miller, *Building Poe Biography* (Baton Rouge: Louisiana State University Press, 1977), 50, 53.

50. Quoted in J. C. Derby, *Fifty Years among Authors, Books and Publishers* (New York: G.W. Carleton, 1884), 548; Oakes Smith did not identify the letter snatcher or mention the date of the incident. Mary E. Phillips, quoting the ancedote in *Edgar Allan Poe, the Man,* 2 vols. (Chicago: John C. Winston, 1926), 2:1143–1144, asserted that the third woman was Ellet. The first systematic Poe biographer, John H. Ingram, considered Oakes Smith unreliable, and most later biographers have overlooked or ignored her reminiscences.

51. Dates from Walsh, *Plumes,* 136, 139; and James B. Reece, "A Reexaminatin of a Poe Date: Mrs. Ellet's Letters," *American Literature* 42 (1970): 157–164.

52. *Letters,* 2:407–408.

53. Sidney P. Moss relates, in *Poe's Major Crisis: His Libel Suit and New York's Literary World* (Durham, N.C.: Duke University Press, 1970), and *Poe's Literary Battles,* how the affairs of the Osgood and Ellet letters reactivated and engendered various unsavory rumors about Poe.

54. *Letters,* 2:408.

55. Josephine Poe January, "Edgar Allan Poe's 'Child Wife,'" *Century Magazine* 78 (1909):895.

56. *The Complete Poems of Edgar Allan Poe,* ed. J. H. Whitty, (Boston: Houghton Mifflin, 1917), 271–272; *Collected Works,* 1:386–90.

57. Ellet to Frances Osgood, 8 July [1846?], Boston Public Library; quoted by permission of the Trustees of the Boston Public Library. Poe's reputation was sullied not only by talk of adultery but also by his treatment of Ellet, the "Longfellow War" (Quinn, *Poe,*453–455), the Boston Lyceum hoax, and his controversial "Literati" sketches published in *Godey's Lady's Book,* May-September 1846 (Moss, *Poe's Literary Battles*). On the Osgoods' reconciliation(s), see Walsh, *Plumes,* 47–48, 91, 101, 143–146.

58. *Complete Works,* 15:105, 101.

59. *Columbian Lady's and Gentleman's Magazine* 5 (June 1846):246. The word "charm," missing in this text, is supplied from Osgood's *Poems* (Philadelphia: A. Hart, 1850), 123. Although the addressee is not necessarily or simply Poe, the title links this poem with "Ida Grey," and the use of quotations in stanzas 1, 8, and 16 suggests a connection with "Lines from an Unpublished Drama" (see below).

60. *Graham's Magazine* 30 (February, 1847):90, 91. The narrator of Osgood's "Kate Carol to Her *" explicitly states, "Kate is my other self" (*Sartain's Union Magazine of Literature and Art* 1 [July 1847]:56).

61. *Graham's Magazine* 30 (March 1847):177, 178, 179.

62. H. F. Harrington, "Poe Not to Be Apotheosized," *Critic,* 3 October 1885,

157–158. The Rev. Mr. Harrington was reacting against a perceived trend to gloss over Poe's moral failings. Both Mabbott (*Collected Works,* 1:563–564) and Walsh (*Plumes,* 85–86, 142–143) question his account. The latter argues, however, that Poe did visit Osgood some time before Fanny Fay's sudden death in October 1847.

63. *Letters,* 2:384; Caroline Ticknor, *Poe's Helen* (New York: Chas. Scribner's Sons, 1916), 42–48.

64. Whitman letter of 11 May 1874, quoted in *Poe's Helen Remembers,* ed. John Carl Miller (Charlottesville: University Press of Virgina, 1979), 154–155.

65. Whitman letter of 10 October 1850, quoted in Stanley T. Williams, "New Letters about Poe," *Yale Review* 14 (1925):769.

66. *American Metropolitan Magazine* 1 (January 1849):45.

67. Whitman recalled, "He had seen them in ms (at the publisher's, I think) and believed them to be addressed to himself. With his impressible & impulsive temperament I can see that they must have deeply affected him & have revived remembrances which, for the moment, prevailed over every other feeling" (Whitman to Mary E. Hewitt, 4 October 1850, quoted in Williams, "New Letters about Poe," 768. Her letter quoted on p. 769 confirms that Whitman was referring to Osgood's "Lines").

68. *Letters,* 2:419.

69. *Ibid.,* 2:447. He may have been responding to a query prompted by Mrs. Clemm's 11 January letter to Mrs. Richmond, which mentions "the lines to Eddy in . . . the *Metropolitan.* They are by Mrs. Osgood, and very beautiful" (quoted in John H. Ingram, *Edgar Allan Poe: His Life, Letters, and Opinions,* 2 vols. [London: John Hogg, 1880], 2:202). On Poe's other relationships, see Richard P. Benton, "Friends and Enemies: Women in the Life of Edgar Allan Poe," in *Myths and Realities: The Mysterious Mr. Poe,* ed. Benjamin Franklin Fisher IV (Baltimore: Poe Society, forthcoming).

70. Joy Bayless relates that on 23 January 1849 Griswold wielded Ellet's 1846 letter of retraction to Osgood "and threatened to publish it if she did not cease maligning the innocent Fanny" (*Rufus Wilmot Griswold: Poe's Literary Executor* [Nashville: Vanderbilt University Press, 1943], 153).

71. *Sartain's Union Magazine of Literature and Art* 4 (March 1849):180. The March issue came out on 15 February (*Collected Works,* 387).

72. *Southern Literary Messenger* 15 (April,1849):220–221.

73. *Complete Works,* 13:175, 176, 188. All four reviews of Osgood, first published in December 1845, March and September 1846, and August, 1849, are included in the *Complete Works.*

74. *Letters,* 2:396, 410.

75. *Ibid.,* 2:353n, 413–414, 450–451; Quinn, *Poe,* 563, 611–12.

76. Osgood to Mary Ingersoll Locke, Anthony Collection, Rare Books and Manuscripts Division, The New York Public Library, Astor, Lenox, and Tilden Foundations.

77. Osgood to Martha J. Locke, Brown University Library, Providence, R.I.

78. Quoted in Griswold, "Poe," 342, 343. Whitman, hurt by what seemed to

be a gibe at her, was assured by Osgood's close friend Mary Hewitt that Fanny intended to deflate Sarah Anna Lewis, whom Mrs. Clemm had complimented as the inspiration of "Annabel Lee" (Ticknor, *Poe's Helen*, 132–133; Miller, *Poe's Helen Remembers*, 144).

79. Mabbott discusses the poem's provenance, *Collected Works*, 1:468–478. See also Jones and Ljungquist, "Poe, Mrs. Osgood, and 'Annabel Lee.'"

80. Quoted in *Correspondence of Griswold*, 256 (the "mother" referred to here was Mrs. Clemm; it was standard usage to drop "in-law" from these relations by marriage).

81. Bayless, *Griswold*, 144–146, 156–160, 174–175, 179, 203; Griswold, "Frances Sargent Osgood," *International Magazine* 2 (December 1850): 136.

82. Griswold, "Osgood," 133, 135, 139–140. The sketch also appeared in *The Memorial: Written by Friends of the Late Mrs. Osgood*, ed. Mary E. Hewitt (New York: Geo. P. Putnam, 1851), reprinted as *Laurel Leaves* (New York: Lamport, Blakeman, and Law, 1854).

JOYCE W. WARREN

Subversion versus Celebration: The Aborted Friendship of Fanny Fern and Walt Whitman

WHEN FANNY FERN AND WALT WHITMAN MET early in 1856, she was, at forty-four, the author of four very successful books and the highest paid newspaper writer of the time. The thirty-six-year-old Whitman, on the other hand, was an unemployed newspaper writer and housebuilder who, the year before, had published at his own expense a slim volume of poetry, of which few copies had been sold. The meeting was fortunate for Whitman. During the year that they were friends, Fern was to exercise all of her influence—and it was considerable—on his behalf. She invited him to her home, introduced him to her friends, and wrote about him in her column in the *New York Ledger*. But most important, on 10 May 1856, she wrote a remarkably courageous review unqualifiedly praising *Leaves of Grass*, which till then had received very little public praise and a great deal of censure. In later years, Whitman never acknowledged the boost that Fern had given him, but at the time he must have been jubilant, and her review was promptly copied the following week in the 17 May issue of *Life Illustrated*, which was published by Fowler and Wells, the distributors of Whitman's book. Not only did Whitman not acknowledge his debt to Fanny Fern, but, embittered by her insistence that he repay a loan her husband had made to him, he made a disparaging comment about her in print three weeks after her husband's collection agent called at his house. Nor, apparently, did he afterward speak kindly of her in private.

Whitman was probably familiar with Fern's work before he met her, and he may have taken the idea for the title and cover design of *Leaves of Grass* from Fern's first book, *Fern Leaves from Fanny's Portfolio*, published in 1853.[1] Both books were bound in dark green cloth with gold lettering and decorated with tendrils intertwined on the cover and

59

spine, with a triple-lined border stamped in gold. Whitman's book was larger, however, in keeping with the magnitude of his claims, or, as has been suggested, to allow for the easier printing of the unusually long lines in his poetry.[2] The immediate fate of the two books was dramatically different. Whereas *Fern Leaves* sold fifty thousand copies in six months, *Leaves of Grass* sold fewer than ten.[3] The history of the two books since then has been different also, but in reverse: whereas *Leaves of Grass* has been reprinted many times since Whitman first brought it out and is known throughout the world, *Fern Leaves* has not been reprinted since the period of its original fame and is little known today.[4]

It cannot be said that either Fern or Whitman was influenced by the other or that one was the disciple of the other. Rather, theirs was a literary friendship that grew out of their apparently common attitudes and beliefs. In her newspaper columns, Fanny Fern was an outspoken critic of sham and pretense, and a firm believer in the democratic man and woman. She eschewed stilted, artificial language and abhorred hypocrisy and the superficial dandies of her time—both male and female—and apparently thought that she had found in Walt Whitman, the man and his work, the kind of unpretentious honesty that she extolled in her columns.

The Fern-Whitman friendship ended in mid-1857 when Whitman failed to repay the two hundred dollars that he had borrowed from Fanny Fern's husband, James Parton, the biographer. Whitman had promised to repay the money in full in a few months, claiming that he was soon to receive a sum of money for a literary project. When Whitman was unable to repay the loan, Parton investigated his claims and found that the project he had mentioned did not exist. Angered by Whitman's apparent dishonesty, the Partons placed the matter in the hands of a lawyer friend who arranged to collect certain goods from Whitman in lieu of cash.[5]

Whitman apparently harbored no ill will toward James Parton, commenting favorably on Parton's *Life of Aaron Burr* in his paper the following year. Instead, he blamed Fanny Fern. When questioned about the debt by Horace Traubel years later, Whitman was vague:

> There were other elements in the story—venom, jealousies, opacities: they played a big part: and, if I may say it, women: a woman certainly—maybe women: they kept alive what I felt James Parton would have let die.[6]

In later years, Whitman's defenders used this quotation and its obscure reference to a woman's "jealousies" to support the contention that

Fanny Fern was in love with Whitman and that, spurned by him, she had urged Parton to pursue the debt.[7]

The innuendos of Whitman's defenders are not only without foundation, they are offensive to any student of Fern's works. They imply that Fanny Fern could not have—perhaps even that no woman could have—appreciated Whitman's poems unless she was in love with him, and contrarily that no woman would have a reason to become angry with him unless she was a woman scorned. The implication is that Fanny Fern is not to be treated seriously as a critic of literature or as a person.

Whitman scholars have made two serious errors in writing of this episode in Whitman's life. First, they have not read Fanny Fern's work and thus, like Fred Lewis Pattee in 1940, they have dismissed her as a writer of "sentimental pap," unworthy to be discussed as an intellectual equal of Walt Whitman.[8] And second, assuming this to be true, they have accepted Whitman's friends' hints that Fern must have been in love with Whitman as the only explanation for her appreciation of his work and her later hostility toward him.[9] What needs to be recognized is that Fanny Fern was one of the most intelligent and perceptive writers of her day. Far from being the sentimentalist they would portray her as (anymore than Whitman can be called a sentimentalist for having written sentimental popular fiction early in his career), she was in most of her writing a plainspoken, delightfully satirical critic of all that was false and pretentious in her culture.

Fanny Fern was born Sara Payson Willis on 9 July 1811, in Portland, Maine, the fifth of the nine children of Nathaniel and Hannah Parker Willis.[10] When she was an infant, the family moved to Boston, where Nathaniel Willis founded two religious newspapers, the *Recorder* and the *Youth's Companion*. Sara was close to her mother, whose cheerful warmth and sensitive spirit provided a haven for all of the children from their father's somber religiosity. An impulsive and imaginative child, Sara was sent to Catharine Beecher's Hartford Female Seminary to complete her education and subdue her high spirits. Fortunately for the world that later came to know her as Fanny Fern, the latter goal was not achieved, and she earned the nickname "Sal Volatile" among her classmates. In 1830 or 1831 Sara returned home where she was to remain until 4 May 1837, when she married Charles H. Eldredge, a cashier at the Merchants' Bank in Boston. Happily married for nine years, she was left penniless with two children to support when her husband died of typhoid fever in 1846. Her father, who had remarried, and her father-in-law grudgingly contributed a small pension for her support while urging her to remarry. On 15 January 1849, she entered into a marriage of convenience with Samuel Farrington, a widower with two little girls of his own. It was soon apparent that the marriage was a terrible mistake, and in January 1851 she took the unprecedented step of leaving her husband, who was violently jealous and spread libelous scandal about his wife that his own brother sought to retract. In 1853 Farrington obtained a divorce in Chicago on grounds of desertion.[11]

When she left Farrington, her family was scandalized and did not resume the pension. Unable to support her two children, she reluctantly allowed Grace, the elder, to stay with her in-laws while she attempted to support herself and her other daughter by sewing, an experience that provided her with a sympathy for working women whose overworked and underpaid plight she later wrote about with such conviction. She took and passed the teaching exam, but, lacking the necessary influence, she did not receive an appointment. In desperation, she tried writing for the newspapers. Her first piece was published anonymously in the *Boston Olive Branch* on 28 June 1851. She received fifty cents for it. She sent some sample articles to her brother, Nathaniel P. Willis, a successful poet and journalist and editor of the New York *Home Journal*, but Willis's taste was too fastidious for Fern's down-to-earth writing. He apparently also shared his family's anger at her for having brought disgrace upon the family by leaving her husband. In reply to her letter asking for his help, he wrote that there was no market for her work in New York, that her humor ran into "dreadful vulgarity," and that her writing "sometimes touched very close on indecency."[12] Fern persevered without her brother's help, and in the fall of 1851 began writing also for the *Boston True Flag*. Soon her articles were being copied—pirated—by newspapers all over the country and across the Atlantic.

In 1852 Oliver Dyer, publisher of the *New York Musical World and Times*, contacted Fanny Fern through the Boston papers and offered her twelve dollars a column to write for his paper. In October 1852 she began writing a regular column for the *Musical World*, which made her the first woman newspaper columnist in the United States. Although there were other women journalists—editors and correspondents—Fern was the first to write the equivalent of a modern newspaper column. In December 1852 the editor of the *True Flag* reluctantly agreed to match Dyer's offer, and Fanny Fern began a regular column for the *True Flag* as well. She continued to write for the Boston papers until the spring of 1853, when her book, *Fern Leaves from Fanny's Portfolio*, was published. *Fern Leaves* was a collection of her newspaper articles, and, in order to make the volume palatable, the editors had selected a disproportionate number of her sentimental pieces, but there was enough of her satirical, witty articles to ensure the success of the volume. In two years, Fanny Fern had been transformed from an impoverished widow shunned by her family to the wealthy author of a runaway best-seller. In June 1853 she moved to New York.

In 1854 Mason Brothers persuaded her to try her hand at a novel, which they promised to use "extraordinary exertions" to promote, and in December 1854 *Ruth Hall* was published. Thinking that she was protected by her carefully guarded incognita, Fern had written a largely autobiographical novel that revealed the unkind way in which her father, father-in-law, and brother had refused to help her and her children. But the editor of the *True Flag*, William U. Moulton, who had been angered by his loss of Fanny Fern as a contributor and was incensed at her satirical portrayal of himself in *Ruth Hall*, revealed her identity in a series of articles in the *True Flag*; in March 1855 he published a vindictive pseudobiography, *The Life and Beauties of Fanny Fern*. Moulton's revelation and book, although they caused Fern a great deal of personal anguish, helped the sales of *Ruth Hall*, which was eagerly sought after as a roman à clef. Reviewers, however, castigated Fanny Fern for her "unfeminine" portrayal of her relatives and for her want of female delicacy. Among the favorable commentators, however, was Nathaniel Hawthorne, who wrote to his publisher, William Ticknor, in February 1855, that the book was a better book precisely because Fanny Fern was not constricted by the straitjacket of conventional femininity that hampered many women writers:

> In my last, I recollect, I bestowed some vituperation on female authors. I have since been reading *Ruth Hall*, and I must say I enjoyed it a good deal. The woman writes as if the Devil was in her; and that is the only condition under which a woman ever writes anything worth reading. Generally women write like emasculated men, and are only to be distinguished from male authors by greater feebleness and folly; but when they throw off the restraints of decency and come before the public stark naked, as it were— then their books are sure to possess character and value. Can you tell me anything about this Fanny Fern? If you meet her, I wish you would let her know how much I admire her.[13]

It was at this point that Robert Bonner, the enterprising editor of the *New York Ledger*, determined to obtain the services of Fanny Fern for his paper, regardless of what it might cost. He agreed to pay her a hundred dollars a column for a story in ten installments. The story, "Fanny Ford," began in June 1855, and the *Ledger*'s circulation soared. Bonner signed an exclusive contract with Fanny Fern, and in January 1856 she began writing a regular column in the *Ledger*, which continued until the day of her death sixteen years later.

On 5 January 1856, the same day that her column began appearing in the *Ledger*, Fanny Fern married James Parton, who had recently published *The Life of Horace Greeley*. Parton, who was eleven years her junior, had been editor at Nathaniel P. Willis's *Home Journal* when Fern was writing anonymously for the Boston papers. Not knowing that she was Willis's sister, he had clipped her columns to publish in the *Home Journal*. When Willis found out and insisted that Parton stop printing his sister's articles, Parton resigned. When Fanny Fern came to New York, Oliver Dyer introduced her to Parton, who became her constant escort around town. Soon after their marriage in 1856, her husband introduced her to Walt Whitman.

Walter Whitman was born 31 May 1819, in West Hills, Long Island, the second of the nine children of Walter and Louisa Whitman.[14] When he was four years old, his family moved to Brooklyn, where his father worked as a housebuilder. All his life Whitman remained close to his mother, whose warm health and spirit contrasted with his morose father. One of his siblings died in infancy, while four others were plagued with physical and psychological illness. Whitman himself seemed to age quickly, and by his midforties his health had permanently failed. He left school at the age of eleven to become an office boy for a lawyer. Then in 1831 he was apprenticed to a printer. At sixteen, his apprenticeship over, he went to Manhattan where he worked briefly as a printer, until a fire in the publishing district left him without work. For the next five years he worked as a country schoolteacher in a number of schools on Long Island. Then in 1840/1841 he published a weekly newspaper, the *Long Islander*, in Huntington, Long Island. During the next ten years, Whitman edited and wrote for a series of newspapers and wrote pedestrian poetry and sentimental fiction for the magazines. He also wrote a temperance novel, *Franklin Evans* (1842). During this time, Whitman dressed like a gentleman—high collar, frock coat, and cane—and sprinkled his speech with French phrases.

In the early 1850s, Whitman assumed the dress of a workingman and for a while worked as a housebuilder in Brooklyn. He did not remain long at any post, and by 1855, at the age of thirty-six, he was unemployed and living at home. He paid to have *Leaves of Grass* printed at the firm of James and Thomas Rome in Brooklyn, laying ten pages of type himself. Of the almost eight hundred copies printed, two hundred were bound in cloth. Whitman had difficulty finding a bookstore that would sell his book, but the phrenologists Fowler and Wells, whose reading of Whitman's head in 1849 had shown that he was a "born poet," agreed to take the book. It went on sale on 4 July 1855. The reception of the book was not encouraging. Whitman's friend, Charles A. Dana, wrote a favorable review in the *New York Tribune* on 23 July 1855, possibly from Whitman's own notes, but the review was qualified by reservations about the "reckless and indecent" language. Edward Everett Hale praised the book, as did William Howitt in the *London Dispatch*, and Whitman received a laudatory letter from Emerson, which Whitman, without Emerson's permission, had printed in the *Tribune* on 10 October 1855, bound into the remaining copies of the first edition, and included in the second edition of *Leaves of Grass*. But except for the reviews that Whitman himself wrote anonymously, the majority of the reviewers described Whitman's book as indecent: "impious libidinousness," "a gathering of muck" and "beastliness," and a mass of "vulgarity and nonsense."[15] It was at this point that Whitman's path crossed that of Fanny Fern.

Early in 1856 James Parton introduced his new wife to Walt Whitman. Fern reflects her impression of Whitman in a column she wrote on 19 April in the *New York Ledger* as part of a series of columns describing New York celebrities, "Peeps from under a Parasol." After deftly sketching such New Yorkers as Charles A. Dana, Henry Ward Beecher, P. T. Barnum, her husband, James Parton, the actors John Lester and Laura Keene, Horace Greeley, and herself, she included in the third column in the series this sketch of Walt Whitman:

> And speaking of books, here comes Walt Whitman, author of *Leaves of Grass*, which, by the way, I have not yet read. His shirt collar is turned off from his muscular throat, and his shoulders are thrown back as if even in that fine, ample chest of his, his lungs had not sufficient play-room. Mark his voice! high—deep—and clear, as a clarion note. In the most crowded thoroughfare, one would turn instinctively on hearing it, to seek out its owner. Such a voice is a gift as rare as it is priceless. A fig for phrenology! Let

me hear the *voice* of a man or a woman and I will tell you the stuff
its owners are made of.[16]

In order to understand the perspective from which this was written, it
is useful to compare it to Fern's sketch of Bayard Taylor earlier in the
series:

> Now I don't suppose Bayard is to blame for being a *pretty* man, or
> for looking so nice and bandbox-y. But if some public benefactor
> *would* tumble his hair and shirt collar and tie his cravat in a loose
> sailor knot; and if Bayard himself *would* open that little three-cent
> mouth of his a l-i-t-t-l-e wider when he lectures, it would take a
> load off my mind. [*NYL*, 29 March 1856]

To interpret Fern's appreciative description of Whitman as indicative
that she had "cast her eye on Walt in a cherishing way."[17] as so many
Whitman scholars have concluded, can only be done if the passage is
taken out of context—out of the context of the series in which it is only
one short sketch among many, and out of the context of Fern's career,
where it is simply an example of the kind of person that she preferred.
Throughout her writing career she criticized the fashion-conscious
"smirking fops and brainless belles" (*NYL*, 12 November 1853) and advocated practical dress and good health habits. Typical of her attitude is
the following passage from an 1867 article entitled "Fashionable Invalidism," in which she urged men and women to live active, healthy
lives:

> How I rejoice in a man or woman with a chest; who can look the
> sun in the eye, and step off as if they had not wooden legs. . . .
> Heavens! I am fifty-five, and I feel half the time as if I were just
> made. . . . I walk, not ride. . . . I like a nice bit of beefsteak and a
> glass of ale, and anybody else who wants it may eat pap. . . . I
> dash out in the rain, because it feels good on my face. I don't care
> for my clothes, but I *will* be well; and after I am buried, I warn
> you, don't let any fresh air or sunlight down on my coffin, if you
> don't want me to get up. [*NYL*, 27 July 1867]

With this attitude, it is not surprising that Fanny Fern liked Walt
Whitman, whose deliberately casual dress and robust good health must
have been a refreshing contrast to the mincing dandies she criticized in
her column. Nor is it surprising that Whitman responded to Fern's

down-to-earth manner. He said that he "liked her better than any woman,"[18] and he visited her and her husband regularly, first at the Waverley Hotel in Manhattan where they lived after their marriage, and then at the house on Oxford Street in Brooklyn that Fern bought in June 1856. Of course it is possible that since Whitman worked very hard as his own public relations man,[19] he may also have been motivated by the hope that Fern and Parton could be useful to him. When Samuel Wells began to divest himself of *Leaves of Grass* because of what he called "certain objectionable passages" in the second edition, he wrote to Whitman on 7 June 1856 that the Partons' publishers, Mason Brothers, were "rich and enterprizing," and suggested that Whitman get them to publish his book.[20] Moreover, Whitman could not have been unaware of the power of the *New York Ledger* as a publicity tool. In August 1856 he wrote a character sketch of Robert Bonner, editor of the *Ledger*. In an article much like Fern's earlier "Peeps from under a Parasol," describing people he saw on the street, he called Bonner the "hero of unheard-of and tremendous advertising," and lauded the *Ledger* as a "gorgeous and unprecedented sheet."[21] The success of the *Ledger* was a well-known fact at the time, its circulation having jumped from twenty-five hundred to one hundred fifty thousand in one year. And one of the reasons for the *Ledger*'s swift success was Bonner's acquisition of the popular Fanny Fern as an exclusive columnist.

Not only might Whitman have perceived that Fern herself could be useful to him, but her home was a good place to meet other potentially useful journalists and writers. Fern had a wide circle of literary friends, and although she did not like to attend fashionable evening parties, she regularly entertained these friends in her home. The *Boston Chronicle* described her as "the brightest and most entertaining of hostesses," and her friends included such people as Horace Greeley of the *New York Tribune*, who was a frequent visitor.[22]

It is clear, then, that Whitman had much to gain from his friendship with Fanny Fern. However, despite Whitman's "lifelong maneuvering for publicity,"[23] it is unlikely that, given his high opinion of friendship, he would have pursued his friendship with Fern if he had not also genuinely liked her. He was a frequent visitor, and he seems to have enjoyed himself while in her company. Thomas Butler Gunn, a writer and illustrator who had collaborated on a book with James Parton, was another visitor, and his diary entries for 1856 and 1857 provide a revealing picture of the relationship between Whitman and Fern. Gunn, who records first meeting Whitman at the Partons in May 1856, notes that Whitman subsequently called on him, that he liked him "immensely," and says

that he "must put him in pen and ink hereafter." If Whitman was looking for literary contacts at the Partons', he certainly did not waste any
time following up on Gunn, and Gunn did soon thereafter publish a pen
and ink sketch of Whitman.

The following entry from Gunn's diary in June 1856 answers some
important questions about the friendship between Whitman and Fern:

> Parton and his wife have just moved to Brooklyn, where *she* has
> purchased a house. I used, as wont to drop in at the Waverley on
> Saturday nights, always finding Walt Whitman there, and some-
> times Oliver Dyer. . . . Walt Whitman is six feet high, nearer
> forty than thirty, I should say, very much sun-burned and rough
> handed. He is broad in proportion to his height, has a short, par-
> tially grey beard and mustache, and a neck as brown as a berry.
> His face is very manly and placid. He wears a wide brimmed low
> crowned felt hat, a rough, loose coat, striped shirt (with percepti-
> ble red flannel one under it), no vest, loose short pants, and big
> thick boots. Thus accoutered I find him lounging on the sofa be-
> side Fanny Fern, his legs reposing on a stool or chair. . . . Parton
> seated in an arm chair, in short, brown, loose in-doors coat, white
> pants and low shiny shoes, listens, leaning forwards to Walt's
> talk. . . . Dyer will probably be sitting 'tother side of Fanny. . . .
> Parton appears very fond of her. (He, however, isn't jealous of
> Walt's kissing her, which he always does on quitting.) Walt talks
> *well*—but occasionally too much, being led by the interest with
> which his remarks are received into monopolizing the converse. I,
> as a rule, would prefer to play listener, yet it is a violation of good
> taste to find yourself constrained to become one. And nobody
> wishes to become a bucket to be pumped into, let the stream be
> ever so nutritious.[24]

This diary entry tells us three important facts: first, that Whitman was a
regular visitor at the Partons; second, that he was at his ease there; and
third, that rather than Fanny Fern being "sweet" on Whitman, it was he
who played up to her.[25]

On 21 April 1856, after reading the first edition of *Leaves of Grass*,
Fern wrote Whitman a note telling him her opinion of it:

> "Leaves of Grass"
>   You are *delicious*! May my right hand wither if I
> don't tell the world before another week, what *one* woman thinks
> of you.

"Walt" ? "what *I* assume, *you* shall assume!"
Some one evening this week you are to spend with Jemmy
[James Parton] & me — Wednesday? — say.
                    Yours truly,
                    Fanny Fern[26]

This note has been used as evidence for the rumor spread by Whitman's friends that Fern was in love with Whitman. However, this interpretation is only possible if one misreads the beginning of the letter to
mean that she is calling Whitman "delicious." It is clear from the manuscript copy that at the beginning of the letter when she says, "You are
delicious," she is addressing, not Walt Whitman, but *Leaves of Grass*.
The word "You" comes on the next line immediatly after "Leaves of
Grass," which is clearly the salutation. Moreover, this is the same expression she uses in the first paragraph of her review of *Leaves of Grass*,
again addressing the book. Fern had already told the world what she
thought of Whitman in her *Ledger* column of 19 April, so that when she
says she will tell the world "what *one* woman thinks of you," the "you"
again refers to *Leaves of Grass*.

Whatever Whitman's later attitude toward Fanny Fern, the receipt of
this letter must have pleased him greatly. Fanny Fern, the most popular
newspaper columnist in America, whose words in the *Ledger* reached
more homes than any other journalist's, had promised to praise in print
his obscure *Leaves of Grass*. That Whitman kept this little note, although he burned so many other letters and papers, indicates how much
it meant to him.

Fanny Fern kept her promise, and on 10 May 1856, the *Ledger*
printed her review praising *Leaves of Grass*:

"Leaves of Grass"

Well baptized: fresh, hardy, and grown for the masses. Not
more welcome is their natural type to the winter-bound, bed-
ridden, and spring-emancipated invalid. "Leaves of Grass" thou
art unspeakably delicious, after the forced, stiff, Parnassian exot-
ics for which our admiration has been vainly challenged.

Walt Whitman, the effeminate world needed thee. The timidest
soul whose wings ever drooped with discouragement, could not
choose but rise on thy strong pinions.

"Undrape — you are not guilty to me, nor stale nor discarded;
I see through the broadcloth and gingham whether or no. . . .
O despairer, here is my neck,
You shall *not* go down! Hang your whole weight upon me."

Walt Whitman, the world needed a "Native American" of thorough, out-and-out breed—enamored of *women* not *ladies, men*
not *gentlemen;* something beside a mere Catholic-hating Know-
Nothing; it needed a man who dared speak out his strong, honest
thoughts, in the face of pusillanimous, toadeying, republican aristocracy; dictionary-men, hypocrites, cliques and creeds; it needed
a large-hearted, untainted, self-reliant, fearless son of the Stars
and Stripes, who disdains to sell his birthright for a mess of pot-
tage; who does

> "Not call one greater or one smaller,
> That which fills its period and place being equal to any";

who will

> Accept nothing which all cannot have their counterpart of on
> the same terms."

Fresh "Leaves of Grass"! not submitted by the self-reliant author to the fingering of any publisher's critic, to be arranged, re-
arranged and disarranged to his circumscribed liking, till they
hung limp, tame, spiritless, and scentless. No. It were a spectacle
worth seeing, this glorious Native American, who, when the daily
labor of chisel and plane was over, himself, with toil-hardened
fingers, handled the types to print the pages which wise and good
men have since delighted to endorse and to honor. Small critics,
whose contracted vision could see no beauty, strength, or grace,
in these "Leaves," have long ago repented that they so hastily
wrote themselves down shallow by such a premature confession.
Where an Emerson, and a Howitt have commended, my woman's
voice of praise may not avail; but happiness was born a twin, and
so I would fain share with others the unmingled delight which
these "Leaves" have given me.

I say unmingled; I am not unaware that the charge of coarseness
and sensuality has been affixed to them. My moral consitution
may be hopelessly tainted—or too sound to be tainted, as the
critic wills—but I confess that I extract no poison from these
"Leaves"—to me they have brought only healing. Let him who
can do so, shroud the eyes of the nursing babe lest it should see its
mother's breast. Let him look carefully between the gilded covers
of books, backed by high-sounding names, and endorsed by par-
son and priest, lying unrebuked upon his own family table; where
the asp of sensuality lies coiled amid rhetorical flowers. Let him
examine well the paper dropped weekly at his door, in which vir-

tue and religion are rendered disgusting, save when they walk in satin slippers, or, clothed in purple and fine linen, kneel on a damask *"prie-dieu."*

Sensual! No—the moral assassin looks you not boldly in the eye by broad daylight; but Borgia-like takes you treacherously by the hand, while from the glittering ring on his finger he distils through your veins the subtle and deadly poison.

Sensual? The artist who would inflame, paints you not nude Nature, but stealing Virtue's veil, with artful artlessness now conceals, now exposes, the ripe and swelling proportions.

Sensual? Let him who would affix this stigma upon "Leaves of Grass," write upon his heart, in letters of fire, these noble words of its author:

> "In woman I see the better of the great fruit, which is
>   immortality
> . . . the good thereof is not tasted by *rouses*, and never can be.
>   . . .
> Who degrades or defiles the living human body is cursed,
> Who degrades or defiles the body of the dead is not more
>   cursed."

Were I an artist I would like no more suggestive subjects for my easel than Walt Whitman's pen has furnished.

> "The little one sleeps in its cradle,
> I lift the gauze and look a long time, and silently brush away
>   flies with my hand.
> The farmer stops by the bars of a Sunday and looks at the oats
>   and rye. . . .
> Earth of the slumbering and liquid trees!
> Earth of departed Sunset!
> Earth of the mountains misty topt!
> Earth of the vitreous pour of the full moon just tinged with
>   blue!
> Earth of shine and dark mottling the tide of the river!
> Earth of the limpid grey of clouds brighter and clearer for my
>   sake!
> Far swooping elbowed earth! Rich apple-blossomed earth!
>   Smile, for your lover comes!"

I quote at random, the following passages which appeal to me:

> "A morning glory at my window, satisfies me more than the
>   metaphysics of books. . . .

Logic and sermons never convince.
The damp of the night drives deeper into my soul."

Speaking of animals, he says:

"I stand and look at them sometimes half the day long.
They do not make me sick, discussing their duty to God. . . .
Whoever walks a furlong without sympathy, walks to his
    funeral dressed in his shroud. . . .
I hate him that oppresses me,
I will either destroy him, or he shall release me. . . .
I find letters from God dropped in the street, and every one is
    signed by God's name,
And I leave them where they are, for I know that others will
    punctually come forever and ever. . . .
—Under Niagara, *the cataract falling live a veil over my
countenance.*"

Of the grass he says:

"It seems to me *the beautiful uncut hair of graves.*"

I close the extracts from these "Leaves," which it were easy to
multiply, for one is more puzzled what to leave unculled, than
what to gather, with the following sentiments; for which, and for
all the good things included between the covers of his book, Mr.
Whitman will please accept the cordial grasp of a woman's hand:

"The wife—and she is not one jot less than the husband,
The daughter—and she is just as good as the son,
The mother—and she is every bit as much as the father."
                                        [*NYL*, 10 May 1856]

Fanny Fern was the first woman to praise *Leaves of Grass* in print—
and the only woman to do so for many years. Her review was daring and
courageous, written at a time when few men were willing publicly to
praise Whitman's work. And even those who did so would probably
have agreed with Charles Eliot Norton that they "would be sorry to
know that any woman had looked into it past the title-page."[27] Even the
favorable reviewers had qualified their praise with reservations about
Whitman's coarseness and indecent language. But it was typical of Fanny
Fern to "tell the world" what she thought regardless of the opinions of
others. In her columns she spoke out on religion, prostitution, venereal
disease, divorce; why not speak out on *Leaves of Grass*? The editor of
the *Ledger* was willing to print her controversial opinions, though some-

times he made editorial comments on them, and, in the case of her review of Whitman, he subtly qualified her review by printing on the same
page an earlier sentimental article, "Little Benny," whose maternal theme
demonstrated that Fanny Fern was not "unwomanly" despite her questionable views on *Leaves of Grass*.

Why did Fern respond so favorably to Whitman's book? Anyone who
has read her work has no difficulty answering this question. As Emerson
said, he read other books only to see his own thoughts.[28] What Fanny
Fern found in *Leaves of Grass* were her own thoughts. Let us examine
the six major points for which she praises *Leaves of Grass*. Each one
has its counterpart in her own writings.

First of all, the language of *Leaves of Grass* is not stiff and artificial.
Fern's own writing had been criticized as vulgar because she did not use
the delicate language expected of women writers. In an article entitled
"Bogus Intellect," she gives her opinion of such writers:

> There is a class of sentimental women who use up the whole dic-
> tionary in speaking of a pin, and circumlocute about the alphabet
> in such a way, every time they open their mincing lips, that no-
> body but themselves can know what they are talking about.
> [*NYL*, 30 December 1865]

It is no wonder that Fern welcomed the freshness and frankness of
Leaves of Grass.

The second point she addressed was the bold strength that she saw in
the writer. For some time Fern had lamented the hypocritical timidity of
"milk and water" men. In 1853, after seeing a "Men Wanted" sign in a
shop window, she commented: "Well, they have been 'wanted' for
some time, but the article is not in the market, although there are plenty
of spurious imitations."[29] And earlier that year, on seeing "The
Bearded Woman," she wrote:

> As if *that* was a curiosity! I can see legions of them any day . . .
> lisping and mincing aimless through creation, on their patent
> leather toes, behind a dickey and moustache. . . . these
> bewhiskered, bescented, be-cravatted, be-jewelled, be-everlast-
> ingly-despised Lilliputian dandies.[30]

The world, as Fern saw it, had become "effeminate." It needed a
strong man like Whitman, "enamored of *women* not *ladies, men* not
gentlemen."

A third point that Fern commented on was the fearless individualism

and self-reliance of Whitman's *Leaves of Grass*. Fern was particularly
critical of writers who were simply imitators, and in 1853 her article
"Borrowed Light" satirized the writers who lacked the courage or were
too lazy to "take the trouble to light a torch of their own."[31] Throughout her writing career, also, Fern urged individualism in all areas for
both men and women. She detested conformity:

> One may even do a worse thing than to be "odd." One may be un-
> true to one's self, or a mere echo of others, which is to me the al-
> pha and omega of disgustingness. Heaven save us from colorless
> characters, what else soever it inflicts upon us: people who don't
> know what they think till they ask somebody.
>
> [*NYL*, 8 April 1871]

The fourth point that Fern makes is to praise Whitman's democratic
ideal. Fern wrote all her life as a friend of the working man and woman,
urging reform and putting herself in the place of the shop girl, the
housemaid, the factory worker, even the prostitute. Always critical of
the Mrs. Grundys who looked down on "life's unfortunates," Fern
wrote with great understanding of the conditions of poverty and the human dignity of all people. Like Whitman, she would not "call one
greater or one smaller." Thus at the end of the Civil War, she wrote:

> *My* history of the War . . . shall record, not the deeds of our Com-
> manders and Generals, noble and great as they were . . . but *my*
> history shall preserve for the descendants of those who fought for
> our flag, the noble deeds of our *privates*, who shared the danger
> but missed the glory.
>
> [*NYL*, 15 February 1868]

The fifth point that Fern addressed—and the most difficult one for a
woman of her period to discuss—was Whitman's "undraped" portrayal
of sex. She welcomed it, she said, because it was a true picture of sex as
it should be: honest love between a man and woman, not the prurient
sex of the roué and the woman he defiles because he regards her as
worthless. This was a subject Fern wrote on many times, in relation to
the spread of venereal disease and the creation of genetically defective
children. In 1858 she wrote in the *New York Ledger*: "Let every man
look upon every woman, whatsoever her rank or condition, as a sister
whom his manhood is bound to protect . . . and let every woman turn
the cold shoulder to any man of her acquaintance, how polished soever

he may be, who would degrade her sex." Every woman, Fern insisted, had the right to healthy children (*NYL*, 17 July 1858).

Finally, after calling attention to the beauty of some of the images projected by Whitman's words, Fern concluded her review with an appreciation of Whitman's apparent extension of the democratic ideal to women: "the wife—and she is not one jot less than the husband." This was the underlying theme of all of Fern's work. It is not surprising that, believing that she saw her principal ideas reflected in *Leaves of Grass*, she should have responded to it so favorably. On this point, however, she was mistaken, and her mistaken estimate of *Leaves of Grass*—and of Walt Whitman—on this question of the role of women goes a long way toward explaining the falling-out between them later.

In many ways, Whitman might seem to be advocating a new and fairer attitude toward women. He makes a point of speaking to both men and women: "The Female equally with the Male I sing."[32] And, breaking with the tradition that regarded women as natural invalids, he admires the strong, physically active woman. In "Democratic Vistas," he urges that women be raised to be the "robust equals" of men.[33] And in "Specimen Days," he writes of his disappointment with the women of the west. He had hoped they would be strong and vital like the men, but they are as "dyspeptic-looking" as their eastern sisters (*CW*, 1:225–226). He also recognizes the sexual nature of women, which the sexual double standard of his time did not grant to "respectable" women.

If one analyzes Whitman's attitude, however, it becomes clear that, except for this emphasis on woman's physical nature, his conception of women differs little from the conventional one.[34] First of all, although he insists that he is talking to women as well as to men, he does not see woman as the doer, the individualist that he is writing about. In "Children of Adam," Whitman describes the female and then the male. The words he uses to describe the male are the conventional ones: action, power, defiance, pride, knowledge. The female is passive and yielding, acted upon, not acting. Whitman concludes with this image: "See the bent head and arms folded over the breast, the Female I see" (*L*, 96–99).

Even the robustness that Whitman likes in women is part of this conventional picture. For Whitman, the significance of woman lies in her biological function. Thus, even when he praises woman, it is only in her role as mother:

I am the poet of the woman the same as the man,
And I say it is as great to be a woman as to be a man,
And I say there is nothing greater than the mother of men.

[L, 48]

At first this seems to be a recognition of woman as a person in her own right. But Whitman undercuts the independent image of woman by telling us that woman's greatest function is to be a mother—of men. What about her value for herself? one might ask. And if she is to be a mother, why not a mother of daughters? At other times, Whitman does mention daughters as well as sons, but it is clear that the value of the daughter is the same as the value of her mother—her potential motherhood. When Whitman insists that women are important, too, he means that they are important as breeders of men. If we are to have stong, vital men, they must have strong, vital mothers.

For Whitman, motherhood is the most important function of women. Although in his later works there are occasional references to some future idyllic time when women might be "even practical and political deciders with men" (CW, 2;389), Whitman cannot seem to conceive of such a time as a reality, and the overwhelming effect of his work is to entrench women even further in the traditional role—which Whitman portrays as both beautiful and necessary for his democratic vision. In "Democratic Vistas" Whitman writes of women's "divine maternity" and cites as the ideal woman "the perfect human mother" (CW, 2:389, 393). The new literature, he says, can teach and train men and raise them to a higher level. Its effect on women will be to make them better mothers. What this country needs, he says, is a "strong and sweet Female Race, a race of perfect Mothers" (CW, 2:372). Throughout "Democratic Vistas" particularly, Whitman seems to be obsessed with this idea of the glorious race of Americans that will develop and of the need for perfect women, "indispensable to endow the birth-stock of a New World" (L, 401; CW, 2:364). He even suggests the necessity of selective breeding to ensure the development of men with native power and intelligence (CW, 2:397). For Whitman, then, woman does not exist for herself, and she is nothing without a man: "A woman waits for me, she contains all, nothing is lacking, / Yet all were lacking if sex were lacking, or if the moisture of the right man were lacking" (L, 101–103).[35]

The opinions that Whitman expressed editorially during his journalistic career confirm the limited conception of women that emerges from his poetry. Although there are articles in which, like Fanny Fern,

Whitman sympathized with the plight of poor working women,[36] unlike Fern, he did not urge the expansion of career and educational opportunities that would make women less vulnerable to economic exploitation. In fact, he specifically opposed education for women on the basis that women did not need to be educated to become good wives and mothers.[37] And whereas Fern consistently deplored the unfair wage differential between men and women in the same occupation, Whitman, in writing on the low salaries of teachers, for example, advocated an across-the-board raise for all teachers, but saw nothing wrong with the unequal pay scale for male and female teachers.[38] Although he could praise Margaret Fuller's *Papers on Literature and Art*,[39] unlike Fern, who urged that women read as much as possible to broaden their minds, Whitman feared unlimited reading among women and blamed female infidelity on the "evil influence of French and British literature."[40] He could support an isolated issue like the Wisconsin action on married women's property rights,[41] but he did not support women's suffrage or any activity in which women were "unfemininely" assertive. He had no objection, he said, if women interested themselves in politics, so long as they retained their "mildness" and did not "violate the rules of decorum."[42] Like Fern, Whitman advocated good health for women and criticized such fashions as tight lacing, but unlike Fern, he did so primarily because of his concern with woman's role as wife and mother. Poor health, he said, prevents a woman from being cheerful in the "conjugal relation," and tight lacing can make a woman unfit to be a wife and mother.[43]

In all of these articles, although Whitman shows an appreciation of, at times even a reverence for, women, his opinion of them derives from, in fact is inseparable from, a conception of women as wives and mothers. This becomes the criterion for any issue affecting women: if, in his mind, the issue does not contribute to or enhance woman's position as wife and mother, then, no matter how beneficial it might be to women themselves, Whitman does not support it. In his newspaper articles as in his poetry, Whitman's picture of women was the same sentimental idealization of women projected by his contemporaries. Physically stronger, perhaps, and capable of more active labor, Whitman's woman was nevertheless gentle and passive, ultimately limited to and valuable for only one role and in one relation: her relation to man as wife and mother.

Charles Eldridge, who was a close friend of Whitman and a member of the circle that met almost nightly with Whitman at the O'Connors' house in Washington in the 1860s and 1870s, described Whitman as "one of the most conservative of men." Of Whitman's attitude toward women as revealed in these conversations, Eldridge wrote:

> I have never heard him give any countenance to the contentions of the "Woman's Rights" people; thought they were a namby-pamby lot as a whole, and he did not believe that woman suffrage would do any particular good. Susan B. Anthony was far from his ideal of a "fierce athletic girl." He delighted in the company of old-fashioned women, mothers of large families preferred, who did not talk about literature and reforms.[44]

Over the years, since Fanny Fern first praised *Leaves of Grass*, many women who have read and responded favorably to Whitman's poetry have been impressed by his portrayal of women. However, as Whitman's relationship with Fanny Fern makes abundantly clear, this response is, in fact, a cruel joke on the women who felt that Whitman offered equal recognition of the sexes. The cruelty lies in the promise unfulfilled. For, although he recognized woman's physical nature, which was unusual in his day, he never regarded her as a doer in the way that he did man; he never saw woman as a person independent of her relation to man.

Fanny Fern's conception of women was very different. In 1859 she described the "coming woman":

> Heaven forbid the coming woman should not have warm blood in her veins, quick to rush to her cheek, or tingle at her fingers' ends when her heart is astir. No, the coming woman shall be no cold, angular, flat-chested, narrow-shouldered, skimpy, sharp-visaged Betsey, but she shall be a bright-eyed, full-chested, broad-shouldered, large-souled, intellectual being; able to walk, able to eat, able to fulfill her maternal destiny, and able—if it so please God—to go to her grave happy, self-poised and serene, though unwedded.
>
> [*NYL*, 12 February 1859]

This sounds like a Whitman woman: robust and strong, able to have children. But there are important differences. Fern's coming woman will be "intellectual," and she is a significant person even if she remains unwedded—even if she is never seen in relation to a man.

Moreover, Fern urged the development of women's talents, talents other than childbearing. On 19 December 1857, she wrote in the *New*

York Ledger after seeing the artwork of Rosa Bonheur and Harriet Hosmer:

> I thank the gods, too, that the young sculptress has had the courage to assert herself—to be what nature intended her to be—a genius—even at the risk of being called unfeminine, eccentric, and unwomanly. "Unwomanly?" because crotchet-stitching and worsted foolery could not satisfy her soul! Unwomanly? because she galloped over the country on horseback, in search of health and pleasure, instead of drawing on her primrose kids, and making a lay-figure of herself, to exhibit the fashions, by dawdling about the streets. Well, *let* her be unwomanly, then, I say; I wish there were more women bitten with the same complaint; let her be "eccentric," if nature made her so, so long as she outrages only the feelings of those conservative old ladies of both sexes, who would destroy individuality by running all our sex in the same mold of artificial nonentity. . . . I am glad that a new order of women is arising like the Bonheurs and Hosmers, who are evidently sufficient unto themselves, both as it regards love and bread and butter.

Despite the claims made by some Whitman scholars on this point,[45] it should be clear that the individualist that Whitman celebrated was a man. For Whitman, woman was always the "other," not, as she was for Fanny Fern, an individual, a person in her own right.

Given this misunderstanding of each other's attitudes toward women, it is not surprising that the next episode in the Fern-Whitman friendship took the form that it did. After Fern's review of *Leaves of Grass*, the friendship between them continued. She apparently did not like certain passages in the second edition of *Leaves of Grass*, but there was no break because of it. Some time late in 1856 or early 1857, however, Whitman borrowed two hundred dollars from James Parton and signed a short-term note claiming that he would soon be receiving money for a literary project. There is no evidence to indicate exactly when Whitman borrowed the money, but the note was due on approximately 3 February 1857. If the note was for six months, then the loan was made in early August 1856, which was a month before Whitman published the second edition of *Leaves of Grass*, and this may have been the literary project

that he spoke of. If so, then he was being disingenuous to say that he expected a large sum of money from it, considering the dearth of sales of
the first edition.

On 15 February 1857, Thomas Butler Gunn records in his diary that
he had visited the Partons and was told that Whitman had failed to meet
the note, "since which something like twelve days has elapsed." Gunn
adds, "It would appear there's reason for suspecting the great 'Kosmos'
to be a great scoundrel."[46] On 22 February Gunn reports that Whitman
has called on Parton and "appears *shuffling*." Parton, says Gunn, is going to sue. Gunn indicates that he felt that Parton, who was always "enthusiastic about human nature," had been fooled by Whitman, and notes
that he himself, although originally cynical, had been "carried away
by *his* [Parton's] judgement of Walt Whitman, despite my own
thoughts."[47]

After this incident, Gunn apparently did not have a high opinion of
Whitman. On 17 January 1859, after seeing Whitman in the street, he
wondered:

> How does that man—a unique character in his way—live? He
> has a mother, an industrious brother, and one idiotic. I suppose
> the second maintains the family. Then, too, there is or was some
> middle aged Philadelphian lady, a widow of indifferent character,
> who admired him and whom he spunged from. And Parton's $200
> might have sufficed to let him "loaf and be at his ease" for a long
> time.[48]

And in July 1869, Gunn reported: "Walt Whitman is voted mean [by the
Bohemians at Pfaff's beer cellar] as he never stands drinks or pays for
his own if it's possible to avoid it."[49]

The Partons insisted on repayment of the debt, James Parton having
specifically told Whitman at the time of the loan that the money was a
sum he had saved for a trip to New Orleans to research his forthcoming
biography of Andrew Jackson.[50] They did not sue, but their friend, Oliver Dyer, who was a friend of Whitman also, offered to try to settle the
dispute.[51] He arranged to meet Whitman at his house, where he agreed
to take a painting and some books in payment of the debt. In 1869
Whitman explained the arrangement in a letter to William Douglas
O'Connor, giving the date as 17 June 1857 and enclosing the receipt.[52]

In a letter to William Sloane Kennedy in 1897, replying to his questions about the debt, Ethel Parton, Fanny Fern's granddaughter, made it
clear why the Partons were disturbed by Whitman's behavior: "The

offense was not merely an unpaid debt which the debtor for any unforeseen reason could not pay"; had that been the case, "Whitman would have received only consideration, sympathy, and absolute silence." The problem, she said, was that Whitman had obtained the loan under false pretenses, "solemnly and repeatedly" assuring Parton that he would soon have the money from a literary project he was completing. When the loan was not repaid, and the date for payment several times put off, Parton investigated Whitman's tale and found that it was wholly untrue. At this point, he put the matter in the hands of Oliver Dyer.[53]

Upon first hearing this story, William Sloane Kennedy, one of Whitman's staunchest supporters, indignantly defended Whitman. Just how determined he and other supporters were to defend Whitman at any cost is apparent from his comments on what Ethel Parton said regarding Dyer's visit to Whitman. She had written:

> We both [she and Fern's daughter Ellen] have a very distinct impression that the lawyer friend, when he went in search of Whitman, found him in bed, and his mother scrubbing the floor; and that he also encountered a brother who was a carpenter, and who told him that W.W. had always been lazy, and untrustful, and apt to lump down upon his relatives.[54]

Kennedy commented:

> One is glad to have a good laugh at this point of the little tragedy. No doubt the brothers of Jesus & Socrates (if he had any) thought them both lazy loafers & humbugs, & no doubt Mary & Xantippe scrubbed many a floor (I hope they did it well & left no dirt in corners) while the son & husband were toiling for humanity at large.[55]

That Whitman had assumed the stature of a god or demigod in the eyes of cultists is an indication of why they would be so eager to blame Fanny Fern.[56] Grasping at straws and at the hints of an anonymous friend that Fern was in love with Whitman, his supporters sought to portray the situation as the case of a woman scorned because this would explain the Partons' hostility and exonerate Whitman. However, the only source for this rumor seems to have been Ellen O'Connor,[57] the wife of William Douglas O'Connor, and her credibility is complicated by the possibility that for years she was herself in love with Whitman.[58] James Parton's later comments indicate no ire regarding his wife's behavior, but only indignation that Whitman could have been such a scoundrel as to have no scruples about inventing an "entire fabrication" in order to borrow money that he had no intention of repaying. According to Ethel Parton, Parton "never ceased to resent what seemed to him so peculiarly base an extortion under false pretenses."[59] The Partons' friendship with Walt Whitman ended with the symbolic buring of *Leaves of Grass* in their fireplace.[60] Both Fanny Fern and James Parton believed that they had been "victimized" by a man who was not what he pretended to be.[61]

When the Partons insisted that Whitman make good his debt, Whitman's reaction was to strike out at Fanny Fern. This he did in his 9 July 1857 article in the *Brooklyn Daily Times*, in which he vindictively disparaged Fanny Fern three weeks after his goods were collected by Dyer. In an editorial arguing against the establishment of free academies for girls similar to the ones for boys, he wrote:

> The majority of people do not want their daughters to be trained to become authoresses and poets; but only that they may receive sufficient education to serve as the basis of life-long improvement and self-cultivation, and which will qualify them to become good and intelligent wives and mothers. . . . We want a race of men and women turned out from our schools, not of pedants and blue-stockings. One genuine woman is worth a dozen Fanny Ferns; and to make a woman a credit to her sex and an adornment to society, no further education is necessary.[62]

Whitman scholars have interpreted this to be a disparagement of Fern's writing, which they have characterized as sentimental.[63] But, in fact, it is a criticism of women who are *more* intellectual, rather than less. What Whitman is saying here is that we need earth mothers, not intelligent women like Fanny Fern. Perhaps the implication is that intelligent women are too assertive; they might even be strong enough and smart enough to insist that you pay your debts.

Fern was in Philadelphia when Whitman's cowardly attack appeared in the *Brooklyn Times*, but in later years she never retaliated in kind— that is, she never mentioned Whitman by name in her column. Perhaps, to a man as publicity hungry as Whitman was, this was the worst punishment of all. But in three columns, Fern did make references that are unmistakably to Whitman. These columns help us to understand her attitude toward him. On 3 April 1858, she wrote in the *New York Ledger* in a column entitled "On Voices and Beards":

I once believed in voices as indicative of character; it makes me laugh now to think of it. I was cured of it by a fellow who looked born to express physically "the dignity of human nature." I believe that is the fasionable phrase. Dignity! there's where the laugh comes in; dignity—in a leviathan of muscle and flesh, crawling lazily out of bed at twelve noon to live the rest of the day by borrowing of anybody who could be bamboozled into believing that honesty, honor and manliness were represented in his deep, rich, sympathetic voice—his stock in trade, which it would be next to impossible to associate with cowardice or dishonor! . . .

The dollars that fellow has borrowed on that voice, the drinks he has swallowed on the strength of it, not to mention the strength of the drinks! the oysters he has eaten by virtue of it, and the rides and invitations he has got!—all by those frank, hearty, jolly, musical tones, which it would puzzle a Shylock to resist. No, I believe no more in voices.

In her "Peeps" column in 1856, Fern had commented on Whitman's voice and added, "Let me hear the *voice* of a man or a woman and I will tell you the stuff its owners are made of." In this article two years later, she confesses that she was taken in by the voice. The man that she had thought was a superior man is, she now believes, a lazy charlatan, who takes advantage of other people in order to get what he can out of them. Fern obviously felt not scorned, but used.

That Fanny Fern's reaction to Whitman's behavior did not derive from the ulterior motive of a spurned love, as Whitman's defenders have insinuated, is clear from the fact that she held this opinion of such behavior before she even met Whitman. In her novel *Rose Clark*, published in December 1855, for example, she satirizes in Tom Finels the type of poet who lives wholly off other people. Finels obtains free dinners, free steamboat rides, even presents, and rationalizes his parasitical existence with Whitmanesque references to "the sovereignty of the individual."[64] Given this opinion of poetic spongers, it is not surprising that Fern reacted as she did when she concluded that Whitman was guilty of such behavior. By the summer of 1857 she was determined not to give Whitman any further publicity. The article "Look Aloft" was prefaced by a quotation from Whitman's poetry when it originally appeared in the *Ledger* on 5 July 1856, but when it was published in her book *Fresh Leaves* in September 1857, the Whitman quotation had been eliminated. Similarly, the paragraph describing Whitman in her "Peeps" series was deleted when the articles were published in *Fresh Leaves*. And her review of *Leaves of Grass* was never reprinted in any of her collections.

On 24 September 1864, Fern wrote an article in the *Ledger* called "In Debt," which makes very clear her opinion of Whitman's behavior with respect to the loan:

> How can a man eat, drink, sleep and be jolly under the pressure of debt. Perhaps one of the meanest of these dainty fellows' tricks is to victimize a *friend* who may be supposed to have scruples about refusing monetary compliance, or about reminding the creditor of his protracted forgetfulness of the sum due. Yes—there *is* one lower depth of meanness yet, and that is, when the friend is a woman who, if she be not too smart, may be generally conveniently put off with well-framed excuses, or, at all events be supposed to be too "refined" and "delicate" to press so unromantic a theme. Fortunately, all women are *not* "fools.". . . It is comforting when such an one without compromising her womanly dignity handsomely compels as a man might and would do, immediate restitution, or the alternative penalty.

This article suggests that Whitman had counted on Parton's "scruples about refusing monetary compliance" and on Fern's feminine "delicacy" not "to press so unromantic a theme" as a debt. But Fanny Fern was nobody's "fool," not even Walt Whitman's. She was a practical woman who had learned to take care of herself and to stand up for herself. As she said in 1856 after successfully taking a man to court who had fraudulently published a book in her name, women have got to stand up for their rights: "Are bonnets to be trampled on by boots?" (*NYL*, 2 August 1856).

The final reference to Whitman in Fanny Fern's column appeared in the *Ledger* on 28 October 1865, in an article on "Unprincipled Talent":

> He really did not *mean* to incur debts he could not pay, but he never could keep a cent of money, and he had never the resolution to face those to whom his money was due; but why mention such *little* foibles? How remember them when reading his splendid, etc., etc. . . . A fig for such a genius! Give me in preference the man who *can* face those he owes, with the hard-earned money in his rough palm, though he never read, or owned, a book in all his toilsome life . . . before him whose verses or whose writings are

quoted the world over, and who yet lets any foolish friend who will, pay for the clothes he wears, or for the food he eats because, forsooth, "he can never keep a penny." . . . Genius forsooth! I have yet to learn that when the ten commandments were written, "geniuses" were counted out.

This article provides the key to an important difference between Fern and Whitman. Although they both urged self-realization and self-reliance, although they both were literary people dedicated to their art, Whitman was in the end concerned primarily with Walt Whitman, while Fern, throughout her life, was concerned with the people around her. No matter how much she complained about the distractions that interfered with her work as a writer, she could not conceive of individual concerns taking priority over people. That is what she could not forgive in Whitman; genius was no excuse for treating friends shabbily.

Whitman was probably right: it probably was Fanny Fern who insisted that he repay the debt. He had underestimated her. His bitterness arose from his having found out too late that she was not the passive, voiceless woman that he wrote about. And she realized that she had overestimated him, having believed him to be possessed of the "candor" that he celebrated in *Leaves of Grass*. Nor was he the advocate of women that she had thought him to be.

Had Whitman read carefully the note that Fern sent him on 21 April 1856, he would not have made the mistake that he did about her. Quoting from *Leaves of Grass* the lines, "What I assume you shall assume," she wrote. "What *I* assume, *you* shall assume!" The significance is in her italics. By italicizing the words that she did, she pointed out to him that they could have the reverse meaning as well—that she, too, was the self, the "I" of the poem. Like Margaret Fuller in her resistance to Emerson's overwhelming attempt to absorb her personality into his own,[65] Fern refused to be the passive other of the poem.

In the context of this situation, there is something very sad about Fern's concluding statement in her review of *Leaves of Grass*, where she asked Whitman to accept the "cordial grasp of a woman's hand." She extended her hand in friendship, but Whitman, although he seemed to portray woman as the equal of man, did not regard her in this light. And his defenders—with his encouragement—turned an honest friendship between them into a sorry tale of unrequited love.

The irony of this aborted friendship is that, although Whitman's name lives on, the name of Fanny Fern—so well known in her own day—has in the twentieth century been heard only in reference to Walt Whitman. Fanny Fern, who insisted that woman should be regarded as an individual in her own right, has come to be known only in relation to a man. It is Whitman's picture of woman that has survived.

The question is, Why has Whitman been remembered when Fern is not even a memory? There are many reasons. Whitman's own lifelong search for publicity and his devoted disciples who turned the man into a myth during his own lifetime—these are two reasons. In contrast, Fanny Fern shunned personal publicity and, after her death, her family, in seeking to counteract the unfavorable publicity spread by such sources as the author of *Life and Beauties*, preferred to foster the image of her as a domestic woman. The literary value of their work is not comparable, perhaps. Whitman was a journalist, but it is as a poet that he is remembered; Fern's major contribution was as a journalist. Yet, in their respective fields both were remarkable. Fanny Fern's frank satire, down-to-earth language, and sharp prose were as unique in her field at the time as Whitman's poetry was in his. Both were innovators who opened the doors to a new tradition in literature.[66]

But there is one major difference between the work of Fanny Fern and Walt Whitman, a difference inherent in the metaphors suggested by the titles of their two books, *Fern Leaves* and *Leaves of Grass*. The titles are similar, but they are also different—and the difference is significant. Ferns grow only in hidden, shady nooks; grass grows in the open sunlight. Fern's message was couched in socially acceptable language and imagery, but the message itself was indeed radical. Fanny Fern was projecting a message that was radically un-American at the time: individualism for women. The year before Fern began to write, James Fenimore Cooper wrote of the ideal woman: "a kind, gentle, affectionate, thoughtful creature, whose heart is so full of you, there is no room in it for herself."[67] This was the credo of nineteenth-century Americans; it was heresy for Fanny Fern to insist that a woman could exist *for herself*.

Fern's message to women was the opposite of Whitman's for women. She insisted that woman existed for herself alone, not merely as wife or mother in relation to man. This is the underlying theme of her newspaper articles, and the theme of her novel, *Ruth Hall*, which was almost unique among nineteenth-century American novels is portraying a woman who succeeds on her own, who fulfills the American Dream previously reserved for men. Following the pattern of Fanny Fern's own success, the heroine of her novel succeeds—becomes rich and powerful—without the help, and in spite of the hindrance, of the men in her life. And the novel ends, not with a wedding, but with the heroine going off to conquer new worlds.

The difference between Fern's and Whitman's messages can be described as the politics of subversion versus the politics of celebration. Fern's writing was political in its message to women to adopt the individualism of American culture, yet her message was conveyed in acceptable language and imagery that made it publishable. Although her language was called indelicate by her more fastidious contemporaries, it never exceeded the limits of what was regarded as the language of a respectable woman. And her message was always given in a safely domestic setting. Like the ferns in the title of her first book, her message, if it was to flourish in her day, had to be kept in the shade of acceptable language and imagery.

Whitman, however, used language and imagery that were daring in his day, but his message to and celebration of the American male were not new; they were simply a restatement of that individualism articulated by Emerson which had long been the cornerstone of American culture.[68] His message, therefore, like the grass in his title, could grow and flourish in sunny soil.

It is this difference that helps to explain the disappearance of Fanny Fern from American literature, and the simultaneous growth of Walt Whitman's reputation. Once Whitman's language and imagery were found to be acceptable, his message was no threat; Fern's message, on the other hand, was a threat, and once her columns stopped appearing after her death, there was no one in the literary establishment—except, as was proper, her husband—willing to champion her. She was popular in her day because the people—mostly women—who read her caustic, thought-provoking barbs at men and institutions responded overwhelmingly in her favor. But her admirers were ordinary people, not literary Brahmins. Who among her supporters—the factory women, the shop girls, the overworked farm wives, the tired mothers—had the knowledge or the time to create a Fanny Fern cult, to ensure that her works were printed and reprinted, to bring her un-American message to succeeding generations? It was not Walt Whitman who was the rebel against American society; it was Fanny Fern. Damned as a sentimentalist, however, she was effectively removed from discussion, and her work—along with her subversive message—remained hidden for over a hundred years.

Notes

1. The similarity between these two books was first suggested by Clifton Furness and Alfred Goldsmith and has been noted by successive Whitman scholars. See Clifton J. Furness, introduction to Walt Whitman, *Leaves of Grass* (New York: Columbia University Press, Facsimile Text Society, 1939), ix–x. See also Walt Whitman, *I Sit and Look Out: Editorials from the "Brooklyn Daily Times,"* ed. Emory Holloway and Vernolian Schwartz (1932; reprint, New York: AMS Press, 1966), 211; and Clara Barrus, *Whitman and Burroughs: Comrades* (New York: Houghton Mifflin, 1931), 178. More recently, it has been noted by Justin Kaplan, *Walt Whitman: A Life* (New York: Simon and Schuster, 1980), 216; and Paul Zweig, *Walt Whitman: The Making of the Poet* (New York: Basic Books, 1984), 42. Zweig comments that Whitman "almost surely" got the idea for the cover and title from *Fern Leaves*. There had been other "Leaves" books prior to Fanny Fern's (e.g., Grace Greenwood's *Greenwood Leaves* in 1850), but *Fern Leaves* was so well known and so unusual in its satiric content that it seems most likely that it was the principal source for Whitman's cover and title, if only because Whitman, who was an eager promoter of his own book, would not have been unaware of the benefits of such an association.

2. See, e.g., Zweig, *Walt Whitman*, 231.

3. For sales figures for *Fern Leaves*, see John S. Hart, *The Female Prose Writers of America* (Philadelphia: E. H. Butler, 1857), 472. As of 1 June 1854, there were 70,000 copies of *Fern Leaves* sold in the United States and 29,000 sold in Great Britain. *Fern Leaves*, second series, published May 1854, had sold 30,000. Whitman's own comments regarding the sales of *Leaves of Grass* appear in Horace Traubel, *With Walt Whitman in Camden*, 6 vols. (Boston: Small, Maynard, 1906–1982), 2:471–472; 3:115–116.

4. Fern's novel *Ruth Hall* (1855) was reprinted in 1986 by Rutgers University Press. The edition contains approximately a hundred of her newspaper articles. See *"Ruth Hall" and Other Writings*, by Fanny Fern, edited by Joyce W. Warren.

5. The receipt and Whitman's explanation are printed in Traubel, *Whitman in Camden*, 3:235–239. For a detailed analysis of the Whitman-Parton debt, see Oral S. Coad, "Whitman vs. Parton," *Journal of the Rutgers University Library* 4 (December 1940):1–8; and Milton Flower, *James Parton: The Father of Modern Biography* (Durham, N.C.: Duke University Press, 1951), 48–49, 240–241. See also the letters of Ethel Parton and William Sloane Kennedy, and others, in the Rutgers University Library, New Brunswick, N.J.

6. Traubel, *Whitman in Camden*, 3:235–236.

7. See, e.g., Whitman, *I Sit and Look Out*, 211; and idem *New York Dissected*, ed. Emory Holloway and Ralph Adimari (New York: Rufus Rockwell Wilson, 1936), 153.

8. Fred Lewis Pattee, *The Feminine Fifties* (New York: D. Appleton-

Century, 1940), 110–118. Gay Wilson Allen, *The Solitary Singer* (New York: Grove Press, 1955), 177, calls her a "purveyer of sentimental pap." Other Whitman scholars who have accepted this opinion of Fern's work apparently without reading it include Henry Canby, *Walt Whitman: An American* (Westport, Conn.: Greenwood Press, 1943), 122, 301; Frances Winwar, *American Giant: Walt Whitman and His Times* (New York: Harper and Brothers, 1941), 183–184; and Kaplan, *Walt Whitman*, 216.

9. This has been the assumption of almost every Whitman scholar. See, e.g., Barrus, *Whitman and Burroughs*, 178; Whitman, *I Sit and Look Out*, 211; idem, *New York Dissected*, 153; Winwar, *American Giant*, 183–184, 202; Canby, *Walt Whitman*, 122; Kaplan, *Walt Whitman*, 216; Zweig, *Walt Whitman*, 279–280.

10. The facts about Fanny Fern's life are drawn primarily from her private papers in the Sophia Smith Collection at Smith College, Northampton, Mass.; her *Ledger* columns; James Parton, *Fanny Fern: A Memorial Volume* (New York: Carleton, 1873); Ethel Parton, "Fanny Fern: An Informal Biography," unpublished manuscript, Sophia Smith Collection.

11. For information about the Farrington marriage, see documents in the Sophia Smith Collection.

12. N. P. Willis's undated letter is in the Sophia Smith Collection, with comments in Fanny Fern's handwriting indicating how cruel it seemed to her at the time, she being "destitute."

13. Nathaniel Hawthorne, *Letters to William Ticknor, 1851–69*, ed. C. E. Frazer-Clark, Jr., 2 vols. (Newark, N.J.: Carteret Book Club, 1972), 1:78.

14. The facts of Whitman's life are taken primarily from Traubel, *Whitman in Camden*; Allen, *Solitary Singer*; Kaplan, *Walt Whitman*; and Zweig, *Walt Whitman*. I have also taken relevant information from other biographies, e.g., R. M. Bucke, *Walt Whitman* (1883; reprint, New York: Johnson Reprint, 1970), which was partially written by Whitman himself; John Burroughs, *Whitman: A Study* (1896; reprint, New York: AMS Press, 1976); and Whitman, *New York Dissected*.

15. For the text of some of these reviews of the first edition of *Leaves of Grass*, see Bucke, *Walt Whitman*, 193–236; Whitman, *New York Dissected*, 145–176.

16. Printed in the *New York Ledger*, 19 April 1856 (hereafter cited as *NYL* in the text).

17. Kaplan, *Walt Whitman*, 216.

18. MS biography of Walt Whitman by Clifton Joseph Furness (cited in Flower, *James Parton*, 48).

19. Whitman, for example, wrote his own anonymous reviews of *Leaves of Grass* and flattering articles about himself. Kaplan, *Walt Whitman*, 207–209, comments that Whitman had learned his lessons from P. T. Barnum. Quentin Anderson, in his introduction to Walt Whitman, *Walt Whitman's Autograph Revision of the Analysis of "Leaves of Grass"* (New York: New York University Press, 1974), 11, comments that "Whitman threw himself into the effort to

make himself known with a single-mindedness unexampled among great writers."

20. See letter from Samuel Wells to Walt Whitman, 7 June 1856, Feinberg Collection, Library of Congress. The passage from this letter is quoted incorrectly by Kaplan, *Walt Whitman* (p. 216), and Edwin Haviland Miller, *Walt Whitman: The Correspondence* (New York: New York University Press, 1961), 2:44, both of whom say that Wells had called the Partons "rich and enterprizing," whereas it is clearly the Partons' publishers that Wells refers to.

21. Whitman, *New York Dissected*, 130–131 (from *Life Illustrated*, 16 August 1856).

22. Undated clipping in Sophia Smith Collection; also Greeley to Fern, 11 May 1870, Houghton Library.

23. Zweig, *Walt Whitman*, 271.

24. MS in Missouri Historical Society, St. Louis, Missouri: see section published by John Francis McDermott, "Glimpses from the Diary of Thomas Butler Gunn, 1856–1860," *American Literature* 29 (November 1957):316–319.

25. McDermott also comes to this last conclusion; see ibid., 316.

26. MS of letter reproduced in William White, "Fanny Fern to Walt Whitman: An Unpublished Letter," *American Book Collector* 11 (May 1961): 8–9.

27. Norton had written a quasi-favorable review of *Leaves of Grass* for *Putnam's Monthly* in September 1856, but he made this comment to his friend, James Russell Lowell, confessing that he himself had trouble with the book's "disgusting" coarseness; see Charles Eliot Norton, *Letters*, 2 vols. (Boston: Houghton, 1913) 1:135.

28. Ralph Waldo Emerson, *Complete Works*, Centenary Edition, ed. Edward W. Emerson, 12 vols. (Boston: Houghton Mifflin, 1903–1904), 3:231–233.

29. Printed in the *New York Musical World and Times*, 24 September 1853.

30. Ibid., 7 May 1853.

31. Printed in the *Boston True Flag*, 9 April 1853.

32. Walt Whitman, *Leaves of Grass*, Norton Critical Edition, ed. Sculley Bradley and Harold W. Blodgett (New York: Norton, 1973), 1 (hereafter cited as *L* in the text).

33. Walt Whitman, *Collected Writings: Prose Works, 1892*, ed. Floyd Stovall, 2 vols. (New York: New York University Press, 1963–1964), 2:389 (hereafter cited as *CW* in the text).

34. Among the critics who have recognized Whitman's limited view of women are D. H. Lawrence, *Studies in Classic American Literature* (1932; reprint, New York: Viking, 1971), 167; Leadie Mae Clark, *Walt Whitman's Concept of the American Common Man* (New York: Philadelphia Library, 1955), 95–107; Nina Baym, "Portrayal of Women in American Literature, 1790–1870," in *What Manner of Woman: Essays on English and American Life and Literature*, ed. Marlene Springer (New York: New York University Press, 1977), 220–221; and Arthur Wrobel, "'Noble American Motherhood':

Whitman, Women, and the Ideal Democracy," *American Studies* 21 (Fall 1980): 7–25.

35. I have not discussed the question of Whitman's ambivalence about his sexual identity here because it does not seem to have had a significant effect on his attitude toward woman's role. Although one might argue that it was his ambivalence about his own sexual identity that enabled Whitman to recognize in women the same physical nature that he felt in himself, there is no evidence that it enabled him to transcend the conventions of his time with respect to his conception of the role of women in society.

36. See the *Brooklyn Daily Eagle*, 19 August 1846, 11 September 1846, 20 November 1846, 29 January 1847. Some of these articles are reprinted in *The Uncollected Poetry and Prose of Walt Whitman*, ed. Emory Holloway, 2 vols. (Gloucester, Mass.: Peter Smith, 1972), 1:137; and Cleveland Rodgers and John Black, eds., *The Gathering of the Forces of Walt Whitman*, 2 vols. (New York: Putnam's, 1920), 1:148–151. For a discussion of Whitman's work on the *Eagle*, see Thomas Brasher, *Whitman as Editor of the "Brooklyn Daily Eagle"* (Detroit: Wayne State University Press, 1970).

37. *Brooklyn Daily Times*, 19 July 1857, reprinted in Whitman, *I Sit and Look Out*, 53–54.

38. *Brooklyn Daily Eagle*, 11 February 1847, reprinted in Florence B. Freedman, *Walt Whitman Looks at the Schools* (New York: King's Crown Press, 1950), 165–166.

39. *Brooklyn Daily Edge*, 9 November 1846; see *Uncollected Poetry and Prose*, 132.

40. *Brooklyn Daily Times*, 2 September 1857, reprinted in Whitman, *I Sit and Look Out*, 113–114.

41. *Brooklyn Daily Eagle*, 18 February 1847, reprinted in Rogers and Black, *Gathering of the Forces*, 1:73–74.

42. *Brooklyn Daily Eagle*, 8 September 1846.

43. See *Brooklyn Daily Times*, 13 March 1859; and *Brooklyn Daily Eagle*, 13 April 1846, 11 September 1846, 12 March 1847, and 29 May 1847. See also Whitman, *I Sit and Look Out*, 117–118.

44. Charles W. Eldridge, "Walt Whitman as a Conservative," *New York Times*, 7 June 1902.

45. Justin Kaplan, for example, claims that the "I" of *Leaves of Grass* "is almost as often a woman as a man" (*Walt Whitman*, 63). Other critics have attempted to make a case for Whitman as a proponent of women, even a feminist. See Judy Womack, "The American Woman in 'Song of Myself,'" *Walt Whitman Review* 19 (June 1973):67–72; Kay F. Reinartz, "Walt Whitman and Feminism," *Walt Whitman Review* 19 (December 1973):127–137; Lottie L. Guttry, "Walt Whitman and the Woman Reader," *Walt Whitman Review* 22 (September 1976):102–110; Muriel Kolinsky, "'Me Tarzan, You Jane': Whitman's Attitudes toward Women from a Women's Liberation Point of View," *Walt Whitman Review* 23 (December 1977):155–165; and Harold Aspiz, *Walt Whitman and the Body Beautiful* (Urbana: University of Illinois Press, 1980), chap. 7.

46. McDermott, "Diary of Gunn," 319.
47. Ibid., 318–319.
48. Ibid., 319.
49. Ibid.
50. Ethel Parton to William Sloane Kennedy, 10 February 1897, Rutgers University Library.
51. Whitman met Dyer frequently at the Partons', but he had first known him ten years earlier when they both worked on the *Brooklyn Daily Eagle*.
52. Whitman's letter and the receipt are printed in Traubel, *Whitman in Camden*, 3:237–239.
53. Ethel Parton to William Sloane Kennedy, 10 February 1897, Rutgers University Library.
54. Ethel Parton to Kennedy, 15 February 1897, Rutgers University Library.
55. William Sloane Kennedy, "Did Walt Whitman Leave a Debt Unpaid?" unpublished manuscript, n.d., Rutgers University Library.
56. Kaplan, *Walt Whitman*, pp. 33–38, describes how Whitman accepted the role of guru, or head of an apostolic church whom his disciples exalted to Christ-like proportions.
57. Most Whitman scholars who have made the assumption that Fanny Fern was in love with Whitman have either cited no source or have cited an anonymous "intimate friend" of Whitman as the source. See, e.g., Whitman, *I Sit and Look Out*, 211. That this intimate friend was Ellen O'Connor is clear from the letters of William Sloane Kennedy in the Rutgers University Library. See also Barrus, *Whitman and Burroughs*, 178; and Kaplan, *Walt Whitman*, 224–225.
58. That Ellen ("Nelly") O'Connor was in love with Whitman is apparent from her letters in the Feinberg Collection at the Library of Congress, 1864 to 1870, culminating in the letter of 20 November 1870, (printed in full in Florence B. Freedman, *William Douglas O'Connor: Walt Whitman's Chosen Knight* (Athens: Ohio University Press, 1985), pp. 246–248:

> I always know that you know that I love you all the time, even though we should never meet again, my feelings could never change, and I am *sure* that you know it as well as I do. I do flatter myself too, that *you* care for *me*,—not as I love you, because you are great and strong, and more sufficient unto yourself than any woman can be.

Whitman was critical of the way O'Connor treated his wife; he lived for ten years as part of the O'Connor family, helping Nelly O'Connor with household chores, exploring Washington with her, and she darning his socks and stitching the little notebooks he kept notes in. When he was seriously ill in 1873, she was his constant visitor and nurse. In 1872 Whitman's friendship with O'Connor ended in a violent quarrel. Although the reason for the quarrel has been given out as having to do with black civil rights or the Franco-Prussian War, it is clear that there was more involved than an abstract argument. That O'Connor urged his friend John Burroughs to maintain secrecy about the quarrel suggests that the reason was personal, and the fact that O'Connor left his wife on the night of the quarrel suggests that the reason for the quarrel somehow involved Nelly. One clue is found in O'Connor's short story, "The Carpenter," published in *Putnam's* in January 1868. The story portrays a man who is "tortured by the deep suspicion that his beloved wife is drifting from him into love with his bosom-friend." See Freedman, *William Douglas O'Connor*, 149–150, 210, 246–260, 340; idem, "New Light on an Old Quarrel: Walt Whitman and William Douglas O'Connor, 1872," *Walt Whitman Review* 11 (June 1965):27–52; Jerome Loving, *Walt Whitman's Champion, William Douglas O'Connor* (College Station: Texas A&M University Press, 1978), 99–102; Traubel, *Whitman in Camden*, 3:509; Edwin Haviland Miller, *The Correspondence*, 2:193–198, 204–207.

59. Ethel Parton to William Sloane Kennedy, 15 and 10 February 1897, Rutgers University Library.

60. This was told to me by James Parton II, the great-grandson of Fanny Fern. He learned it from Ethel Parton, Fern's granddaughter, who was present at the time.

61. Ethel Parton to Kennedy, 10 February 1897, Rutgers University Library.

62. Walt Whitman, "Free Academies at Public Cost," *Brooklyn Daily Times*, 9 July 1857, reprinted in *I Sit and Look Out*, 53–54.

63. For example, Holloway and Adimari (in Whitman, *New York Dissected*, 152) say that the disparaging reference to Fanny Fern "may have been only Whitman's opinion of her as a writer"; and Allen (in *Solitary Singer*, 210) explains it by saying that Whitman was "probably contemptuous of her sentimental journalism."

64. Fanny Fern, *Rose Clark* (New York: Mason Brothers, 1856), 321, 354–355.

65. *Memoirs of Margaret Fuller Ossoli*, ed. Ralph Waldo Emerson, William Henry Channing, and James Freeman Clarke, 2 vols. (1852; reprint, New York: Burt Franklin, 1972), 2:67.

66. For comments regarding Fanny Fern's original style, see, e.g., *Harper's Monthly*, 9 (July 1854):277: "She dares to be original. She has no fear of critics or of the public before her eyes. . . . It shows that the day for stilted rhetoric, scholastic refinements, and big dictionary words, the parade, pomp, and pageantry of literature, is declining."

67. James Fenimore Cooper, *The Ways of the Hour*, in *Complete Works*, 32 vols. (New York: Putnam, 1893), 24:312.

68. For a discussion of individualism in American culture and Emerson's expression of it, see my book, *The American Narcissus: Individualism and Women in Nineteenth-Century American Fiction* (New Brunswick, N.J.: Rutgers University Press, 1984).

SHIRLEY MARCHALONIS

A Model for Mentors?:
Lucy Larcom and
John Greenleaf Whittier

BIOGRAPHERS OF JOHN GREENLEAF WHITTIER have dealt competently with his abolitionism, his Quaker background, and his poetry. They have been less comfortable in protraying his relationships with his "protégées"—the women writers in whom he took a real and active interest. A variety of biographical approaches seem to avoid the questions that these relationships raise.[1]

Although treatments of the protégées vary according to each biographer's thesis or perspective, they reduce all the women to the status of objects existing only in relation to Whittier. Alice and Phoebe Cary, Lucy Larcom, Gail Hamilton, Elizabeth Stuart Phelps, Celia Thaxter, Sarah Orne Jewett, and others are usually treated as a lump of women writers whose careers Whittier somehow encouraged.

Naturally a biographer concentrates on his subject; however, by presenting the protégées as if they were paper cutouts, the scholar finally projects an incomplete, if not false, picture. These women, all very popular and widely read in their day, were a part of the literary world of the latter half of nineteenth-century America; without consideration of them and their work, the account is not complete.

Furthermore, failure to examine these relationships closely leaves unanswered a great many questions about Whittier himself. In crudest terms, what did he get out of his role as mentor to talented, aspiring young women? What led to his interest in them and their needs? Was his reward a sense of power and the enjoyment of the admiration, sometimes verging on adoration, that he received? Was it a trade-off for the sexual life he apparently denied himself? Was his behavior an extension of the Quaker beliefs that led him almost to sacrifice his poetic career in the abolitionist cause? Were these relationships love affairs, or was he simply the too-kind-hearted victim of women's importunities? On the other side of the picture, what did it mean to be a Whittier protégée? What effect did he have on the career of any one writer?

Whittier and the very popular poet Lucy Larcom had a personal and professional friendship that lasted nearly fifty years.[2] Larcom, usually identified as a "former mill girl," appears in most of the biographies; her adult status as a well-known magazine editor and a leading poet is seldom mentioned. She is the recipient of letters (Pollard), a languishing lady (Warren), or a lovesick idiot (Mordell). Seldom is she presented as a person with her own identity.

From almost any study of Whittier, one thing is very clear. He liked women, was comfortable in their company, and enjoyed their admiration of him. His biographers often claim that his Quaker upbringing taught him to see women as equals; in reality, he treated his protégées as daughters, over whom he had some paternal control that permitted him to tell them what to do and how to do it. That attitude hardly reflects equality, but it is more enlightened than the then-prevailing patriarchal attitudes toward women writers. Whittier never told talented women that their real work was to marry and produce young.

Whittier's warm relationships with women began at home. He was extremely close to his mother and his sister Elizabeth, both of whom supported and encouraged him through the years of near-poverty, ill health, and the intense dedication to the abolitionist cause that dominated much of his life. Their Quaker moderation did not inhibit the free use of intelligence and expression of ideas, and Whittier respected their opinions. Visitors to Amesbury, Larcom among them, commented on the beauty of the intense love between brother and sister. However a more psychologically oriented age interprets the kind or degree of such a relationship, it did exist, and it served to educate him to women's identities and talents. His own youthful career was encouraged by the famous poet, Lydia Sigourney.

Whittier and Larcom first met in the spring of 1844 at Lowell, and it is important to understand the status of each at the time. He came to Lowell as the editor of the Free-Soil and abolitionist *Middlesex Standard*. While he had a reputation as a poet, he was far better known as an antislavery activist and writer. Everything—career, health, sexual energy—had been repressed and channeled into the abolitionist cause. He had dedicated, perhaps sacrificed, his pen to the cause; editors without the abolitionist commitment feared his work. His income from editing jobs, articles, and poems was barely enough to support him, his mother, and his sister. One of the reasons he gave in later years for not marrying when young was his extreme poverty and his responsibility for his dependents. At thirty-five he was, according to both male and female contemporaries, strikingly handsome, tall and spare and dark, with a rather bony face dominated by intense dark eyes, which glowed and burned and shot fire and pierced like an eagle's when his emotions were evoked.[3]

The romantic attachments of his young manhood, differentiated from the protégées, were certainly inhibited by his poverty, poor health, and the intensity of his commitment. Letters to them often seem to attract and then repel, but his behavior can be more simply explained as normal attraction that had to be limited by physical and financial circumstances.

By the time he came to Lowell, his image was that of a crusader. Among the mill girls, who were stongly abolitionist in their sentiments (perhaps because the cotton mill owners were so definitely not), he was a hero. He spoke for the bright, well-read, and upright farm girls whose recruitment made the Lowell experiment internationally famous.[4] Most of them could recite, for example, his poem, "The Yankee Girl," about a lovely Northern girl who rejects a marriage proposal and a life of luxury with a Southern plantation owner. She tosses back "the dark wealth of her curls, / With a scorn in her eye which the gazer could feel," and orders, "Go back, haughty Southron!":

> Full low at thy bidding thy negroes may kneel,
> With the iron of bondage on spirit and heel;
> Yet know that the Yankee girl sooner would be
> In fetters with them, than in freedom with thee.

One evening Harriet Farley, a neighbor of Whittier's, brought him to a meeting of the Improvement Circle that produced the monthly magazine called the *Lowell Offering*. The girls in their white dresses were awed at the poet's visit; Larcom, a major although very youthful contributor to the magazine, was embarrassed to have her verses read aloud. When he came to talk to her, she could barely speak.[5]

For a long time awe overshadowed friendship, for Larcom was never very self-confident. Her secure, happy childhood in Beverly, Massachusetts, dominated by her remote, austere, but loving father, ended when his death sent the family to Lowell, where Mrs. Larcom became a boardinghouse keeper. Larcom went to work as a doffer at eleven. She loved school, but financial pressures sent her back to the mill; at about thirteen she was exhausted and ill and was sent to stay with a married sister in Beverly. When she came back to Lowell, her brilliant older sister Emeline's friends, Harriet Farley and Harriott Curtis, had started the *Lowell Offering*; Larcom, although she was much younger than the others, began to write for it. She was an avid reader, had written verses since she was seven, and took every opportunity Lowell offered to educate herself.

At twenty she was a tall, stately young woman, attractive rather than beautiful, with rich light brown hair and bright blue eyes that, according to one of her friends, seemed always to be laughing.[6] She was a compulsive reader with an insatiable love of learning, a talent for verse making, and no real goal for the future. She had a curiously divided personality: cheerful, outgoing and affectionate among friends; reserved, diffident, and barely able to assert herself among strangers.

Larcom called once or twice at the Whittier home, but in 1846 she went west, at that time the Illinois prairie, with her sister Emeline, Emeline's husband, and her brother-in-law, Frank, to whom Larcom was engaged. For them, as for many young people, the west seemed to offer the future.

Larcom took with her from eleven years in the mills the habit of reading and study, a great deal of unfocused knowledge gained from books and lectures and unrelated courses—when she could not find any way of learning English literature, for example, she went to the Lowell library and read and outlined her way through the canon—the self-discipline to make herself work even when she did not want to, and an accompanying belief in the sanctity of work. She also took a hatred of crowds and noise that was almost pathological, and the seeds of disease.[7] Although diffident outside her circle of friends, she had confidence in her ability to take care of herself.

The west was disappointing, but she remained for six years. She acquired an excellent education at Monticello Seminary under its remarkable headmistress, Philena Fobes, and she made some close friends in a family of transplanted New Englanders who encouraged her writing and study, but there were few other positive elements. She watched her brilliant sister Emeline abandon all her talents for a life that seemed to consist of dirt, drudgery, and dead babies. (Emeline bore twelve children altogether, of whom three reached adulthood.) Prairie marriage disgusted the younger sister; she was careful not to say so, but the poems she sent back to the *New England Offering*, successor to the *Lowell Offering*, cannot conceal under their humor her consistently negative feelings.

Larcom described her childhood self as stubborn rather than aggressive; she could never confront, but she developed protective strategies to evade what she did not want. One of the things she managed to evade for the moment was her own marriage.

It was on her return to Massachusetts in 1852 that her real friendship with the Whittiers began. She had called at their home several times while she still lived in Lowell, and after she went west had occasionally written to Elizabeth. Whittier, now corresponding editor for the *National Era*, the Washington, D.C., abolitionist newspaper, once or twice reprinted some of her essays from the *Offering*, like her amusing but rueful account of a district teacher's life. The *Era* published a poem of hers called "The Burning Prairie," in which the sudden prairie fires are compared to the fire in the nation's soul that would burn away slavery, and Whittier wrote a biographical and critical introduction praising her work. He probably recommended her to Rufus W. Griswold, for two of her poems appeared in the 1850 edition of *Female Poets of America*, with Whittier's biographical sketch.

By 1852 Whittier was approaching the point in his career when he was beginning to move away from his role as political activist to become more and more the poet. His belief in the antislavery cause had not changed, but he was forty-five, and most of his energies up to this point had gone into his abolitionist efforts. It was, as J. B. Pickard says, time now for younger men to take over, and for him to concentrate on poetry that celebrated nature, goodness, and the New England past.[8]

His initiative in developing their friendship was one of the bright spots of Larcom's return; she herself was still far too diffident to do more than make the proper formal call on his family. He visited her in Beverly, and gave cordial invitations, backed up by his mother and sister, to visit in Amesbury. His interest in her writing made it more valuable in her eyes, for it never occurred to her to doubt his judgment; she still regarded him with awe. He was as dynamic and compelling as ever, and to have some of that intensity directed on her and her work was flattering; if he chose to set himself up as mentor, she was too dazzled to respond with anything but happiness and gratitude. He was the Master and she the humble pupil—in both their eyes.

Obviously, there were other grounds for compatibility. They were both great readers and shared their love of books, especially poetry. They had the same dry, straight-faced New England humor.[9] Both of them had a love of the natural world—landscape, flowers, trees, water—and this love of nature is reflected in her letters to him. They shared the same morality and background. The early years of Larcom's life as she described them in *A New England Girlhood*, though spent in a village rather than on a farm, resemble the world that Whittier was to evoke in *Snow-bound* in both the mechanics of daily living and the strong family orientation. Their values—work, honesty, duty, love of God—were rooted in the same New England past.

In none of Larcom's letters and journals is there the slightest hint that she ever expected any more of him than friendship. No relationship between complex people is ever simple, and there was certainly a romantic element in their friendship. But it was the romance of hero worship rather than of sex; he was for years the glorious Mr. Great-Heart of *Pilgrim's Progress* and her ideals, and in that sense she remained a little in love with him all her life. The approval of her and her work, the attention and concern from this commanding older man, satisfied something in her that had ached since her father died. She was happy to write as he suggested, and not for many years did she grow restless and uncomfortable with his guidance. The relationship was so much that of master and pupil that she was more comfortable with his sister and saw herself as Elizabeth's friend who was also Whittier's protégée.

Five of her poems were published in the *National Era* in 1853, but Whittier urged her to do more than verses. She had, ever since her days in Lowell, written short essays that she called "Similitudes": a child, in a beautifully described natural setting, learns a religious truth. Whittier was enthusiastic when he read them, and decided that they should be published as a book. He began by urging his own publishers, Ticknor and Fields, to accept them, writing about the "unique and beautiful little book" that "I am quite sure that if it was an *English* book of equal merit and beauty, it would not lack republication here at once."[10] Fields felt that it was not for his house (Larcom herself had been modestly horrified at the idea of submitting her book to the most prestigious of all publishers), but Whittier kept on; a few weeks later he wrote her, "I have seen J. P. Jewett and he is quite ready to publish it. . . . I am certain he is the best publisher for it. He will make a handsome little volume of it."[11]

The book, called *Similitudes: From the Ocean and the Prairie*, came out in autumn and sold for fifty cents (fifty-eight in gilt). Larcom was quietly proud of it, and it had comfortable sales; Whittier, of course, gave it favorable reviews in the *Era*.

Once the book was out, Whittier had other ideas for his protégé:

When ever I take up *Similitudes*, or read a letter of thine, I am impressed with the notion that thou shouldst write a story of

sufficient length for a book by itself. It vexes me to see such a
work as *The Lamplighter* [by Maria S. Cummins] having such a
run, when you cannot remember a single sentence or idea in it
after reading it. I am sure thee could do better—give plesaure to
thy old friends and make a thousand new ones—and "put money
in thy purse" if I may be permitted to speak after the manner of a
Yankee. Pray think of it—study thy plan well and go ahead.[12]

Although Larcom dutifully thought about a novel, or a long story, as
they both called it, it is unlikely that she did much more than that at this
point. She certainly did not think of herself as a writer, as a letter to an
intimate friend shows:

Writing gets a poor remuneration in "lucre" unless one can create
a sensation by some sudden flash, which I, with my disposition to
peace and quietness, will never do. Mr. Arthur [the editor of *Arthur's Home Magazine*] wishes to pay me for all I write for him;
but he feels poor and I suppose has met with many reverses.[13]

This solicitude for the welfare of a publisher is hardly characteristic of a professional writer. She liked to write her poems, and she was
grateful for the ability; expressing her feelings in verse brought great
satisfaction. But it might be unladylike to thrust oneself in the public
eye, and she did not see herself as a writer, although she did expect her
verses to be read seriously for their message. It would, indeed, be hard
to see oneself as a writer when payment was usually gratitude, a magazine subscription, or at most one or two dollars a poem.

Larcom had evaded a decision about her marriage, and the question
was still undecided when in December 1854 she took a position at
Wheaton Seminary, a fine school for young ladies in Norton, Massachusetts. It was a temporary measure, she thought; actually, she stayed
there for nine years, the most difficult time of her life.

The whole period at Wheaton was full of interlocking conflicts,
which, although they are specific to Larcom's life, are representative of
what intelligent and talented women of the time went through if they attempted to use their brains or themselves for anything beyond the accepted role of women. Simply, the question for these women was,
What did God want them to do with their lives?[14] Victorian women's
roles were clearly (male) defined; a woman was to be the queen of her
home, to give up self to the nurture of others—her family, or, if she had
none, perhaps other women's children. Woman in her purity, piety,

submission, and obedience was a quiet force for good.[15] Out of the world she would remain untouched—and, of course, uncompetitive. Her role was to be invisible and silent.

Although Larcom always gave lip service to this view, her own life quitely contradicted it. When she went to Wheaton she was just beginning to face the problem of marriage or possible alternatives. There was always the picture of her sister, diminished to household drudge, before her. Teaching was an acceptable substitute nurturing, but, as hard as she tried and as much as her pupils praised her, she disliked the life. Even on the prairie she had distinguished between teaching and "keeping school"; at Wheaton the latter meant living among the girls and being a kind of surrogate mother: noise, bustle, constant interruptions, and lack of privacy. What she really loved to do, although she hestitated to confess it, was to read books, write her verses, go for long walks and talk to friends.

Her background was so different from that of the average middle-class woman that it was doubly difficult for her to disappear into a stereotype, no matter how much she might want to. From age eleven she had contributed to the family income or supported herself, experience that gave her an unusual independence. Her mind had been challenged and developed during the Lowell years, when young women were distinguishing themselves by their intelligence and participation—there had even been Lowell girls who had bank accounts of their own! The west, with its comparative openness and newness, had standards and rules of propriety for women, but Larcom rejected some of them and could stay detached from the rest. Monticello Seminary, whose curriculum then sounds comparable to today's small liberal arts colleges, widened her mind, taught her to use it more efficiently, and gave her a great deal of confidence in her own intelligence. All of these environments had created a young woman of independence, but at Wheaton (in what she called sedate New England) her confidence in herself weakened.

For several years she was greatly influenced and her problems were intensified by a strange young woman named Esther Humiston, who carried womanly silence and invisibility to an extreme. Humuston, who was probably tubercular, had taken to her bed and her room to wait for death, refusing to see anyone except her family and an assortment of ministers. Apparently she and Larcom met only once, but their correspondence lasted from 1856 to 1860 (she died in 1861). Humiston preached resignation, self-effacement, contempt for the world, piety, and other saintly attitudes. All Larcom's religious belief and much of her early conditioning supported these views, although her temperament and experience did not, and her letters to Humiston were tortured and morbid as she tried to force herself into a life she did not want. Intensifying the difficulties was the fact that she could no longer mindlessly accept the Calvinism into which she had been born; she was moving toward a kind of Christian transcendentalism, reflected in so much of her poetry, but to reject orthodoxy was terrifying. Much of her reading was theological as she attempted to give her feelings legitimacy.

All these conflicts showed themselves in a variety of ways: wide extremes of mood from exhilaration when her naturally cheerful temperament was in control to dark and morbid depression, restlessness, and dissatisfaction with her physical surroundings; increasing bouts of psychosomatic illness characterized by a heavy pain in her head accompanied by almost total apathy; and finally a near nervous breakdown and briefly a questioning of her own sanity.

Through all this mental turbulence, Whittier was, consciously or not, a steady voice that repeated that she and what she had to say were important. At a very bad point in her life he wrote, "I see nothing of thine lately. I am sure thou must have found something to say in thine own clear simple and beautiful way during this long winter. Does not the voice say to thee as formerly to the Exile of Patmos, *Write!*"[16]

She never did stop writing, although in her worst moments she could do little, and then her inability increased her illness. To be fanciful, Whittier and Humiston are like two allegorical figures: a light angel and a dark angel fighting for a soul. His praise and belief in her was an enormous source of strength; her visits to Amesbury when she and Elizabeth and "Greenleaf" sat before the fire and talked or stared into the flames, or the walks she and the poet took in the natural world they both loved, were shining and serene moments in a troubled existence. Elizabeth's friendship and encouragement was as important as her brother's; Larcom's place in their home and family gave her more confidence in herself. She was pleased, for example, that she was invited to use Whittier's family name, Greenleaf. She described Whittier and Elizabeth to Esther Humiston:

> He was never married; that perhaps is one reason why there is such depth to his poetry, for if ever a man was capable of love stronger than death, it must have been he. One cannot help feeling that he has been through the deep waters, through the furnace-heat, and so is cleansed and purified. The calmness of some great self-conquest rests upon his life. Lizzie seems like a meek, timid bird that one would brood under motherly wings, and yet she has much mental and moral strength and is a most lovely character.[17]

Paradoxically, Whittier's support and encouragement deepened her conflict. When she went to Wheaton she was working on the "long story" he had suggested in the leisurely way in which she liked to do things; to her horror, he announced in the *Era* that Miss Larcom would soon produce a long American story. "I wonder if you can guess how frightened I was when I saw the announcement in the *Era*, that a book of mine would be published this season!" she wrote him. "I had begun to count it among the impossibilities, my time is so completely broken into little bits here. But when I saw that notice, I said, 'Now it *must* be done.' Will it be a 'breach of promise' if I shouldn't succeed in finishing it?"[18]

To her friend Harriet Hanson Robinson she wrote much more emotionally, "How that book is ever going to get written I don't know. I could have cried, when I saw that Mr. Whittier had mentioned it, in the paper; for I had given it up in discouragement, myself. And then I didn't mean to have my name to it. Indeed, I should not have dreamed that I could write a long story, if Mr. Whittier had not told me I could, and advised me to try."[19] The pressure of attempting to live up to Whittier's expectations for her, adjusting to a new world that she did not really like, trying to find time to do any writing at all, and other personal problems plunged her into mental turmoil at the very beginning of her time at Wheaton. In fact, the book that was to outdo the best-selling *Lamplighter* eventually dwindled into *Lottie's Thought Book*, letters from a young girl to her mother—similitudes in another form.

Clearly Whittier felt that he had every right to tell her what and how to write; there is never a hint of apology as he suggests corrections in words or lines. Nor in these early days did Larcom mind. If he wanted to correct her poems and send them to editors without asking her first, she did not feel herself in a position to object. "I received a few days ago, the poem 'Across the River,' with a 'respectfully declined' from the new Maga.," she wrote him, referring to the *Atlantic Monthly*. "I was not at all surprised, only that I did not certainly know that you had sent it. With all deference to the gentlemen editors, I think it is quite a decent little poem, with the changes you made."[20] Comments in both their letters indicate that for years she sent him copies of her poems, and he approved or edited them to fit his moral vision of poetry. Perhaps the most extreme example is the following letter from Whittier:

"On the Beach" is admirable in conception and so very felicitous in some of its lines and verses that I wanted to have thee work it over until it took a perfect shape. I have ventured to alter the copy sent me, by way of hint of what I think would tersely and clearly express the idea: and I send the marred manuscript back to do with as pleases thee best. Even as it stands it is one of thy best poems, and should go to the *Atlantic* for the Nov. number, before it comes out in the book.

There are lines in it that will live always: "The bands of green and purple light" *"The broad refreshment of the sea"* "My thoughts o'er float these murmurous miles" "They add to tenderness divine / Unto this tremulous sea." But the last verse rises into sublimity and is worth fifty pages of ordinary verse.

I don't quite like the line, "Around us daylight gently dies." It seems common-place as compared with the verbal felicities of the poem. The "gently dies" don't suit me. It would be better to say "Around us slow the daylight dies," perhaps. . . .

In the Prelude to thy book, when thee get the proof-sheet of it, see if "Its pines are tennanted" is quite the thing. Squirrels and crows run and roost in the pines, and suggest *themselves* at once as their *tennants* But I must let criticism alone. I'm not able to correct my own verses.[21]

Ironically, the person to whom the letter was sent was no longer a novice poet but a magazine editor (to whom writers submitted their work) and a poet with an established reputation of her own. In spite of her personal crises through the 1850s, she had produced four small books and a steady stream of poetry that usually had no trouble in finding a publisher. She appeared often in the *Crayon*, a prestigious but short-lived journal of the arts (1855–1861) whose editors liked her work and paid well; less prestigious (and less well-paying) outlets were newspapers and some of the "family" magazines like *Arthur's Home Magazine*.

The kind of fame that makes one's name a household word came, unexpectedly, early in 1858, when the *Crayon* published a poem of hers called "Hannah Binding Shoes." Its appearance was followed almost at once by charges of plagiarism from the *New York Tribune*. Larcom was able to defend herself by telling a story that illustrates the perils of midcentury publication: She had sent the poem to that paper four years earlier, with a letter requesting payment if the paper used it. When she never heard from them, she assumed the poem had not been accepted. Years later she pulled it out of her files and sent it to the *Crayon*, only to discover that the paper had published it (under the pseudonym "Mercy More") and neither paid nor informed her.

The controversy called attention to the poem, which became instantly popular, surprising no one more than its author. It was a story poem, picturing a scene thoroughly familiar in the fishing and shipping villages of the New England coast: a young woman waiting faithfully for her sailor husband who would never return. It was set to music and became a concert song; several paintings represented Hannah at her window, waiting for the ship that never came. Hannah had all the womanly virtues: love, fidelity, quiet uncomplaining courage. William Dean Howells thought of it as a great poem, one that could confer immortality on its writer.[22] The poem followed her all her life, when she would much rather have been judged by more important and more characteristic work.[23]

The poem opened editorial doors for her, as well as calling forth a great deal of fan mail. For a small but regular salary she became unofficial poetry editor of the *Congregationalist*, a denominational paper with a wide circulation. The patriotic verses she wrote as the Civil War approached also gained attention, and in 1861 she had her first acceptance from the *Atlantic Monthly*.

It was still the *Atlantic*'s custom to publish poems anonymously and not to reveal authors until the yearly index came out. This practice made a pleasant guessing game for the literati; Larcom's poem "The Rose Enthroned" (June 1861), involving evolution, the growth and perfectability of the human race, and the horror of civil war, was briefly attributed to Lowell, but then firmly given to Emerson. The poem added prestige to Larcom's fame; it also brought her to the attention of James and Annie Fields, who promptly made her part of the literary world that they dominated. There were other *Atlantic* poems, including the much-anthologized "A Loyal Woman's No" (December 1863).

Whittier was not, however, the only person from whom she sought advice. She frequently sent her verses to William S.Robinson, political activist, writer, editor, later clerk of the Massachusetts House of Representatives, and husband of her friend Harriet Hanson.[24] He liked her work and published it in whatever paper he happened to be editing at the time. He was temporarily a reader for the *Atlantic* when she sent him "The Rose Enthroned," and he promptly showed it to the editor, James Russell Lowell, who accepted it. Nor did Whittier see "A Loyal Woman's No" before publication. That poem was written in Wisconsin and sent directly to Annie Fields: "Will you care to look at the enclosed, as you have glanced at other verses of mine? They can be returned to Beverly if not the thing for the Maga.—I wrote from a sudden feeling of how I wished some women would feel."[25]

In 1863, as a result of some personal and family tragedies that caused a real examination of her life, Larcom finally broke away from Wheaton. A year later she became one of the editors of *Our Young Folks Magazine*, whose first issue came out in January 1865. The magazine was one of the new projects that Fields launched when Ticknor's death gave him control of the firm, and it was set up in a way that could not work unless Fields himself were involved.[26] There were three editors who apparently never saw one another. Larcom did most of her work at home; the tempestuous Gail Hamilton (Mary Abigail Dodge) wrote for the magazine and occasionally gave advice; John Townsend Trowbridge was sent off almost at once to travel through the South and write about Civil War battlefields. Howard Ticknor was the office manager, and apparently Fields made all final decisions about what went into the magazine. At the end of two years, Hamilton left, to begin the controversy with Fields that would drag on for several years and end with her *Battle of the Books* (1869) and Fields's retirement from publishing in 1871.[27] Larcom became the sole editor in 1868 and remained so for two years, although Trowbridge's name remained on the title page, and he took over for the last years of the magazine's life.

As an editor Larcom had financial security, time, and a recognized position in the literary world. Fields could call on the best writers of the day; Larcom met them, of course, and her circle of friends widened.

The kinds of new friends she made are significant. Her chief model for a writer was Whittier; now she began to meet women who wrote. She corresponded with Lydia Maria Child, as one editor to another; she met and enjoyed talking with Harriet Beecher Stowe, who greatly admired her work; Grace Greenwood (Sara Lippincott) spent time with her when the latter visited in Boston. Best-selling novelist Adeline Dutton Train Whitney and the author of the *William Henry Letters*, Abby Morton Diaz, who had grown up at Brook Farm and as part of an antislavery activist family, became her close friends. Mary Bucklin Claflin, wife of a governor and herself influential in the establishment of women's degrees at Boston University, was another good friend at whose gracious home Larcom was a frequent visitor. These women — busy, active, and yet "ladies" — provided new models for Larcom; it would be hard, if not impossible, for her to go back to pupil status, even if she wanted to.

Whittier's letter (quoted above) concerned selections from her published verses for Larcom's first collection, called *Poems* (1868); the poem he talks about, which referred to Elizabeth Whittier, appeared in the collection, although probably nowhere else. Whittier has been given credit for having her book published; how much influence he had cannot be determined (he had certainly tried twice before).[28] If there was a motive for its publication beyond the fact that the public liked Larcom's poems and therefore a book of them would sell, it is more likely that James and Annie Fields wanted to reward her for her loyalty during the controversy that Gail Hamilton was now creating. Harriet Hanson Robinson's journal records Larcom's confidence that she still had never received any money from Fields for her devotional book, *Breathings of a Better Life* (1866), although it had steady sales and several revisions.[29]

At some point Larcom stopped sending copies of her poems to Whittier, and he wrote her wondering why. Anxious not to hurt his feelings, but clearly wanting to go her own way now, she wrote back, tactfully, "But you have taught me all that I ought to ask: why should I remain a burden on you? Why should I always write with you holding my hand? My conscience and my pride rebel. I will be myself, faults and all."[30]

Although his mentorship was ended, Whittier remained supportive. After the publication of her third book of poems, *Wild Roses of Cape Ann* (1880), a book with strong local color and Essex Country flavor, he wrote to Oliver Wendell Holmes, "Has thee seen Miss Larcom's *Cape Ann*? I like it, and in reading it I thought thee would also. Get it and see if she has not a right to stand with the rest of us."[31]

Just as their professional relationship changed over the years, so did the quality of their friendship. Until Elizabeth Whittier's death in 1864, the primary relationship was that of mentor and pupil. Larcom herself had gone through a heartbreaking year in 1863, and the death of Elizabeth the following summer was another deep hurt, but one she shared with Whittier, who turned to the people his sister had loved. She visited Amesbury as often as she could during the autumn, and they read "In Memoriam" together.

Larcom's job as editor allowed her to organize her life as she wanted it: she rented an "apartment" in Beverly Farms, the first home of her own that she had ever had; she spent the winter in "rooms" in Boston where she could enjoy her fill of exhibitions, concerts, and social life and give some time to the North End Mission and various working-girls' clubs; spring and early summer she spent at home in Beverly, and in August, just before her hay fever arrived, she left for New Hampshire, taking her work with her and sometimes staying well into November. Generally her stay included Bearcamp (a small hotel in West Ossipee that Whittier and his friends virtually took over for a few weeks each summer), various resorts, and a quiet farmhouse where she could relax and write. Mountains came to mean a great deal to her, for themselves and for their symbolic closeness to God. The years at *Our Young Folks* were the happiest and most productive of her life.

She wrote the kind of poems she had established as hers, with the theme of nature's beauty leading to God and celebrating a kind of Christian transcendentalism. She also wrote poems about children, most of them for her own magazine, and collected as *Childhood Songs* (1875), and for a while some poems about women and marriage. Although she had long since rejected her engagement and the kind of life it offered, circumstances now forced her into defining her position as an unmarried woman; the poem "Unwedded" (*Poems*) justifies her choice. It grew out of her own feelings and a conversation on the subject with Harriet Beecher Stowe. She was a regular contributor now to the *Independent*, a nominally Congregationalist newspaper with great prestige and circulation; it published all the "great" writers and paid them very well.

James T. Fields retired from publishing in 1871, leaving the firm in the hands of the charming but not very competent Osgood, who ran into more and more trouble until eventually he was rescued and eased out by Henry O. Houghton.

Osgood sold *Our Young Folks* to Scribner's in 1873. Larcom was not at first worried; she had money in the bank and sources of income from her writing. As time passed, however, she missed the dependable income, and she went to Osgood to ask that some kind of editorial position be found for her. She had had seven years of experience, and of living the kind of life that truly satisfied her; she dreaded the thought of going back to teaching but feared dependence on her writing. Osgood, unmarried and very much "one of the boys" responded with a letter of charming callousness, cheerfully suggesting that of course she could teach and write at the same time.[32] Somewhat grimly, she took a teaching job at Bradford Academy. She lasted only one dreadful year; she hated it, her teaching was bad, and all the symptoms of illness that had virtually disappeared when she left Wheaton returned. After that year she never again had a steady position or a secure income, but it is clear that she would have preferred dependence on her family or starvation to another regular teaching job.

She had money from her poems, and from another source: beginning in 1870, she and Whittier had collaborated on three anthologies for Osgood, *Child Life* (1871), *Child Life in Prose* (1873), and *Songs of Three Centuries* (1875). The division of labor can be pieced together from her letters: Whittier, whose name was given as editor, made the final choice of poems, wrote the preface, was paid for his work, and received all the royalties; Larcom read, found poems, copied them out, discussed the choice with Whittier, then made copies of the poems, dealt with the publisher, and read and corrected proof. For this she was paid a flat sum, either three hundred or five hundred dollars. At first the inequality did not matter; it was a pleasure to work with Whittier and she was still in the editorial offices anyway. The second collaboration was not quite so easy.

In *Child Life* she was acknowledged in the preface by name as a kind friend "who has given him the benefit of her cultivated taste and very thorough acquaintance with whatever is valuable in the poetical literature of Child Life." In the second collaboration her name was not mentioned at all.

"*The Hearth and Home*'s notice of 'C.L. in Prose' gives me all the credit for this last volume. I deferred to what I thought was thy wish in not directly using thy name in the Preface, but I ought in justice to both of us to have given it," Whittier wrote her.[33] Earlier, however, he had written: "I've got the sheets of our *Child-Life* and like it hugely. But I think now I shall take all the credit to myself. If it had not looked nice and good, I should have shirked it, and left it all on thy shoulders."[34]

However Larcom felt about the omission of her name, she said nothing to Whittier. The return to teaching and anonymity seemed to negate all she had achieved. Her health did not improve, and she may have been suffering the discomforts of menopause as well. Anxiety about her finances drove her to work harder than she should have. As pressures increased, so did her tense, nervous state and the bouts of illness.

The third collaborative volume, *Songs of Three Centuries*, was more elaborate than the former ones. It contained about five hundred fifty poems, ranging through three hundred years of English and American literature. Larcom and Whittier planned on doing the final selection of material during their stay at Bearcamp House. Before her delayed arrival there, however, she wrote a friend, "I have scarcely walked to the beach this summer,—for why? I have been so busy about a book, Mr. Whittier's book—a compilation of English poetry which Mr. Osgood wished him to make and which he agreed to do with my help. It is to be published this fall, and there is the hurry and fatigue of it; my head has been nearly used up, through the warm weather. If I had supposed it would be one third as hard, I would have refused to do it, without a year's time. . . . I have lost the beauty of the summer, poring over books."[35] Knowing that Whittier was enjoying himself at Bearcamp did not help her mental state.

That there was some kind of quarrel is confirmed by two letters from Whittier, apologizing and blaming "the matter" on his "nervous excitability."[36] The other letter, undated, says they were both to blame and ends, "I dare say I was a fool, but that's no reason thee should make thyself one, by dwelling on it. Lay it all to dyspepsia, Ben Butler, or anything else than intentional wrong on the part of thy old friend. We have known each other too long, and done each other too many kind offices, to let it disturb us."

Larcom's valuable suggestions and aid were noted in the preface, and Whittier assigned her half the copyright and royalties; he received the money directly, however, then gave her her share. Although on the surface everything was patched up, and the following summer found the Whittier circle again happily at Bearcamp House, the relationship was never the same.

It is difficult to understand what comes across as an incredible piece of exploitation, except to assume that, regardless of Larcom's gentle attempts to break away from the role, he still regarded her as his protégée long after she stopped seeing herself that way. Her work on the books was both decision-making and secretarial drudgery, with neither money nor credit enough to reward her for her task, and was done under pressure from her own precarious financial situation, her illness, and the unsympathetic Osgood, who saw her only as the person who could keep Whittier working.

It is also difficult to understand Whittier's miserliness, since it extends in some directions and not in others. For fifty-eight years he lived close to poverty until the publication of *Snow-bound* in 1866 brought the popularity that made all subsequent volumes sell, and made him rich. Like a canny New Englander, of course, he kept quiet about money in the bank, but he was quite generous to his nieces, and he tried, as Larcom told Lizzie Whittier Pickard years later, many times to pay her expenses in the mountains. Her pride would never let her accept the offers, of course, and besides, "I thought he was as poor as I was."[37]

Yet the flat sums paid her certainly do not reflect the proportion of work she did, and while the second and third volumes were being done, she had no steady income. Whittier must have known that; there is a curious blindness and insensitivity in his failure to make sure that she was adequately and fairly paid and credited.

Perhaps the breach would have been healed sooner, but other circumstances intervened. In the spring of 1876, his niece and housekeeper, Lizzie Whittier, married Samuel T. Pickard and moved to Portland, Maine. After a delightful stay at Bearcamp,[38] Whittier left Amesbury to live with cousins in Danvers.

There are conflicting reports about Oak Knoll and Whittier's residence there. Some of his friends found him less accessible and the atmosphere less welcoming. He did, perhaps, need protection from all the strangers who felt they had the right to visit this venerable institution —Whittier called them the Pilgrims—but an account from Edmund Gosse, British critic and scholar, suggests that the protection may have been overdone.

Gosse describes the place as "sinister. . . . After a long pause the front door opened slightly, and a very unprepossessing dog emerged, and shut the door (if I may say so) behind him." After a few tense minutes assuring the dog that they were friends, he rang again. The door was "slightly opened, and a voice of no agreeable timbre asked what we wanted." He explained an appointment with Whittier, and the door was closed again. "But at length a hard-featured woman grudgingly admitted us, and showed us, growling as she did it, into a parlor."[39]

Friends saw him only in the most formal way. Larcom wrote Lizzie Pickard that she had been to tea at Oak Knoll and had seen Whittier again at the Claflins:

Sometimes I wish the old times could come back, as when I used to be so at home with you all at Amesbury, and saw him so often,—for you know how I value his friendship. But he almost never calls on me now, and I never was one who could run after even my best friends, when they seemed to be having a better time without me. . . . The spirit of anything good can never be lost, so I shall always be grateful for that pleasant share of mine in the Amesbury life, in your Aunt Lizzie's time, and after.[40]

After a while, however, Whittier began spending more time away from Oak Knoll, going back often to Amesbury, which was still his legal residence, staying with his Cartland cousins in Newburyport, visiting friends like Mrs. Claflin in Newtonville or Annie Fields in Manchester, or staying in Boston. Gradually he sought out his old friends, and several of Larcom's letters in the 1880's mention having met him, usually by arrangement, at friends' houses.

Not until 1877 did Larcom feel well again, although she worked steadily. Learning from the collaboration with Whittier that anthologies paid, she edited two small books designed to accompany the traveler: *Roadside Poems for Summer Travelers* (1876) and *Hillside and Seaside in Poetry* (1877). Another book, *Landscape in American Poetry* (1879), was a commission; it is a handsome art book for which she wrote the text. She frequently taught classes for schools or private groups; she worked up several lectures, mostly on literature or women in literature, which she gave to women's groups or lyceums and for which she was paid twenty-five dollars (men were paid more); she wrote a commissioned article for the *Atlantic* on the Lowell mill girls (November 1881); she wrote a newsletter for Samuel Pickard's *Portland Transcript*. In 1881 she published her collection of local-color poetry called *Wild Roses of Cape Ann* and the new firm, Houghton Mifflin (in the break between Osgood and Houghton, she had wisely gone with the latter) brought out a *Household Edition* of her poems in 1884. At their request she wrote what is undoubtedly her best work, *A New England Girlhood* (1889). That was followed by three very popular small devotional books in which she tried to sum up and communicate all that she had learned about life and religion. From 1875 on, her letters to her Houghton Mifflin editors show no sign of the amateurishness that had characterized her earlier dealings with publishers; they are pleasant but firm, and concerned with typeface, arrangement, texure of paper, color of covers, price, advertising, and availability in bookstores—the letter of a professional regarding the details of her career.[41]

Nevertheless, life was precarious. Her ability to write depended entirely on her health. When she was seriously ill in the autumn of 1883, Whittier immediately set about raising money for her. Many of their common friends contributed, but it all had to be done very quietly for, as Harriet Minot Pitman, a close friend of both, wrote Whittier, everyone knew that Lucy was too proud and independent to accept charity.[42]

They met fairly often, but the mentorship was long past. In the late 1870s, at the time when Larcom felt that Whittier was turning away from his old friends, she met Phillips Brooks, the young rector of Trinity Church, Boston, famous for his superb preaching as well as for his nondogmatic Christianity. The two became very close friends; he was the last of the father figures in her life, although their relationship was not so much that of mentor and pupil as of friends who shared a religious vision.

Her last three books were dedicated to the three people she felt had most influenced her life: Philena Fobes (her headmistress at Monticello), her sister Emeline, and Whittier. The dedication to Whittier in *The Unseen Friend* (1891) calls him "Most beloved and most spiritual of American poets whose friendship has been to me almost a life-long blessing." In June 1892 came news of her sister's death, and in September of the same year, Whittier died. She hurried back from the mountains to be an honorary pallbearer, along with Elizabeth Stuart Phelps, Mary Bucklin Claflin, and Alice Freeman Palmer, at his funeral.[43] He left an estate of over one hundred thirty thousand dollars; to Larcom he left five hundred dollars and the copyrights of their three collaborations. "I am very glad he left me the copyrights of the books I compiled with him," she wrote Lizzie Pickard, "and indeed, it was only right, as I worked hard on them. The *Songs of Three Centuries* nearly cost me my health, the publishers rushed it so. I was good for nothing for three or four years after, as far as writing went. But he never knew the cause."[44]

Samuel Pickard was Whittier's literary executor, and he set to work at once to collect material and find a suitable biographer, finally deciding, with the approval of friends, to do the job himself. He and Larcom corresponded about the project:

> Mr. Whittier many times said to me—apparently in earnest and jest both—"Don't *thee* ever go to writing about me!" It used to hurt me a little, as if I *would* parade his friendship for me in any way! I could not do after he died what I would not when he was alive—unless I knew he was willing—and he never hinted any wish of the kind, certainly. I have already been asked to furnish "Recollections" for two periodicals, and have declined. I may be over-particular in this matter, but I do feel a delicacy about it —almost as if I had not the right.[45]

Her delicacy also meant a financial sacrifice, since she would have been paid well for her memories, and she seems to be the only one of Whittier's women friends who did not write about him. But she offered Pickard letters and all the help she could give him.

> I think Mr. Whittier had a wish that just a straight-forward story should be written about him, the plain facts of his life, and he put the material into your hands as the person he could be surest of, to tell just the truth. He may have feared that his women-friends idealized him too much,—and some of his men-friends, too. At any rate, he did want you to write his life, and he knew you so well that he knew what to expect of you. I think he was wise in his choice, and the book will be better for being entirely yours. —But if, by talking things over with you, I can help, I shall be glad to do so. I shall look up his letters soon.[46]

Larcom had very little time to help or to profit by the royalties. In the autumn of 1892 she was ill with heart disease; she recovered and, re-fusing to rest, went back to Boston to get on with her work. Her illness returned in the winter, and after the sudden death of Phillips Brooks in January 1893, she seemed to give up. Her last weeks were spent in Boston, where her window looked out to Trinity Church, and she was cared for by family, loving friends, and a number of former students from Wheaton. She died 17 April 1893. After a memorial service in Boston, attended by personal friends and most of the literary world, her body was taken home to Beverly for burial.

The two-column headline in the *Boston Globe* announcing her death called her "The Best of Our Minor Poets." Her poems continued to be anthologized. In 1924 the *Boston Evening Transcript* did a half-page article on her life and work, and in the 1930s a Lowell paper asked in its headlines whether Lucy Larcom would have approved the strike then going on. When Whittier and the other nineteeth-century giants were swept from poetic eminence, Larcom went with them.

During the years of her fame—from 1858 to 1893—she, like Whittier, spoke in a voice that appealed to a wide public. Even in the last years, when they were beginning to be old-fashioned, they somehow retained their popularity. She was usually classed with him as a New England poet, and the classification was a logical one up to a point. They wrote on many of the same themes and out of the same moral vision. Both were deeply religious, and both wrote public poetry.

Technically, she was a better craftsman than he. She is far more consciously experimental about verse form, using everything from the sonnet and Spenserian stanza to ballad meter and the unfortunate fourteener. Her lines are more consistently metrical. She wrote from a coherent theory of what poetry should be: "I believe in but one Beauty, the twin of truth, and the subtle essence of all that is sweet and deep and noble, in letters, morals, religion, and everyday life. I think that poetry would lose its very soul, if it ceased to breathe out *moral* lessons; though, of course, no one wants it to be '*preachy*.'"[47] This moral vision of poetry (and, indeed, of art in general), was one she shared with other poets of her time, and certainly with Whittier, who had, after all, used his poetry as a weapon in the abolitionist cause. Her ideas are not in themselves original; they were part of the intellectual climate in which she lived. Her work and ideas were acceptable because, for the most part, they did not deviate from the patriarchal tradition; she was a part, if a minor one, of the nineteenth-century literary establishment of New England.

Even when she writes about women, few of her poems are gender marked; her subjects are women in a patriarchal world. Like Hannah, binding her shoes and faithfully waiting, they celebrate the male-defined womanly virtues: fidelity, patience, quiet suffering, and enduring love. Even in "A Loyal Woman's No" the attack is not against men and marriage, but against one kind of man and one kind of marriage, and the poem assumes that the "right" man should lead a woman to the sublimity of the mountains, not keep her in the valleys. (There is a bit of subversion here in the implication that if a man does not lead her to the mountains, she will get there by herself.) "Unwedded," about a woman who chooses to remain single, justifies that choice to a patriarchal system, as later poems, "Woman's Christmas" and "Woman's Easter," justify woman's importance in Christianity.

Yet there are a few hints of dissatisfaction, as if suppressed feeling occasionally burst out of her. The poems that show this feeling stem from her experience on the prairie, the same experience that set her permanently against marriage. One often-repeated theme is loss of identity: in some very early verses and in "Sylvia" (*Atlantic Monthly*, 1873) the subject becomes, after marriage, "Old Woman" or "Wife." In Sylvia's case, the loss of her identity weakens and destroys her; not until she is dying does her husband again think of her as a person with a name of her own.

Probably her most antiestablishment poem appears, surprisingly, in her *Childhood Songs*. Called "A Little Old Girl," it is the tale of Prudence, who is taught to bake, sweep, sew, milk, plant, and go to school and meeting. She is also taught to fear the beauty and magic of nature, which might distract her from work. Her reward is the approval of her elders: "What a good wife she will make!"

A contemporary review of *Childhood Songs* calls this poem a light and pleasant picture of childhood; I find it the most cynical poem Larcom wrote. Given her own free and happy childhood and her concern as an adult for young girls, her love of freedom, and above all, her belief that it is through the perception of natural beauty that we grow in our souls and toward God, it is clear that the inhibiting of the child's instinctive playfulness and attraction to beauty will result in a wasted life and an unhappy woman.

Larcom did not think of herself as a "woman poet." In fact, it was being a woman that first kept her from thinking of herself as a writer and then, during the time at Wheaton, caused so much conflict. Even late in her life she rejected the word *career*.[48] It was here, I think, that she owes her greatest debt to Whittier; his influence slowly turned her into a professional.

As a young woman she was far too unsure of herself, and far too buried in the tradition of womanliness to bring herself deliberately to public notice. Like so many women writers, she used pseudonyms or initials to sign her poems; "Angelina Abigail" or "L.L." wrote the light verses, essays, and stories she sent back from Illinois to the *Offering*; "Culma Croly," an anagram of her name, wrote for *Arthur's Magazine*; "L.L." sent material to newspapers. Her *Era* poems are signed; Whittier used her full name. He knew the value of public familiarity with a specific name while Larcom was still picturing herself as a person who liked to write verses. When she did use her own name she was amused to find that many people assumed it was a pen name (like Grace Greenwood, Fanny Fern, and other alliterative women); once she moved into the literary world in 1865, name and identity came together. By the end of her career her name had become important to her on her own terms; in 1884, when the Houghton Mifflin Household Edition of *Larcom's Poetical Works* was published, she was horrified. "I feel naked without my prefix," she wrote her editors. "It makes me sound like one of 'them literary fellows'—and I'm not."[49] Later editions are of *Lucy Larcom's Poems*.

A single woman who wrote for a living could stay womanly by a life of service to others. Larcom came to believe, and letters from her admirers supported her belief, that her verses were her contribution, that by using the talents given her to tell her readers what she knew about life and nature and religion, she was indeed doing what God wanted her to do with her life.

Beyond that she could not go. Although she was committed to the abolitionist movement, and a great many of her early poems are propaganda pieces for it, she could never allow herself to be involved with the struggle for women's rights. Her friend Harriet Hanson Robinson was an active feminist, and there are several letters in which Larcom refuses to help the cause. Her excuses are that she has no time, or is working on something else, or, finally, that she had not made up her mind what was right, or whether women were ready for such a responsibility as the vote. She was certainly in favor of education for women. Perhaps because her own happy childhood had been so sharply curtailed and she had never had a "girlhood," she felt and showed a strong interest in young women, but that interest did not overtly include voting rights. The end of *A New England Girlhood* has a long passage directed to girls, telling them to prepare themselves for their futures, since as women they will be the upholders of morals, goodness, and truth for future generations.

The paradox is, of course, that she had rejected the very womanly role that she praised and supported. She could disguise herself, how-

ever, under her support and her womanly behavior. Aside from the fact
that earning a living took most of her time and energy, women's activ-
ism was threatening; her hold on the place she had won for herself and
the life she so enjoyed was at all times precarious. Because she had no
strong base other than her own efforts, she was vulnerable to public disapproval. Whatever her deep feelings, she had to remain within the establishment to be safe.

Her need for security also explains her writing of verse. Having read
all her published work and as much of her unpublished writing as is
available (letters, journals, rough drafts), I feel a sense of regret for a
lost vocation. She was most comfortable with the length and shape of
the essay, and her prose is better than her verse. Her style is clear, direct, and unadorned; it flows smoothly and with some elegance to its
point. *A New England Girlhood*, although it suffers to many modern
readers from its messages about religion, is still a book that can en-
chant. She had a gift for making pictures for the reader, perhaps
because she was also a painter and a lover of painting. Her visual imagination and her perception of natural detail make the beauty she describes very real. She enjoyed writing articles and stories, spending
time lovingly crafting her prose—and that fact made the writing of
prose a luxury that she literally could seldom afford.

Her verses had brought her approval as a child, even from her awe-
some father, and brought her approval as an adult, for it was perfectly
acceptable for women to write poems. The inspirational messages of
these sweet singers were, indeed, womanly. Larcom's poems were as
much a guide as was Agnes's lamp.

To return finally to the question with which this study began, What
was the nature and extent of Whittier's influence on her and her work?
She did not, even though her poetry is like his, imitate his content and
themes. She herself, in fact, named as the chief influence on her poetry
not Whittier, but William Cullen Bryant; they all wrote within one tradition of nineteenth-century poetry that connected man and God and nature. Nor did she learn the techniques of poetry writing from him; she
was a far better crafter than he was.

Nevertheless, Whittier made her a writer, not so much by editing her
work and submitting it to publishers as by building up her confidence in
herself and her abilities, by giving his approval to the image of Lucy
Larcom as a writer, by forcing her to act as a professional. In that
way he was the most important figure in Larcom's life, and she never
stopped being grateful to him, even after she eased away from his guidance. Perhaps the other protégées benefited in the same way, getting

from the poet not so much the tinkering with their work that he liked to do, but the confidence to see themselves as writers through the approval of the institution that Whittier had come to be and represent.

Notes

1. Most of the information on which this paper is based comes from letters: Whittier's from John B. Pickard, ed., *The Letters of John Greenleaf Whittier*, 3 vols. (Cambridge: Harvard University Press, 1975); and Larcom's from various manuscript collections (see note 2 below). I also use Samuel T. Pickard, *Life and Letters of John Greenleaf Whittier*, 2 vols. (Boston: Houghton Mifflin, 1895); and idem, *Whittier-Land* (Boston: Houghton Mifflin, 1904). Whittier letters quoted here are from J. B. Pickard and identified by date, unless otherwise noted. Other biographies mentioned are John A. Pollard, *John Greenleaf Whittier: Friend of Man* (Boston: Houghton Mifflin, 1949); Robert Penn Warren, *John Greenleaf Whittier's Poetry* (Minneapolis: University of Minnesota Press, 1971); Edward Wagenknecht, *John Greenleaf Whittier: A Portrait in Paradox* (New York: Oxford University Press, 1967); and Albert Mordell, *Quaker Militant: John Greenleaf Whittier* (Boston: Houghton Mifflin, 1933). For an excellent account of Whittier biographers and critical attitudes, see Jayne Kribbs, introduction to *Critical Essays on John Greenleaf Whittier* (Boston: G. K. Hall, 1980).

2. Nearly two thousand letters, some autobiographical writings, and contemporary personal reminiscences are my sources of information about Lucy Larcom. Frequently statements in published works are modified by comments in letters; when that happens, I follow the letters. Location and dates of letters are given in the notes; I would like to thank the various libraries for permission to quote from their holdings.

Larcom's own autobiography, *A New England Girlhood* (Boston: Houghton Mifflin, 1889), is an obvious source of information, although it is impressionistic rather than factual. I have not used the only biography, Daniel Dulany Addison, *Lucy Larcom: Life, Letters, and Diary* (Boston: Houghton Mifflin, 1894), except when he quotes material not available anywhere else; Addison allows his thesis to shape his selection and interpretations.

Since I am working from a background of much research, and since this is a short paper, I have not traced all my steps to the conclusions I have reached. They will be available in the biography of Larcom on which I am working.

3. All Whittier's biographers talk about his eyes; the adjectives I use here are typical.

4. Benita Eisler, *The Lowell Offering* (New York: Lippincott, 1977), is the best modern account of the mill girls and has a bibliography of important works in the subject. Contemporary accounts are Harriet Hanson Robinson, *Loom and Spindle* (New York: Thomas Y. Crowell, 1896); Larcom's *A New England Girl-*

hood; and her "Among Lowell Mill-Girls," *Atlantic Monthly* 48 (1881): 593–612.

5. Larcom, *Girlhood*, 254–255.
6. Robinson, *Loom*, 109.
7. She had scrofula, a form of tuberculosis also called the king's evil, and probably had a susceptibility to respiratory ailments.
8. J. B. Pickard, *Letters of Whittier*, 2:207–208.
9. Both Larcom and Whittier have been accused of being humorless, a charge that S. T. Pickard, Elizabeth Stuart Phelps, and other contemporaries deny.
10. J. B. Pickard, *Letters of Whittier*, 2:221, 8 July 1853.
11. Ibid., 2:222, 28 July 1853.
12. Ibid., 2:256–257, 14 May 1854.
13. Lucy Larcom to Ann Spaulding and Rebecca Danforth, 15 May 1854, Lucy Larcom Papers (7006-b), Clifton Waller Barrett Library, University of Virginia, Charlottesville.
14. Elaine Showalter, *A Literature of Their Own: British Women Novelists from Brontë to Lessing* (Princeton: Princeton University Press, 1977), 24. Showalter is talking about British women, but American women certainly felt the same question of vocation.
15. Barbara Welter, "The Cult of True Womanhood, 1820–1860," *American Quarterly* 18 (1966):151–174.
16. J. B. Pickard, *Letters of Whittier*, 2:323, 20 February 1857.
17. Larcom to Esther Humiston, 1 May 1859; quoted by permission of the Massachusetts Historical Society, Boston.
18. Larcom to John Greenleaf Whittier, 22 February 1855; quoted by permission of the Wheaton College Library, Norton, Mass.
19. Larcom to Harriet Hanson Robinson, 16 February 1855; quoted by permission of the Arthur and Elizabeth Schlesinger Library, Radcliffe College, Cambridge, Mass.
20. Larcom to John Greenleaf Whittier, 30 October 1857; quoted by permission of the Wheaton College Library.
21. J. B. Pickard, *Letters of Whittier*, 3:178, 22 August 1868. For evidence that Larcom was not the only poet with whose work Whittier "tinkered," see S. T. Pickard, *Life of Whittier*, 2:535.
22. William Dean Howells, *Literary Friends and Acquaintance: A Personal Retrospect of American Authorship* (New York: Harper and Brothers, 1900), 123.
23. The Beverly, Massachusetts, Historical Society has the journal of Sarah Trask, whose story is like Hannah's; it was almost a commonplace in coastal towns. See also Mary Blewett, "'I Am Doom to Disappointment': 1849–51," *Essex Institute Historical Collections* 117 (1981): 191–212.
24. The story of Harriet Hanson and William S. Robinson is told in Claudia Bushman, *A Good Poor Man's Wife* (Hanover, N.H.: University Press of New England, 1981). Her journal is in the Schlesinger Library, Radcliffe College, Cambridge, Mass.

25. Larcom to Annie Adams Fields, 11 September 1863; quoted by permission of the Houghton Library, Harvard University, Cambridge, Mass. Whittier wrote James T. Fields, asking, "Who wrote 'A Loyal Woman's No!'—Was it Lucy Larcom? I though it might be" (J. B. Pickard, *Letters of Whittier*, 3: 54–55, 25 December 1863).

26. My statement contradicts Warren S. Tryon, *Parnassus Corner: A Life of James T. Fields, Publisher to the Victorians* (Boston: Houghton Mifflin, 1963), 290, but everything I have read in the letters leads me to believe that Fields and Annie Fields kept firm control over the magazine.

27. See Tryon, *Parnassus Corner*; and James C. Austin, *Fields of the "Atlantic Monthly": Letters to an Editor, 1861–1870* (San Marino, Calif.: Huntington Library Press, 1953), for accounts of the controversy from Fields's point of view.

28. Generally scholars have mixed up Larcom's first book, *Similitudes*, 1853, with her first book of poems, 1868; usually they add that the earlier book was published by Ticknor and Fields, when the publisher was in fact John P. Jewett.

29. Robinson journal, 8 November 1868.

30. Addison, *Lucy Larcom*, 68. He gives no date; I assume the letter was written after 1868 because there are no more editing letters from Whittier and because Larcom's attitude about her work changed at this time.

31. Ibid., 198. The letter was written by Whittier to Oliver Wendell Holmes; Holmes quoted the passage in a letter of congratulations to Larcom.

32. James R. Osgood to Larcom, 25 July 1873; by permission of the Massachusetts Historical Society. The letter, pleasant enough in tone, is very patronizing; it also reveals Osgood's belief that only Larcom could get Whittier involved in these anthologies, and it suggests plans for further books by Larcom.

33. J. B. Pickard, *Letters of Whittier*, 3:307–308, 19 November 1873.

34. S. T. Pickard, *Life of Whittier*, 2:575; the letter is dated November 1871.

35. Larcom to Mary B. Claflin, 25 August 1875; quoted by permission of the Rutherford B. Hayes Presidential Center Library, Fremont, Ohio.

36. J. B. Pickard, *Letters of Whittier*, 3:338–339, 22 September 1875; the undated letter is given in a note on the same page.

37. Larcom to Elizabeth Whittier Pickard, 16 October 1892; quoted by permission of the Houghton Library.

38. S. T. Pickard, *Whittier-Land*, 110–118.

39. Gosse is quoted in Edwin Watts Chubb, *Stories of Authors* (New York: Macmillan, 1926), 317–318. For the more usual view, see Richard P. Zollo, "Oak Knoll—Whittier's Hermitage," *Essex Institute Historical Collections* 117 (1981): 27–42.

40. Larcom to Elizabeth Whittier Pickard, 19 April 1877; quoted by permission of the Houghton Library.

41. Most of this active correspondence is in the Houghton Library.

42. Harriet Minot Pitman to John Greenleaf Whittier, 13 October and 2 November 1883; quoted by permission of the Houghton Library.

43. Elizabeth Stuart Phelps (Ward), "The Bearer Falls," *Independent*, 4 May 1893.

44. Larcom to Elizabeth Whittier Pickard, 16 October 1892; quoted by permission of the Houghton Library.

45. Larcom to Samuel T. Pickard, 11 November 1892; quoted by permission of the Houghton Library.

46. Larcom to S. T. Pickard, 21 November 1892; quoted by permission of the Houghton Library.

47. Larcom to John Greenleaf Whittier, 30 October 1857; quoted by permission of the Wheaton College Library.

48. Larcom, *Girlhood*, 274.

49. Larcom, to Frank Garrison, 13 November 1884, and to Henry O. Houghton, 11 November 1884; quoted by permission of the Houghton Library.

RAYMOND A. MAZUREK

"I Have no Monarch in My Life": Feminism, Poetry, and Politics in Dickinson and Higginson

AMONG NINETEENTH-CENTURY AMERICAN Women writers, Emily Dickinson holds a unique place. Although almost completely unknown in her own lifetime (1830–1886), by the 1930s and certainly by the 1940s, Dickinson was widely considered a major American poet, even "a great poet."[1] While the rise of feminist criticism has led to a revaluation of Dickinson's achievement, it has not been necessary for feminist critics to perform the initial step of getting her work accepted in the canon, for Dickinson has long been considered one of the dozen or so major writers of nineteenth-century American literature.

The relationship between Dickinson and Thomas Wentworth Higginson, the nineteenth-century critic who has sometimes been considered Dickinson's mentor, is similarly peculiar. For although Higginson was considered an important critic in his own time, he has long been overshadowed in the literary histories by Dickinson, and is in fact remembered by literary scholars chiefly for his failure to recognize her talent. Long before the resurgence of feminist criticism, Higginson, with his nineteenth-century whiskers and avuncular pose, had been reduced to playing an awkward Polonius to Dickinson's leading role. In writing about their literary relationship, it is therefore as necessary to rediscover the male critic as the female poet. Both Higginson and Dickinson have often been reduced to caricatures—she as the crazed and lonely poet of romantic fantasy, he as the pedantic fool of Victorian criticism.

But while historical reconstruction is needed, more than that is of interest in this literary relationship. Dickinson remains one of the most enigmatic figures of American literature. Not only is her life and work a source for rediscovering the dynamics of gender and art in nineteenth-century America, it is also a battleground for articulating major categories of contemporary criticism, including modernism, postmodernism, and feminism. To encounter Dickinson's poetry is to come to terms with a difficult interweaving of socially and philosophically subversive meaning and modernist literary form; the more we know about her work, the easier it is for us to understand Higginson's inability to comprehend it. Although a sympathetic figure—he was one of the leading abolitionists of the 1850s and was also an early feminist—Higginson was a very limited literary critic, and it is of less interest today to blame Higginson for failing Dickinson that it is to understand the dynamics of their literary relationship and its significance to her. For with all his limitations, Higginson represented Dickinson's major encounter with the world of literary criticism, and looking at the gulf between them can help us to understand the uniqueness of Dickinson's literary project in her own time and the difficult choices her world presented to her. Moreover, the critical discussions that surround their literary relationship draw us back to the central issues of Dickinson criticism, which today include the attempt to understand both the aesthetic and social implications of her poetry and to synthesize the insights of postmodernist and feminist readings of Dickinson.

When the thirty-one-year-old Dickinson sent Thomas Wentworth Higginson her first letter and four poems in 1862, the response she received is unknown, though it was apparently not completely encouraging. The relationship with Higginson that was thus begun came at a time of personal crisis in which Dickinson seems to have been attempting to define her role as a poet. By the time of the first letters, she had already written some of her best poems and had, as Wendy Martin notes, also gone through three of the four major struggles of her life: her resistance to Christian conversion while a student at Mount Holyoke; her conflict with her father over continuing her studies and being allowed the time and space to write; and a romantic crisis, the details of which remain obscure, but which probably involved an intense passion for a man who did not reciprocate. The fourth crisis, according to Martin, was "waged with her preceptor Thomas Wentworth Higginson over the value of her poetry. In each contest, the adversary is a male figure—Christ, her father, a potential husband, and a poetic mentor."[2]

The encounter with Higginson needs to be placed in the context of these other crises. While too much maudlin prose has been written about Dickinson's life, the romantic crisis that she experienced shortly before the letters commenced was apparently significant, regardless of the identity of the potential lover (Bowles or Wadsworth, male or female) toward whom her energies were directed.[3] And while the strangeness of her life-style has, like the romantic crisis, been exaggerated both in her own time and since, there is a core of truth to the Dickinson of popular legend. She herself indirectly encouraged the gossip of the people of Amherst concerning her life, for she consciously lived at the center of a personal mythology that emphasized the wonder and sacredness of nature and of ordinary life. Thus Dickinson dressed habitually in white; she sent ritual gifts of flowers with poems to friends; she sent glasses of wine and sometimes poems to visitors who sang in the parlor for her, while she, unlike her sister Vinnie, remained unseen. Sandra Gilbert suggests that visitors and townspeople were not completely to blame for mythologizing Dickinson's life. Instead, "observers were responding to a process of self-mythologizing that led Dickinson herself to use all the materials of daily reality, and most especially the details of domesticity, as if they were not facts but metaphors, in order to recreate herself-and-her-life as a single, emblematic text, and often, indeed, as a sort of religious text."[4]

The complex relation of Dickinson's life and work creates special problems and possibilities for readers—it helps us to see why her contemporaries had such difficulty in understanding her, for not only was she writing a difficult, emblematic poetry, composed of disjunctive flashes of insight; that poetry was also connected to a life that might be described, following Gilbert, as consciously sacramental (but not Christian), creating an original aesthetic and religious response outside of the conventional structures of nineteenth-century society. But to just as great an extent the relation of her life to her work helps to warn twentieth-century critics of the difficulties of Dickinson. The twentieth century attempt to respond to her poems as poems-in-themselves, artistic structures cut off from a life, a social matrix, a set of personal and social struggles, also fails to lead to an understanding of Dickinson's work. Thus, although she was recognized as a major poet by the New Critical generation, and as an American poet in the spiritual traditions of Edwards, Taylor, and the transcendentalists by postwar Americanists, the rise of feminist criticism has led to a new understanding of her poetry as part of a particular woman's struggle for identity, autonomy, and meaning.

The radical novelty of her poetry was a source of difficulty for the few contemporaries, such as Higginson, who read it during her lifetime. As a poet, Dickinson has long been appreciated as an early explorer of later tendencies. Like Whitman, Hopkins, and Baudelaire, she was a prefigurer of literary modernism and, more recently, of postmodernism (both of which terms are notoriously difficult to define). Her emphasis on showing rather than telling, on concrete images rather than discursive explanations, on disjunctive leaps rather than continuity, on extreme states of consciousness rather than conventional wisdom, on language as an almost autonomous field of play, on paradox rather than simplicity, on openness and acceptance of contradiction rather than on closure, on the profundity of the mundane and the ludicrous banality of the supposedly sacred—all of these features make Dickinson appear peculiarly modern. They have also led some critics to associate her with postmodernism, which can be described as extreme or "terminal modernism"[5] with a special emphasis on the autonomy of language, the inevitability of disjunction, and the impossibility of closure. Postmodernism is also associated with the postwar (postmodern) era, with its repudiation of the grand mythological continuities of modernists such as Yeats, Eliot, Lawrence, and Faulkner, and with the breakdown of notions of the coherent self and of related social continuities.

While Dickinson does prefigure contemporary literary movements, she was also very much a nineteenth-century poet and person. And yet there are interesting relations between Dickinson's artistic modernity and her significance for contemporary feminism. For, clearly, the desire to demolish and transform (or, to be fashionable, to deconstruct) the mythologies of patriarchal society, and the willingness to accept discontinuity as a given condition of existence to be suffered and played through, are quite easily reconciled with one another. As Sandra Gilbert once suggested, postmodernism probably has different connotations for male and female writers—what may be a threat of nihilism for one may be a welcome annihilation of oppression for another.[6]

A full treatment of Dickinson is obviously beyond the scope of this essay; however, if we are to understand the difficulties Thomas Wentworth Higginson faced in understanding Emily Dickinson, we must at least hint at the complexity of the Dickinson he tried and failed to understand. The story of Dickinson and Higginson is more than the story of, in Karl Keller's words, "the entrepreneur [who] could not see, for almost thirty years, the starlet."[7] It is also the story of Emily Dickinson's relationship to and misunderstanding by the world of criticism, as is indicated by Higginson's recurring prominence, sometimes almost as a metaphor, in critical studies of Dickinson. Higginson, as first critic, stands in for us (especially the male critical establishment, but perhaps also for all who have been baffled by Dickinson), embarrassed as we are to acknowledge him.

Who was the Higginson that Emily Dickinson wrote to in April 1862? Whatever his limitations, he was a more interesting figure than those who know him only through his relationship with Dickinson realize. By

1862 Higginson had become famous as one of the most radical of abolitionists. Ordained a Unitarian minister in 1847, Higginson was influenced by the transcendentalists, especially reformer Theodore Parker, as well as by abolitionist William Lloyd Garrison. In 1851 he led a failed attempt to rescue the fugitive slave Thomas Sims in Boston, and in 1854 he led a violent mob in an assault on the Boston Court House in an effort to free another fugitive slave, Anthony Burns. It was this second incident that made Higginson an abolitionist hero; he was wounded and a policeman killed, and for a time it appeared that Higginson and others would stand trial. Later, Higginson took arms to Kansas and befriended John Brown, becoming one of the secret supporters in the unsuccessful plot to start a slave insurrection at Harper's Ferry.[8]

As a minister, Higginson was controversial, and he held only two pulpits in his life, during the first ten years after ordination—a brief stay at Newburyport (which found him too radical), and a longer one in Worcester, where his ideas were more welcome, but which he resigned in 1857. During the war, he commanded for a time the First South Carolina Volunteers—the first black regiment in the Union army, a post he took up shortly after his correspondence with Dickinson began. After the war, Higginson supported himself chiefly by writing and editing, although he also served briefly in the Massachusetts legislature.

This brief history may seem to make Higginson a very strange poetic mentor for Emily Dickinson to have sought out—for Dickinson had little interest in politics at any time in her life, while politics had been Higginson's chief interest. However, she wrote to him shortly after an essay of his, "A Letter to a Young Contributor," had appeared in the *Atlantic*. Higginson wrote the essay during a period of disappointment when it appeared that he would not receive a military appointment, and it extols the virtues of the life devoted to the "higher" world of the arts, warning readers not to be "misled by the excitements of the moment into overrating the charms of military life"[9] and asserting that "war and peace, fame or forgetfulness, can bring no real injury to one who has formed the fixed purpose to live nobly day by day" (*AE*, 92). The emphasis of "A Letter to a Young Contributor" on the transcendental virtues of solitude and patience in the practice of one's art, plus its hint of a personal disappointment with the public world and a consequent turning inward, might well have appealed to Dickinson. But for the most part, Higginson's essay is a discussion of the practical matters of writing and publishing, directed especially at women who seek to publish. In addition to encouraging patience and dedication, the essay has practical advice on preparing a manuscript, revision, style, diction, and audience.

Most of his advice is similar to what one would find in any standard rhetoric text. The overall tone is encouraging, while informing readers that their works, regardless of their good intentions, must speak for themselves: "Do not waste a minute, not a second, in trying to demonstrate to others the value of your own performance. If your work does not vindicate itself, you cannot vindicate it" (*AE*, 84). Such words were the sort that Dickinson was apparently eager to hear by 1862, when she had already written hundreds of poems, including some of her best.

But there is another reason why Higginson may have appeared to be a congenial adviser: his feminism. Like other reformers of the 1850s, he became interested in women's rights as a consequence of his involvement with other movements: abolitionism and temperance (he was also long an admirer of the work of Margaret Fuller, whose *Woman in the Nineteenth Century* had appeared when Higginson was a divinity student). In 1853 Higginson was one of the members who walked out of the planning committee of the World Temperance Convention when other members refused to seat Susan B. Anthony on the committee because she was a woman. An alternate group was formed, the Whole World Temperance Convention, led by reformers including Higginson, Wendell Phillips, Anthony, Elizabeth Cady Stanton, Lucy Stone, Horace Greeley, and Theodore Parker.[10] Dickinson might not have known of these events (or taken much interest if she had), but she may have read Higginson's 1859 essay in the *Atlantic*, "Ought Women to Learn the Alphabet?" This essay discusses the aspect of feminism that seems to have been most important to Dickinson: women's equal right to education and opportunity in their chosen careers. Higginson begins this essay with a comment on the question posed by the French satirist Maréchal in 1801, in his "Plan for a Law Prohibiting the Alphabet to Women" (*AE*, 94). Higginson asserts that this question of basic eduction is a crucial one: "Concede this little fulcrum, and Archimedea will move the world before she has done with it: it becomes merely a question of time. . . . Woman must be a subject or an equal; there is no middle ground" (*AE*, 96). He goes on to discuss the gains made by women in America, where some states had given women "control of their own earnings" (*AE*, 98), and all the free states had allowed some control of property. Suffrage, Higginson believed, was gradually being accepted. But the root of women's continued oppression was the contempt in which they were held: "If contempt does not originally cause failure, it perpetuates it . . . woman begins under discouragement, and works under the same. Single, she works with half-preparation and half-pay; married, she puts name and wages into the keeping of her husband" (*AE*, 103–104). He argues that reformers should not suggest that women were already in every way men's equals, but rather that they would be equal in achievement if they received the same material advantages of education and encouragment that men received. While like many nineteenth-century reformers, Higginson overestimated the importance of education, he is very insightful about the disadvantages women worked under and the role of societal pressure and prejudices in shaping women to fit nineteenth-century roles.

> We deny woman her fair share of training, of encouragement, of remuneration, and then talk fine nonsense about her instincts and intuition. . . . If an outstanding male gymnast can clear the height of ten feet with the aid of a spring-board, it would be considered slightly absurd to ask a woman to leap eleven feet without one; yet this is precisely what society and the critics have done. Training and wages and social approbation are very elastic spring-boards; and the whole course of history has seen these offered bounteously to one sex, and as seduously withheld from the other. Let woman consent to be a doll, and there was no finery so gorgeous, no baby-house so costly, but she might aspire to share its lavish delights; let her ask simply for an equal chance to learn, to labor, and to live, and it was as if that same doll should open its lips, and propound Euclid's forty-seventh proposition.
>
> [AE, 106–107]

Higginson's scathing words on the contempt with which women's abilities were treated are tempered by reassurances that he has no wish to eliminate domestic labor for women—he only wishes to allow them the chance to aspire to something higher as well. Such attempts to reassure were common to nineteenth-century feminists, who tried to parry the accusation that they were destroying the home. He notes the success of women like Margaret Fuller and Elizabeth Barrett Browning who were "educated 'like boys'" (*AE*, 109) by their families, and assumes that such successes would be widespread if women were given an equal chance.

As to the causes of women's oppression, Higginson assumes that in the past, the rule of force was inevitable in human societies, and that women's inferior status—like slavery—was once legitimate, because inevitable. However, as society has become increasingly ruled by "the higher reason of arts, affections, aspirations" (*AE*, 114), women's oppression is no longer legitimate. While he sometimes idealizes women, he is also remarkably modern in his analysis, asserting the material base for ideological change—"Everybody sees that the times are altering the whole material position of woman; but most people do not appear to see the inevitable social and moral changes which are also involved" (*AE*, 114). Finally, as a militant abolitionist, Higginson sees the need for women to assert themselves in concrete struggle, noting that "will, not talent, governs the world" (*AE*, 121) and that those who hold privilege do not concede rights without being compelled to: "Men can hardly be expected to concede either rights or privileges more rapidly than they are claimed, or to be truer to women than they are to each other" (*AE*, 121).

Higginson the early feminist was hardly free from chauvinism, anymore than Higginson the militant abolitionist was free of racism. A member of the American Suffrage Association after the war and for fourteen years the coeditor of its *Woman's Journal*, he sometimes thought of both women and blacks as innately childlike and domestic, and was capable of suggesting that women avoid wearing eyeglasses because they were unbecoming and unsuitable.[11] Nevertheless, he was a clear and articulate supporter of women's rights as well as an encourager of women writers, and it was thus not inappropriate for Dickinson to seek him out for advice in her career as a writer. Higginson's main limitations were neither his politics nor his intentions; unfortunately, he was a hopelessly bad judge of poetry, as were most of his nineteenth-century peers, if judged by twentieth-century standards.

It is unfortunate that, with the exception of a few letters and journal entries, only Dickinson's side of the correspondence with Higginson has survived. The spring and summer of 1862, along with 1870 (the year the two met for the first time), is the crucial period in the flow of letters that Dickinson maintained until her death in 1886. Richard Sewall, the major Dickinson biographer, calls these letters "among the most thoughtful (as they are the most literary) of her correspondence."[12] But in addition to their literary significance, Sewall notes that the amount of self-revelation Dickinson put into these early letters to a complete stranger is astonishing;[13] if she attached great importance to Higginson as a friend, this is probably as much due to the personal revelation she had invested in their friendship as it is to the literary significance of their communication.

In April 1862 Dickinson was emerging from her most serious personal crisis and apparently ready to test the strength of the poetry on which she centered her life. The first letter, written after she had read in the April issue of the *Atlantic* Higginson's "Letter to a Young Contributor," is very brief, containing six short sentences, beginning, "Mr. Higginson, Are you too deeply occupied to say if my Verse is alive?"[14] The envelope contained four poems, as well as an envelope containing her name (the letter was not signed). The poems represented a range of Dickinson's styles, including the difficult #216, beginning "Safe in their Alabaster Chambers," as well as two easier poems (#318, "I'll tell you how the Sun rose," and #319, "the nearest Dream recedes—unrealized"), and #320,[15] a brief poem of great economy, of which many twentieth-century imagists would have been proud:

> We play at Paste—
> Till qualified, for Pearl—
> Then, drop the Paste—
> And deem ourself a fool—
>
> The shapes—though—were similar—
> And our new Hands
> Learned *Gem*-Tactics—
> Practicing *Sands*—

The movement from paste to pearl, sands to gem, is typical of Dickinson's discovery of wonder in the everyday, of significance in the apparently lowly. The form of the poem is irregular; the condensation ("*Gem*-tactics") modern. While she follows Higginson's advice and chooses to let her work speak for itself, this poem, obviously about writing, hints at considerable experience, though her next letter, dated ten days later, falsely asserts "I made no verse—but one or two—until this winter" (*L*, 2:261). Perhaps Dickinson was her own harshest critic; perhaps, as Karl Keller suggests, she was posing as the inexperienced female here.[16] Clearly, the letters contain a considerable amount of pose, and all statements within them cannot be taken at face value, though there is also an intensity and sincerity, especially in these early letters.

Higginson must have replied quickly and addressed many questions to Dickinson about herself. His praise of the poetry was apparently qualified, though she says, "Thank you for the surgery—it was not so painful as I supposed. I bring you others—as you ask—though they may not differ" (*L*, 2:261). Higginson obviously hit upon the comparison that so many subsequent critics have made, for she says, "You speak of Mr. Whitman—I never read his Book—but was told that he was disgraceful—" (*L*, 2:261). Higginson probably cited Whitman as an example of the dangers of looseness of form, a criticism he leveled at Dickinson's poetry throughout her life (his comments on Whitman were far more scathing, which should indicate to modern readers his lack of qualifications as an adviser to Dickinson).

The bulk of this letter, so familiar to modern critics, is about Dickinson's life—her recent crisis, her male friends or "tutors" (Ben Newton and probably Samuel Bowles are alluded to), her family, her religious skepticism, and the joy and wonder of her solitary life:

> I had a terror—since September—I could tell to none—and so I sing, as the Boy does by the Burying Ground—because I am afraid . . . When a little Girl, I had a friend, who taught me Immortality—but venturing too near, himself—he never returned—Soon after, my Tutor, died—and for several years, my Lexicon—was my only companion—Then I found one more—but he was not contented I be his scholar—so he left the Land.
>
> You ask of my Companions Hills—Sir—and the Sundown—and a Dog—large as myself, that my Father bought me—They are better than Beings—because they know—but do not tell—and the noise in the Pool, at Noon—excels my Piano. I have a Brother and Sister—My Mother does not care for thought—and Father, too busy with his Briefs—to notice what we do—He buys me many Books—but begs me not to read them—because he fears they joggle the Mind. They are religious—except me—and address an Eclipse, every morning—whom they call their "Father." But I fear my story fatigues you—I would like to learn—Could you tell me how to grow—or is it unconveyed—Like Melody—or Witchcraft?
>
> [*L*, 2:261]

This letter is itself an astonishing literary composition, and more than one critic has expressed surprise that Higginson did not immediately go "packing off to Amherst,"[17] considering the poems that were also sent. The poems also included were probably, according to Thomas H. Johnson (*L*, 2:262), #86, "South Winds jostle them," #321, "Of all the Sounds despatched abroad," and also #322, "There came a Day at Summer's full," which, Sewall notes, is regular enough in form that it should have pleased Higginson's conventional standards.[18] But as the next letter, dated six weeks later, indicates, Higginson's comments

were again mixed. Dickinson is very thankful for his praise and begins, "Your letter gave no drunkenness, because I tasted Rum before—
Domingo comes but once—yet I have had few pleasures so deep as
your opinion, and if I tried to thank you, my tears would block my
tongue" (L, 2:408). However, he had apparently badly underestimated Dickinson, who writes (apparently adopting a conventional
pose of modesty, as Keller claims),[19] "I smile when you suggest that I delay 'to publish'—that being foreign to my thought, as
Firmament to fin—" (L, 1:408). But she also notes, with apparent
confidence and calm, "if fame belonged to me, I could not escape
her—if she did not, the longest day would pass me on the chase—and
the approbation of my Dog, would forsake me—then—My Barefoot-
Rank is better—" (L, 2:408).

However, Dickinson also resists her critic with playful sarcasm.
"You think my gait 'spasmodic'—I am in danger—Sir—You think me
'uncontrolled'—I have no Tribunal" (L, 2:409). Although she includes
conventional feminine self-deprecation ("I have a little shape—it would
not crowd your Desk") and ends with the request, "But, will you be my
Preceptor, Mr. Higginson?" (L, 2:409), she has clearly stuck stubbornly
by her poetry and her standards, despite the poignant claiming of the
"Barefoot-Rank."[20] The next two letters continue a wavering tone,
mixing requests for help and advice with mild sarcasm. The fourth contains the famous remark: "Will you tell me my fault, frankly as to
yourself, for I had rather wince, than die. Men do not call the surgeon,
to commend—the Bone, but to set it, Sir" (L, 2:412). The fifth letter,
written in August, reveals the conflicting emotions she continued to experience. It begins with the conventional request for advice, "are these
more orderly? I thank you for the Truth" (L, 2:414), but continues, "I
have no Monarch in my life, and cannot rule myself, and when I try to
organize—my little Force explodes—and leaves me bare and charred"
(L, 2:414). She seems to be still seeking a "master"; her earlier struggles with patriarchal religion, her father, and her intended lover apparently have persisted and resurfaced in a desire for poetic guidance. Her
mild sarcasm continues: "I think you called me 'Wayward.' Will you
help me improve?" (L, 2:415), together with a persistent request for advice, and increasing frustration:

> You say "Beyond your knowledge." You would not jest with me,
> because I believe you—but Preceptor—you cannot mean it? All
> men say "what" to me, but I thought it a fashion—

When much in the Woods as a little Girl, I was told that Satan would bite me, that I might pick a poisonous flower, or Goblins kidnap me, but I went along and met no one but Angels, who were far shyer of me, than I could be of them, so I haven't that confidence in fraud that many exercise.

I shall observe your precept—though I don't understand it, always.

[*L*, 2:415]

Dickinson appears increasingly exasperated by Higginson's lack of understanding; the story she recounts indicates her willingness to question the (often fraudulent) judgment of authorities. Although her attacks on his judgment are mild enough, the next letter is a brief note apologizing and asking him to write (*L*, 2:417). For the most part, the intensity of her discussion of poetry diminishes after this fifth letter—more of the later letters discuss personal matters, such as the deaths of relatives and friends, although the requests for advice on her poetry, and the sending of poems, continues. By the fifth letter, Higginson had in his possession approximately thirteen poems, including some very good ones, and his essential failure to see the value of her poetry continued beyond her death. He was eventually instrumental in getting her poems published, but he was probably less important in this than Dickinson's sister Lavinia, who persisted in believing in Emily, and did less work on the revisions (and alterations) of the poems for publication than did Mabel Loomis Todd (an Amherst woman who was probably the lover of Dickinson's brother Austin).[21]

Higginson's single visit to Amherst, in 1870, is a monument to his failure to understand Dickinson. As Sewall notes, he "seems to have come prepared for oddity and found it."[22] Earlier, he had encouraged her to visit Boston and attend literary gatherings. It is unfortunate that she refused to go, for she might have had literary relationships with others who could understand her better than Higginson did.

Before the visit, Higginson wrote of his hope that "perhaps if I could take you by the hand I might be something to you; but till then you only enshroud yourself in this fiery mist and I cannot reach you" (*L*, 2:462). But the visit did little to dispel the "mist" Higginson complained of; he found Dickinson childlike and exhausting: "She came to me with two day lilies which she put in a sort of childlike way into my hand & said 'These are my introduction' in a soft frightened breathless childlike voice—& added under her breath Forgive me if I am frightened; I never see strangers & hardly know what to say—but she talked soon & thenceforward continuously—& deferentially—sometimes stopping to ask me to talk instead of her—but readily recommencing" (*L*, 2:472). Fortunately, Higginson recorded much of Dickinson's conversation in a letter to his wife, in which he also reported, "I never was with anyone who drained my nerve power so much. Without touching her, she drew from me. I am glad not to live near her" (*L*, 2:476). That many of Higginson's comments on Dickinson come in letters to his wife, where he may have habitually felt the need to deprecate the literary women he associated with, should be remembered when we interpret his words, for there is role playing here, just as there is in Dickinson's letters to him.[23] Nevertheless, Higginson clearly feels a need to dismiss Dickinson as "childlike" (a word he repeats in a single sentence) while unmistakably feeling threatened by her, who "without touching," so "drained" and "drew from" him. The sexual metaphors he unconsciously uses, and his apparent need to recall the incident in detail, suggest that at a deep level he found Dickinson very unsettling. In any case, he seems to have recognized that he could not develop with her the student-mentor relationship that he had with such other women writers as Helen Hunt Jackson.

Higginson seemed incapable of fully responding to Dickinson either as a person or as a poet. Nevertheless, by agreeing to coedit the first two editions of her poetry after her death, and by defending her work in print with qualified praise, he was instrumental in belatedly helping her poetry to gain recognition—a fact that his critics sometimes forget.[24] However, his critical judgment of Dickinson's poetry remained limited by the conventionality of his ideas about literature, which rarely transcended the prejudices of the New England establishment. In his *Reader's History of American Literature* (1903), the poets he praises most highly are Longfellow and Whittier. He apologizes for Longfellow's "simplicity," which he realizes is the source of much of the poet's popularity, for "it is possible that this simplicity was the precise contribution needed in that early and formative period in American letters".[25] Longfellow, he claims, "rendered a service [to American literature] only secondary" to that of Emerson, whom he viewed as the great original thinker of the century (*RH*, 145). Whittier deserved special commendation because "not one of this eminent circle [the Cambridge group] had the keys of common life so absolutely in his hands as Whittier" (*RH*, 147). While he praises the transcendentalists generally, including Emerson, Thoreau, Fuller, and Parker, he has the sharpest criticism for Whitman: "In the stricter sense of the critics, Whitman may not be called a poet" for Whitman "substitute[d] mere cadence for form" (*RH*, 227–228). In addition to charging Whitman with formlessness, Higginson brings the familiar charge of immorality. Even more telling, he praises "My Captain," arguably Whitman's worst poem, and says that "of all our poets, he is really the least simple, the most meretricious; and this is the reason why the honest consciousness of the classes which he most celebrates—the drover, the teamster, the soldier—has never been reached by his songs" (*RH*, 233).

Given Higginson's consistent opposition to formal experimentation and "difficulty" and his praise of simplicity and the ability to reach a wide audience, it is hardly surprising that he could not fully appreciate Dickinson. He does devote several pages of the *Reader's History* to her, saying she was, next to Helen Hunt Jackson, "perhaps the most remarkable" New England woman of the time (*RH*, 130). Next to Jackson, however, Dickinson was "a woman of a far less easily intelligible type: a strange, solitary, morbidly sensitive, and pitifully childlike poetic genius" (*RH*, 130). The ambivalence of Higginson toward Dickinson is evident in these pages. He quotes her on "shunning men and women," and says her "reply is indicative of her weakness and of her strength" (*RH*, 130). It was hard for him to deprecate Dickinson without praising her, or to note her strength without criticizing:

> Emily Dickinson never quite succeeded in grasping the notion of the importance of poetic form. . . . With all its irregularity, however, her poetry preserves a lyrical power almost unequaled in her generation. In remoteness to allusion, in boldness of phrase, it stands at the opposite remove from the verse of Longfellow, for example; but if it can never attain popularity—the last fate which its author could have wished for it—it is likely, in the end, to obtain the attention of the "audience fit, tho' few," which a greater poet once desired of Fate.
>
> [*RH*, 131]

While Higginson observes some of the same qualities later critics find in Dickinson's poetry, he thinks of most of these qualities as defects, except for her "lyrical power." The revisions he and Mabel Todd made in the Dickinson manuscripts tended to simplify and regularize the poems, adding titles, changing words, regularizing meter and punctuation, and generally reducing the complexity and novelty of her work. Similar editorial liberties with the few poems published in her lifetime infuriated Dickinson and were part of the reason she avoided publication.[26] The sort of revisions Higginson made were understandable in context, however, given his limited ideas about poetry and the liberties taken by nineteenth-century editors—Samuel Clemens' work was posthumously revised every bit as thoroughly and destructively as Dickinson's, although Clemens was a male writer with an international reputation at the time of his death.

Higginson, then, was a conventional critic, and it is probably less important to determine how much praise or blame he deserves than to ask what he meant to Dickinson, and what she sought in her correspondence with him at a crucial juncture in her life and career. As Karl Keller points out, there is an implied inquiry about publication beneath Dickinson's assumed pose as the student who must repeatedly ask her teacher for help in order to "improve"[27]—she first wrote Higginson, we must remember, in response to an essay that sought to help women writers publish. However, she sought more than help with publication. Her refusals to enter Boston's literary circles, and her failure to seek out a second opinion, may be written off to her inexperience or her resolute self-dependence, but these actions also suggest that publication was not so important to her. It is unfair to her not to assume that the decision not to publish was hers. We know she refused the requests that publisher Thomas Niles made for manuscripts, at Helen Jackson's prompting, in 1882 and 1883 (L, 2:725–726, 769). If we view publication as Dickinson's chief motive in writing to Higginson, then their literary relationship was a disastrous mistake, and nothing more—a classic example of the failure of the male mentor to help a female writer. However, while a better critic than Higginson, someone who could appreciate the complexity of her poetic project, would have been a great help to her, the dynamics of their literary relationship were more complicated than this rather simple mentor-protégée model would indicate. It is possible that Higginson came to serve a positive as well as a negative function for Dickinson as she strove to develop and understand her role as a poet.

David Porter suggests that in the correspondence Dickinson was seeking more than publication: she was seeking artistic validation and a sense of purpose that she soon realized Higginson could not provide.[28] Clearly, this absence that Higginson could not fill, the absent "Monarch in my life," is an underlying theme in the 1862 letters, and the "Monarch" has many meanings: It is the inability to find the degree of outward validation she sought, personally or aesthetically. It is also the struggle with and the negation of patriarchy, the absence and negation of a traditional center—ordering principle, patriarchal God, father, male, master, hierarchical form—that is one of the most characteristic thematic and formal elements in Dickinson's work. This complexity is suggested by the very state in which the poetry was left after her death—seventeen hundred untitled poems in forty-four packets and additional manuscripts. Porter is correct in asserting that it is partly this absence that makes Dickinson's poetry appear so modern, together with her obsession with language as a decentering source of insight. But he neglects to stress that her "failure" in finding what she sought from Higginson was a failure that she transformed into a success. In his eagerness to associate Dickinson with the "radical modernism" of contemporary thought, which has "all the pathos of power without a project,"[29] Porter misreads the significance of Dickinson's decentered poetry, criticizing the lack of an overall architectural structure, the lack of social consciousness and history, and the lack of an *ars poetica* in her work. As several feminist critics have noted, the absence of public events in her poetry does not signify a lack of social consciousness—only a redirecting of that consciousness toward the domestic world of nineteenth-century women.[30] Similarly, the apparent lack of architectural structure is itself a kind of antistructure, reacting against the philosophical systems and assumptions of more hierarchical structures. The model of modernism to which Porter assimilates Dickinson needs revision, partly by incorporating the notion that there are different "modernisms" in different historical contexts, and that the same literary forms and techniques may have a different significance for male and female writers. But while there is much justice in the criticisms that have been leveled at Porter by feminist critics, there is also some irony in this debate, for in describing her poetry in terms of "terminal modernism," he is *praising* Dickinson by assimilating her to the most powerful and avant-garde literary movement of contemporary literature, a movement that he nevertheless distrusts as a trap he knows no way out of. But following Sandra Gilbert, we should note that the modernist or postmodernist tendencies of women writers are often subversive, a welcome annihilation rather than a nihilist trap. It is therefore Porter, not Dickinson, who has made the mistake of not being sufficiently historical.

But if the "absent Monarch" is crucial to Dickinson's poetic project, what does this say about her relationship to Higginson? And if Dickinson's poetry was so radical, what does this say about her relationship to the critical institutions of her era, the other Higginsons she might have met? One possibility is that Higginson's absence—on one level, his

physical and geographic remoteness; on another, the fact that he provided a reference point but presented no intellectual threat—made him
well suited for her purposes. Ostensibly, he was her critical "preceptor"; in reality, he was almost irrelevant. Through contact with him she
may have learned something about the radicalness of her own project
and its remoteness from the literary institutions of her America. Her
difficulty was that she found no way to reject the "Monarch" while also
getting her work accepted and understood by nineteenth-century readers
in a form that was also acceptable to her. That this occurred is partly
an accident of history; one can think of others of her contemporaries
(Melville, perhaps Emerson, certainly Fuller, had she lived) who might
have proved better guides. Yet it is also a matter of her own choice, and
of her understanding, perhaps, that she could accomplish her work better with only the most tenuous relationship to literary institutions.
Higginson provided that relationship—a door not closed, but open just
a crack.

Dickinson's strength and significance lies partly in the inward isolation she mapped out for herself in opposition to the gender roles of
nineteenth-century America. To live out such a project on a deep level,
in a way that she herself only partially articulated and understood, was
simultaneously to increase the likelihood of cutting herself off from the
public forum of thoughts and feelings represented by publication. The
personal isolation she experienced, and chose, is thus reproduced in her
relation to the public role of the poet, which she refused, partly through
circumstance, partly through choice. There is tragedy, sarcasm, and anger in the voice that she leaves us, as in the following poem, #1072:

Title divine—is mine!
The Wife—without the Sign!
Acute Degree—conferred on me—
Empress of Calvary!
Royal—all but the Crown!
Bethrothed—without the swoon
God sends us Women—
When you—hold—Garnet to Garnet—
Gold—to Gold—
Born—Bridalled—Shrouded—
In a Day—
Tri Victory
"My Husband"—women say—
Stroking the Melody—
Is *this*—the way?

While the biographical sense that "Wife—without the Sign" had for Dickinson will probably always remain unclear, the irony of the poem and its depiction of marriage is unmistakable. Similarly, as poet, she remained without the sign—the "nomination" she once asked from Higginson[31]—which would have publicly confirmed her vocation. Her world is marked by fissures, the gulf between person/role, word/thing, male/female, public/private. One has only to think of the roles and possibilities that would have been available to a Dickinson today to realize that these separations were, in a sense, tragic—and yet she would probably have considered a split existence inevitable. It is for us, not her, to assert the historical variability of some of the divisions she lived under; a contemporary Dickinson would be a political poet, in part because of the way the historical Dickinson had been a private one.

Notes

1. Yvor Winters, *Maule's Curse: Seven Studies in the History of American Obscurantism* (Norfolk, Conn.: New Directions, 1938), 165; see also Klaus Lubber, *Emily Dickinson: The Critical Revolution* (Ann Arbor: University of Michigan Press, 1968), 161–183.

2. Wendy Martin, *An American Triptych: Ann Bradstreet, Emily Dickinson, Adrienne Rich* (Chapel Hill: University of North Carolina Press, 1984), 84.

3. See Martin, *American Triptych*, 102–103; Richard B. Sewall, *The Life of Emily Dickinson*, 2 vols. (New York: Farrar, Straus and Giroux, 1976), 2:400–420; Vivian R. Pollak, *Dickinson: The Anxiety of Gender* (Ithaca: Cornell University Press, 1984), 59–102.

4. Sandra M. Gilbert, "The Wayward Nun beneath the Hill: Emily Dickinson and the Mysteries of Womanhood," in *Feminist Critics Read Emily Dickinson*, ed. Suzanne Juhasz (Bloomington: Indiana University Press, 1983), 23.

5. David Porter, *Dickinson: The Modern Idiom* (Cambridge: Harvard University Press, 1981), 7.

6. Sandra M. Gilbert made these remarks on feminism and postmodernism in a panel discussion on feminist criticism with Susan Gubar at the Tenth Annual Twentieth-Century Literature Conference, University of Louisville, Louisville, Kentucky, 27 February 1982. As for the particular ways in which Dickinson's poetry subverts conventional notions of gender, I do not discuss them because of limitations of space; however, they are amply discussed in the feminist criticism on Dickinson. See especially Sandra M. Gilbert and Susan Gubar, *The Madwoman in the Attic: The Woman Writer and the Nineteenth-Century Literary Imagination* (New Haven: Yale University Press, 1979), 581–650.

7. Karl Keller, *The Only Kangaroo among the Beauty: Emily Dickinson and America* (Baltimore: Johns Hopkins University Press, 1979), 213.

8. See Tilden G. Edelstein, *Strange Enthusiasm: A Life of Thomas Wentworth Higginson* (New Haven: Yale University Press, 1968), 68–236. Other books on Higginson include Anna Mary Wells, *Dear Preceptor: The Life and Times of Thomas Wentworth Higginson* (Boston: Houghton Mifflin, 1963); Howard N. Meyer, *Colonel of the Black Regiment: The Life of Thomas Wentworth Higginson* (New York: Norton, 1967); and James W. Tuttleton, *Thomas Wentworth Higginson* (Boston: Twayne, 1978).

9. See Edelstein, *Strange Enthusiasm*, 250–251. Higginson, *Atlantic Essays* (Boston: James R. Osgood, 1871), 88 (hereafter cited as *AE* in the text).

10. Edelstein, *Strange Enthusiasm*, 146–148.

11. Ibid., 320, 373.

12. Sewall, *Life of Dickinson*, 2:533.

13. Ibid., 2:543–544.

14. *The Letters of Emily Dickinson*, ed. Thomas H. Johnson, 3 vols. (Cambridge: Harvard University Press, Belknap Press, 1958), 2:403 (hereafter cited as *L* in the text).

15. The poems are referred to by the numbers given them by Thomas H. Johnson in *The Complete Poems of Emily Dickinson* (Boston: Little, Brown, 1955).

16. See Keller, *Only Kangaroo among the Beauty*, 213–215.

17. Sewall, *Life of Dickinson*, 2:553.

18. Ibid., 552–553; also Thomas H. Johnson, *Emily Dickinson: An Interpretive Biography* (Cambridge: Harvard University Press, Belknap Press, 1955), 114–116.

19. Keller, *Only Kangaroo among the Beauty*, 213–215.

20. See Johnson, *Interpretive Biography*, 113–114; Keller, *Only Kangaroo among the Beauty*, 216–217.

21. See Martin, *American Triptych*; and Sewall, *Life of Dickinson*, 1:170–185, 215–228.

22. Sewall, *Life of Dickinson*, 2:563.

23. See Keller, *Only Kangaroo among the Beauty*, 213–215.

24. See Lubber, *Critical Revolution*, 201–202.

25. Thomas H. Higginson and Henry Walcott Boynton, *A Reader's History of American Literature* (Boston: Houghton Mifflin, 1903), 143 (hereafter cited as *RH* in the text). Although revised with Boynton, the book is based on lectures Higginson gave in Boston in 1903.

26. See Johnson, *Interpretive Biography*, 120.

27. Keller, *Only Kangaroo among the Beauty*, 218–219.

28. Porter, *Modern Idiom*, 111, 143–144, 184.

29. Ibid., 236, 138–141, 152–155, 180, 184.

30. See Martin, *American Triptych*, 81; Suzanne Juhasz, introduction to *Feminist Critics Read Dickinson*, 7–9; also idem, *The Undiscovered Continent: Emily Dickinson and the Space of the Mind* (Bloomington: Indiana University Press, 1983), 2–3.

31. Porter, *Modern Idiom*, 143.

RITA K. GOLLIN

Subordinated Power:
Mrs. and Mr. James T. Fields

ON 5 JANUARY, 1915, the *Boston Evening Transcript* carried the headline, "Mrs. J. T. Fields Dies at Her Home," the subheadline identifying her as the "Widow of Former Boston Publisher." The obituary itself begins, "Mrs. Annie Adams Fields, the widow of James T. Fields, widely known more than a generation ago as a publisher in the firm of Ticknor & Fields, friend of Dickens and other leading people of the literary world both here and abroad, died this morning at her home, 148 Charles Street, where she had lived for sixty years."

The woman who had continued to lead an active life throughout her thirty-four years of widowhood would have approved of the wording and even the syntactical ambiguity: "friend" could apply equally well to her husband or herself. She would also have approved of Henry James's memoir of her in the *Atlantic*, entitled "Mr. and Mrs. James T. Fields." In her own memoir of the English writer Mary Cowden Clarke, the widow's identity was defined by the husband who had died decades before; the very title, "Two Lovers of Literature: Charles and Mary Cowden Clarke," suggests the ideal definition of her own marriage—a loving partnership in the service of literature, with the husband in first place.[1] But Annie Fields's role in that partnership was more active and more varied than anyone has yet acknowledged, and it shows how a nineteenth-century woman could assert herself even in a state of genteel subordination.[2]

In the fall of 1854, the Boston publisher James T. Fields invited the English novelist Mary Russell Mitford "please to congratulate me that after an engagement of a few weeks I am . . . to go to church with one of the best Yankee girls of my acquaintance. Indeed she is the best in any body's acquaintance. Just the girl you would choose for me." To the elderly spinster, he stressed the sweet wholesomeness of his twenty-year-old fiancée:

141

She has never written books altho' she is capable of doing that some; never held an argument on Woman's Rights or Wrongs in her whole life, and so full of goodness of heart and beauty that you would say at once "that is the maid of all others for my friend F." . . . In short Annie is a girl after your own heart and she told me to give her love to you and ask you to love her.[3]

His assessment was at once accurate and limited. At thirty-seven, he was beginning an unusually companionate though childless marriage that would last until his death twenty-seven years later, and he was right about the charm of his twenty-year-old bride. But Annie would repeatedly demonstrate her capacity for writing books, and although she "never held an argument on Woman's Rights," she contrived to expand women's personal and professional options, including her own. A few days before their wedding, Fields jauntily told his friend Longfellow, "Nought of news other than that I go into King's Chapel next Wednesday with Miss Annie and bring her out as somebody else."[4] By making Annie "somebody else," Fields brought her into a world populated by the period's major writers, a literary world that centered on Boston but extended to New York and included England. Ticknor and Fields was the exclusive publisher of Longfellow, Emerson, Holmes, Hawthorne, Whittier, and other outstanding American writers, and its English list included De Quincey, Tennyson, Browning, and Thackeray. They all became the friends and admirers of Mrs. James T. Fields.[5]

The wedding took place in King's Chapel on the morning of 15 November, 1854, and the fact that the newlyweds then moved into the family house on Boylston Street suggests a comfortable feeling of mutuality.[6] The new husband was solicitous and protective, sending notes and gifts to his "Dear Love" from his office almost daily. In her wedding portrait, we see a wide-eyed sweet-faced young woman with dark wavy hair and what Henry James later called a "pensive Burne-Jones air," an eminently satisfactory wife for the genial and ambitious publisher.

As a genteel Bostonian, she was already committed to the values of high culture and public service. Her father, Zabdiel Boylston Adams —an eighth-generation descendant of Henry Adams of Braintree and a graduate of Harvard College and Harvard Medical School—was a prominent Boston physician and an active member of cultural and civic organizations until he died, two months after the wedding.[7] Her mother, Sarah May Holland Adams, was also a descendant of prominent early Bay settlers, and also a high-minded and self-reliant nurturer, cherished by Annie for her "active spirit of good."[8] Annie's brother was a doctor; one sister became the translator of Herman Grimm; another became a professional portrait painter; and Annie earned respect as a hostess, a poet, a civic reformer, and a biographer.

Some of the credit belongs to her teacher, George B. Emerson, whose School for Young Ladies provided "the best education possible" and trained students to be "good daughters and sisters, good neighbors, good wives, and good mothers."[9] Emerson urged dedication to literature, service to others, and religious faith; he also urged self-fulfillment. "Whatever faculty you find within you, do not fear to use and cultivate it to the highest degree," he advised in his retirement address. Thus Annie Fields was following the advice of her teacher (as well as his cousin Waldo) whenever she spurred herself to make the most of her "faculties"—whether she was giving a dinner party, writing a poem, choosing manuscripts for the *Atlantic Monthly*, establishing a working-women's residence, lecturing on charity organizations, or chairing an advisory committee on women's admission to medical school.

But throughout her marriage, her steadiest support and encouragement came from her husband. He brought his bride "a tenderness which grew only with the years," she recalled at the time of his death in 1881. Representing herself as "a young girl, a younger member of a large family, with less reason for special consideration than any other person in the household," she virtually ignored her separate identity to stress her fulfillment in marriage; it was "an exceptional experience . . . to be swept suddenly out upon a tide more swift and strong and all-enfolding than her imagination had foretold; a power imaging the divine life, the divine shelter, the divine peace." The passive voice befits the role she was prepared to assume as a wife who floated on her husband's "tide." Yet without relinquishing her submissive role, the young Annie soon became not only her husband's companion but his colleague.[10]

Raised to believe that women's lives centered on the home, Annie could enthusiastically admire a woman like Emily Tennyson, who was wholly devoted to a noble husband and loving children. Yet she more fully sympathized with Harriet Beecher Stowe, who earned literary renown while shouldering heavy domestic responsibilities; her friendships with unmarried professional women—writers like Lucy Larcom, actresses like Charlotte Cushman, and artists like her sister Lissie— provoked unsettling questions about women's needs. She remained all her life what contemporaries called a womanly woman—she believed in the sanctity of the family and woman's nurturing role as thoroughly as she believed that literature should stimulate and record high endeavor. But she also believed in self-fulfillment, and even while remaining within the bounds of convention, she stretched them.

Throughout the twenty-seven years of their marriage, Annie was the poised and conscientious partner of the most eminent publisher in Boston, charming the scores of celebrities who came for breakfast, dinner, an evening reception, or an overnight stay. The firm of Ticknor and Fields paid for the house on Charles Street that the Fieldses occupied from the time it was built, in 1856, and it soon became widely known as a center of hospitality and high culture—the "little ark of the modern deluge," James later called it. There was certainly a tacit understanding that James and Annie Fields would use it as they did, as a social annex of the firm. For years, only close friends knew that their hostess also served as her husband's literary assistant or that she had literary ambitions of her own. Not that she was devious; she was guided by the period convention that required a married woman to appear in public only under the protection of her husband's name. But the title of an article Fields wrote for the *Atlantic*, "My Friend's Library," implicitly comments on their mutuality: his wife was his friend, and the library where they read and entertained together was as much Annie's as it was his.[11]

Aided by a small staff, Annie soon became a consummate hostess, though (as Willa Cather later observed) years of "unruffled" hospitality in a narrow four-story building with a basement kitchen "cost the hostess something—cost her a great deal."[12] It was one of her most important jobs—essentially a gratifying one—to keep Ticknor and Fields writers happy. Thus during the five months of Charles Dickens's reading tour, from November 1867 until the following April—a shrewd business venture for the novelist and his publishers—he was repeatedly Annie's guest of honor at dinners and receptions. One of her greatest social coups was to have him under her roof for four days, and he came to regard her as "one of the dearest little women in the world."[13] If Hawthorne or Stowe spent the night in Boston, it was usually at Charles Street, where they could expect encouragement about whatever literary project they were completing or contemplating. As he left her house one morning, Hawthorne delighted his hostess by saying that he "liked no house to stay in better than this."[14] Stowe insisted that she liked nothing better than an evening with her "dear young angel" Annie, reading her a new story or simply talking until midnight.[15] Whenever Whittier came to town, he anticipated chatty breakfasts with James and Annie; and although he disliked large parties, he often returned for supper with the hostess he considered one of his dearest friends and "the busiest woman in Boston." When Emerson lectured in Boston, he often came for dinner and sometimes for an overnight stay, as in the spring of 1872 when Annie invited about forty friends to hear him read "Amita," his tribute to his "noble stoical" aunt, Mary Moody Emerson.[16]

Of course, Annie Fields's combined social and literary role was never limited to hospitality, whether at Charles Street or (after 1874) at the Fieldses' summer home in Manchester. As her husband had anticipated in his letter to Mitford, she could be counted on to charm everyone she met. "Annie has made a great strike among the English," Fields bragged to his brother-in-law in August 1859, two months into a year-long trip abroad. "They all wish her to stay here and make a home with them. Dickens told his daughter he had not met an American lady he admired so much."[17] During that same trip, she also became the friend of America's most important novelists, Nathaniel Hawthorne and Harriet Beecher Stowe, and all three families returned to America together in June 1860. "We all anticipate so much from the idea of making the voyage with you," Stowe had written the month before.[18] The image of Annie sitting on the boat deck and chatting with Harriet Beecher Stowe and Sophia Hawthorne seems emblematic of her position in American literary circles: both women confided in her about literary and personal matters, eager for intimacy and urging visits. Annie was more often a hostess than a guest, but her diaries include lively records of visits to literary celebrities—to Americans including Hawthorne, Emerson, and Twain, and English writers including Dickens, Tennyson, and George Eliot.

Even in the early years of her marriage, however, Annie maintained a literary identity of her own. Her husband encouraged it. She thought of herself as a poet even when cloaked in anonymity, as in the case of her first major publication—the *Ode Recited by Miss Charlotte Cushman, at the Inauguration of the Great Organ in Boston, November 2, 1863*. "There has been an ode written to be spoken at the organ opening," Annie wrote in her journal the week before. "No one is to know who wrote it. Miss Cushman will speak it." Even granting period conventions and womanly modesty, it seems curious that Annie did not acknowledge authorship even in her diary. But she was proud of having written the ode for that great occasion, and proud that it would be delivered by a close friend who was also the country's most celebrated actress. Presumably with the poet's approval, her husband had the eleven-page poem privately printed, with its cover stamped in gold, and he sent copies to close friends. Warm praise poured in, laced with surprise at the identity of the poet. As an occasional poem celebrating the new organ and Boston itself while espousing the Union cause, the ode is competent if undistinguished. Both the poet and her husband thought so well of it that they were outraged by the unsigned hostile review in the *Commonwealth*, written (they soon learned) by their friend Julia Ward Howe. "That mistress of envy, scandal, and malice has cast the first stone at my wife's beautiful poem," Fields complained to Sophia Hawthorne; in her diary, Annie sweepingly asserted, "Julia Ward Howe has said and sung her last as far as Boston goes. Her jealousy of the Odist got the better of her judgment and she has written out her gall for the 'Commonwealth.'"[19] Nonetheless, for most of her close friends, Annie Fields (with the aid of her husband) had established her credentials as a poet.

Yet her husband's comment that she would never do anything better than the ode conveyed a mixed message. She had been writing poems for years, preserving fair copies of many of them, and seven had already appeared anonymously in the *Atlantic*. "I feel I can do something far more sustained and as truly lyrical,—but not under the ordinary conditions of my city life," she protested. "Too much a woman to be always a poet," she put household responsibilities first. She had "a heart of a singer hidden in me and I long sometimes to break loose—but on the whole I sincerely prefer to make others comfortable and happy . . . and say fie! to my genius if it does not sing to me from the sauce-pan."[20] Aware of the cost, she sometimes worried that her "faculty" might die. Yet she kept writing poems all her life, ranging from brief lyrics to sustained narrative poems. Some—like the "Canticles of Married Love" presented as anniversary gifts to her husband from 1865 to 1868, or birthday poems for her friend Laura Johnson—were never intended for publication. Usually she had publication in mind, though until 1875 she published only anonymously or pseudonymously. Her husband had selected a total of twenty lyrics for the *Atlantic* before he resigned as editor in 1871; subsequently, her poems continued to appear in the *Atlantic* and in other prestigious periodicals including *Harper's Monthly* and *Scribner's*. Two long poems were published in the 1870s—in 1872, *The Children of Lebanon*, a narrative centering on two young Shakers; five years later, *The Return of Persephone: A Dramatic Sketch*, dedicated "to the memory of my mother." Both develop tender mother-daughter relationships and young people's yearning for marriage, and the poet's proud husband arranged to have them both privately printed (the first anonymously and the second attributed to "A.F."). As with

the ode, Fields sent copies to friends, signifying his approval: Annie's
Shaker poem provided "a perfect picture of this strange people," he assured Longfellow.[21] Houghton Mifflin would subsequently publish two
collections of Annie's poems: shortly before her husband died in 1881,
Under the Olive by "A.F."; then fourteen years later, *The Singing Shepherd*, by "Annie Fields." Both were well reviewed, and not just out of
courtesy. Although "too much a woman to be always a poet," Annie
Fields had worked hard to earn her reputation for technical skill, occasionally revealing the "heart of a singer."

She was far less successful as a writer of fiction, but here, too, she
had her husband's support and espoused ideals they both shared. Although there is no way of knowing if she hoped to publish her slight if
high-minded sketches, her only novel—*Asphodel*—was anonymously
published by Ticknor and Fields in 1866. Its reception by two of her
closest friends might well explain why she never again attempted prose
fiction. "How very naughty you were not to tell me about Asphodel and
to let me say that provoking thing," Laura Johnson wrote, though the
letter with the "provoking thing" has not survived (not surprising, given
Annie's tender skin). Laura managed only faint praise: the book was
graceful and included interesting thoughts, and she was glad "to have a
book of yours . . . in my hands."[22] By contrast, Sophia Hawthorne's
response to the novel was so harsh that Annie never admitted authorship. "I began but *could not* read 'Asphodel' on account of its lack of
nature, truth, simplicity, vraisemblance," Sophia asserted. Granting
that it might get better as it went on, she nonetheless declared, "I think I
could not ever read it." Then she said with unintentional irony, "I hope
you do not like it yourself well enough to care whether I like it or not,"
and inquired, "Is it some new young authoress, whom you are trying
to befriend and bring forward?" If Annie felt hurt, perhaps she was
mollified by her friend's praise of a long narrative poem she had copied
out for "S.H." The novelist "is no novelist certainly," Sophia asserted;
"I would rather have your Florentine mosaic (as I call it) than a library
of such books as this."[23]

Asphodel presents interrelated but disjunctive episodes in the lives of
a married couple and two of their friends, many of them tedious and a
few heavily melodramatic. Perhaps Fields's editorial judgment was im-
paired by the novel's images of conjugal affection, or perhaps by its
promise of healing love in the aftermath of the Civil War. One statement by the unmarried Erminia about her friend Alice's wedding con-
veys the story's basic sentiment: "In my girlish weakness, I feared I had
lost something, being ignorant of the divine mystery of married love to

enlarge the possibilities of life."[24] Bayard Taylor praised the novel and
told Annie that Lowell's copy was well worn, yet it offers more to the
biographer than the literary critic. Through lively conversations between the two heroines, Annie affirmed her deepest convictions: despite
the constraints of presumed subservience, women had to nurture not
only their families and friends, but themselves.

Although she showed most of her works in progress to her husband,
sometimes reading them aloud (one of the many ways marriage helped
"enlarge the possibilities of life" for her), she also looked elsewhere for
criticism. She often sent copies of poems to friends, including Longfellow, Whittier, Larcom, and Thaxter, and they in turn sent theirs. Praise
was assumed, and for Annie it was an emotional necessity, though she
welcomed and offered minor suggestions for revision. In 1877 her desire for a sympathetic critical forum led her to inaugurate "a club of
about ten ladies who meet here every Tuesday each one to read something of her own" (as she told her friend Laura Johnson), a venture she
repeated the following year.[25] Throughout her long period of intimacy
with Sarah Orne Jewett that began in 1881 and ended with Jewett's
death in 1909, each of them routinely read the other's manuscripts. But
while James T. Fields was alive, he was his wife's primary literary
critic.

Fields always encouraged his wife's endeavors as a writer, but he had
his own uses for her literary skills. In July 1861, while actively continuing his other publishing responsibilities, he also began editing the
magazine that Ticknor and Fields had recently purchased, the *Atlantic
Monthly*, turning it into one of the country's most important periodicals. Effectively, Annie served as an assistant throughout the decade of
his editorship, although only a handful of friends knew it. "What ex-
cellence in the Atlantic generally!" Thomas Starr King wrote from
California. "No wonder when we remember the publisher & his
wife!"[26] Some *Atlantic* writers addressed letters about literary and social matters to both of them: Rebecca Harding Davis once began a letter
without a salutation, explaining, "I don't know which to write to—I
cannot separate you."[27] Elizabeth Peabody was one of many contribu-
tors who tried to influence the editor through his wife: after praising
Annie's ode in December 1863, Peabody told her to read the enclosed
essay about a projected art school and "get Mr. Fields to read it before
the March number is made up—& I want you to take care that it is not
mislaid."[28] Occasionally a writer complained to Annie about her husband's editorial butchery. More frequently, a contributor would casu-
ally include a message for the editor in a letter to his wife, as when

Anna Waterston told Annie that Fields would receive her article the following week.[29]

But some of their friends specifically requested Annie's editorial help. It is relatively easy to understand the humble submissiveness of a fledgling like Abby Morton Diaz, who wrote diffidently about her stories to both Fieldses, urging them to "have no hesitation in altering or amending anything of *mine*, for I am a novice in writing, and know nothing of rules, or fitness."[30] But important and well-established writers like Whittier and Stowe also respected Annie's advice. It was not unusual for Whittier to send Annie a poem, asking her to transmit it to her husband if she thought it was good enough. Nor was it unusual for Whittier to recommend a writer to both of them, as when he successfully urged them both to accept Charlotte Forten's account of teaching former slaves in South Carolina, "Life on the Sea Islands."[31] Even more frequently, Harriet Beecher Stowe included a message to one Fields in a letter to the other and sometimes asked them both for editorial assistance. On one occasion when she sent Fields an essay encouraging Americans to buy native products, she asked, "Please let Annie look it over & if she & you think I have said too much of the Waltham watches make it right." After suggesting that he might want to insert a paragraph about American glass, she added, "If Annie thinks of any other thing that ought to be mentioned & will put it in for me she will serve both the cause & me."[32] Another letter to Annie simply conveyed the news that an essay would arrive a week after deadline.[33] Like Whittier, Stowe also tried to enlist Annie's support for an unknown writer: she sent Fields a story by a Mrs. Ruggles in the hope that he "& Annie will read it with care & see what can be done with it."[34] An even more characteristic letter asked her editor to "give my love to Annie. I should like to say many things to her & read her now & then a scrap as I go on."[35] It might be argued that Stowe did not expect massive assistance or profound criticism, but clearly, one of the country's most important writers trusted Annie's critical acumen.

Occasionally Annie took her own editorial initiatives, as when she proposed an appropriate subject to a friend. Thus Anna Waterston told Fields she had written her essay on Jane Austen for the *Atlantic* because of her "love for Miss Austen—and my dear Mrs Fields."[36] Sometimes Annie intervened in the editorial process with even more enterprise, particularly on behalf of talented young friends. One such beneficiary was her cousin Louisa May Alcott, who wrote her poem "Thoreau's Flute" soon after the death of Thoreau in May 1863; her proud father showed the stanzas to their next-door neighbor, Nathaniel Hawthorne, who in turn sent them to Fields—"to sit among high places where they hardly belong," Louisa told Annie. Annie promptly sent suggestions for revision, and Louisa wrote to thank "Dear Cousin Annie" for the "'Flute's' promotion," deferentially saying, "if any one takes the trouble to criticize it seems to prove that the thing is worth mending."[37] The mending was evidently satisfactory: the poem was published in the *Atlantic* three months later. Another beneficiary of Annie's advocacy was Henry James, though he probably never knew it. One summer afternoon at the seashore, Annie enthusiastically read "Compagnons de Voyage" to her editor-husband and he agreed to include it in the *Atlantic*.[38] Of course, Annie's power was limited, but she was Fields's ideal assistant. A casual journal entry in September 1867 suggests that consultation about manuscripts was an ordinary occurrence: "I lay down to read a Mss J wants to know of."

The "Mss J wants to know of" might have been for the *Atlantic*, but it might also have been for book publication. One of the manuscripts sent to Fields in the mid-1860s was *The Gates Ajar*, the passionately religious first novel of a young woman named Elizabeth Stuart Phelps, a book with a strong narrative voice and two strong heroines. By advising her husband to accept it, Annie helped launch an enormously successful career. In the memoir she wrote three decades later, Phelps recalled the long period of suspense before her manuscript was accepted:

> I have the impression that the disposal of the book . . . wavered for a while upon the decision of one man, whose wife shared the reading of the manuscript. "Take it," she said at last, decidedly; and the fiat went forth.[39]

While today's readers may well be disconcerted by the book's sentimentality, especially its assertion that everything we love in this world survives in the next, Annie correctly anticipated the country's eagerness for such reassurance in the aftermath of the Civil War. The novel was an astonishing success: four thousand copies printed in November 1868 sold out within a month, and it would remain popular for three decades. Phelps soon became Annie's friend, and for the rest of her life counted on her companionship and advice.

Almost certainly, Annie "shared the reading" of other manuscripts by unknown writers, women in particular. Almost certainly, she put merit ahead of gender (as with the Henry James story), and it is a good guess that (as with *The Gates Ajar*) her advice was validated by public response. Unfortunately, we know nothing about the Fieldses' discussions of particular manuscripts, including Annie's poems (nor whether he paid her for any of them). But there is no doubt that James T. Fields trusted his wife's literary judgment: as the title of his essay "My Friend's Library" suggests, she was his other self.

As a letter to Laura Johnson indicates, Annie was sometimes assigned the delicate task of rejection. "Dear Laura you understand about the little book," Annie wrote in the spring of 1864. "How glad JTF would be to print it if it were possible. But the expense of making a book now-a-days is something *frightful* (what a word that is to use but the price acts as a bar to keep publishers from the path of book making) therefore we stop in a degree."[40] Tactfully, she attributed the rejection entirely to financial problems, but it is important to notice the word *we*.

Undoubtedly Fields consulted his wife about staffing problems. In 1865, when Fields started the children's magazine *Our Young Folks*, Annie's intimate friends Gail Hamilton and Lucy Larcom became two of its three editors. And although Annie's approval was not the main reason Fields asked William Dean Howells to become assistant editor of the *Atlantic* the following year, it was probably a contributing cause.

The publication of Nathaniel Hawthorne's notebooks is a more important instance of Annie's effectiveness as the editor's (and publisher's) collaborator. Soon after Hawthorne died in May 1864, she advised his widow to go through his manuscripts and transcribe whatever seemed suitable for publication. Sophia was reluctant to violate her husband's privacy and felt unworthy to be his editor, but financial straits made her yield to the arguments of "darling Annie." She agreed to "copy out all that is possible" from his American notebooks: "I think there may be a good deal for the Atlantic . . . and then we three will decide what to do," she wrote.[41] The Fieldses encouraged her to expand her idea of what was "possible" and "we three" decided to publish all of Sophia's transcriptions, first in the *Atlantic* and then in book form. Sophia finished preparing her edition of the American notebooks in 1867, though by that time the friendship was strained: Annie thought Sophia was a weak parent and an imprudent financial manager, and Sophia resented her increasing coolness. Soon the writer Gail Hamilton convinced Sophia that Fields had cheated them both, and Annie bitterly resented their allegations. They were "implacable," she wrote in her diary in December 1868; "having conjured up a fancied wrong, they nurse it well." Nonetheless, if not for Annie's urging, Sophia might never have agreed to transcribe or publish any of Hawthorne's notebooks or his unfinished romances.

After Fields's retirement, husband and wife continued to collaborate on many projects—practical ventures like building their summer house in Manchester, but also a wide range of cultural ventures and civic initiatives (including his lecture tours). One of several joint efforts on behalf of women's education will serve as an example. "We are at present full of starting a university for women in Boston," Annie wrote in her journal in the spring of 1872. "To this end Jamie intends having a course of free lectures on English literature in the last trimester of the year in order to bring the audience together."[42] Then less than two weeks later, she reported, "Today appeared our prospectus for the lectures for women which are to forerun a university we hope for women in this city."[43] A key word is "our." "Our" prospectus announces a "Free Course of Lectures on English Literature for Ladies" every Saturday from October through December, given by some of the most distinguished men in Boston, Holmes and Emerson among them, all of them friends of the Fieldses and all of them published by Ticknor and Fields.[44] Boston University had just been established as a coeducational institution, the "Annex" that became Radcliffe College would soon begin, and Annie would serve on advisory boards for them both.

Increasingly, she took her own initiatives in civic and cultural projects, and though her husband sometimes disapproved, he usually bent to her inclinations. "So, my dear love, do not let me stand in the way of your happiness," he wrote in the course of a lecture tour in 1875, "but if you think you can . . . do that work . . . I must not interfere."[45] Evidently he had urged Annie not to work so hard at the North End Mission, where she organized living arrangements and cultural activities, but she had balked. Protesting that his only concern was her health, he declared, "It is not for me ever to put a bar between you and inclination. It has always been my desire to see you contented and happy in your duties in life, and to help on so far as I could see wisdom in the helping. The Mission seems to be your magnet, and in God's name, I say, go on and do all the good you can everywhere." Since he had decided not to interfere, Fields could resume his usual role of supportive companion. "I know you got handsomely over your talk to the ladies," he later wrote, then urged, "Tell me all about it though please."[46]

However paradoxical it may seem, one of the most important ways Annie Fields helped her husband—and the least known—was through her diary. Through the dozens of journals she kept between 1859 and 1877, Annie was simultaneously developing her separate identity and serving as her husband's collaborator. In June 1859, at the beginning of her first year abroad, Annie dutifully inaugurated a travel diary and made detailed entries for the entire trip; then after a three-year lapse, she kept a journal more or less regularly for over thirteen years. As her teacher George Emerson had urged, she included meditations and personal experiences, but a major purpose is suggested by the title she set down when she resumed journalizing in July 1863: "Journal of Literary Events and glimpses of interesting people." She mused, "I wonder much how I have already allowed so many years to elapse without making an attempt . . . to record something of the interesting events in literature which are constantly passing under my knowledge." Then she summarily reported on such friends as Hawthorne, Emerson, and Longfellow, and throughout the ensuing volumes, she preserved intimate glimpses of their activities and records of their conversation. She also set down her husband's reports of conversations at the men-only dinners of the Saturday Club and the Dante Club and his accounts of "interesting events" at the Old Corner Bookstore. She was consciously serving as chronicler for the two of them, preserving privileged knowledge of the most important writers of the time. It was a personal record, though probably compiled with further purposes in mind.

Charged by Annie Fields not to make her life "a subject of record — 'unless . . . for some reason not altogether connected with myself,'" her literary executor Mark De Wolfe Howe extracted from her diaries a chronicle of famous writers and artists entitled *Memories of a Hostess.*[47] Essentially, he was following her lead: she had drawn on those diaries in the same self-effacing way when she compiled her own memoirs of writers who had been her friends—including her husband, Stowe, Thaxter, Whittier, Hawthorne, Longfellow, Emerson, Holmes, and Sarah Orne Jewett. What is not generally known is how her husband used her journals. Her entries about Charles Dickens are a prime example.

Both of the Fieldses had been devoted to Dickens, and that devotion knit them more closely together. It is no exaggeration to say that they loved him. They wept together when he left for England in April 1868; they prayed for him at night, then dreamed of him; Annie could vent her emotions with nobody "except with my beloved." Dickens was their main reason for going to England in 1869, and their two visits to his home at Gad's Hill were the high points of their journey. When the telegram announcing his death arrived in June 1870, they were both devastated. "Our dear friend Charles Dickens died last night June 9th at 6 o'clock," she lamented in her journal. A world without Dickens seemed intolerable: friends from all over the country sent them letters of condolence; together, she and Jamie mourned the death of their "best friend."

But in coping with that loss, she took an important initiative: she and

Jamie prepared an essay together. "We occupied ourselves during Sunday in making up a short paper for the A.M.," she wrote. "We know some one must do it and I thought it better that we should." Both the *we* and the *I* are worth noting. "Some Memories of Charles Dickens" appeared in the *Atlantic* in August 1870, later listed as the work of James T. Fields.[48] It was the beginning of Annie's long series of memoirs. The following year, she would again collaborate with her husband on an expanded memoir of Dickens, drawing heavily on her journal record of their visits to Gad's Hill. It appeared in the *Atlantic* and was later incorporated in Field's most successful book, *Yesterdays with Authors*. But it includes with only slight modification over fifty pages from Annie's journal.

The following year, Fields again drew from Annie's journal for his essay on Hawthorne, which would also appear in the *Atlantic* and then in *Yesterdays*. Annie wrote in her journal for 1 November 1871 that she had resolved "to write less than ever on personal matters," more on "the great men and women" she entertained, but declared, "Still the poor little diary with all its imperfections has answered many a good turn." The Hawthorne essay was among those good turns: many of the passages about his last months come directly from Annie's diary (and the quotations from Sophia Hawthorne are from letters to Annie). As her husband's helpmeet, Annie Fields expected to have her name subsumed by his. She never expected such recognition, but the name of James T. Fields on the title page of *Yesterdays with Authors* must be understood to include his wife as coauthor.

When Fields died in 1881, his widow went into a period of deep mourning. Her "dear partner" was dead. She saw virtually no one for months, and recovered emotionally only in the course of going through his papers for her *Biographical Notes* of his life. Before the year was over she began to share a rich life with her "dear companion" Sarah Orne Jewett, but she always maintained the friendships and activities of the life she had shared with her husband.

The way she grew as a woman of letters is evident from even a brief summary of her publications in the 1880s and 1890s. In the 1880s ten of her poems appeared in *Harper's Monthly*, three in the *Atlantic*, five in *Scribner's*, and two in the *Century*, in addition to her prelude to the collaborative novel *A Week Away from Time*, a birthday tribute to Harriet Beecher Stowe read aloud at a large celebration and then published in the *Boston Advertiser*, and a collection of her poems entitled *Under the Olive*. Even more poems would be published in the following decade, as well as her final collection, *The Singing Shepherd*.

Annie's charitable activities increased during the 1880s and so did her publications about them, ranging from brief reports on such topics as "Work for Paupers and Convicts" in the *Nation* to a book entitled *How to Help the Poor*, published by Houghton Mifflin in 1883 and reprinted in 1884 and 1885. Drawing on over a decade of experience as a founder and director of the Associated Charities of Boston, Annie produced a handbook that charity workers could put to immediate use: over twenty-two thousand copies were sold within two years. On a humbler level, her four publications in the children's magazine *Wide Awake* also gave practical advice based on private experience, including a paper, "About Clothes," which urged each younger reader to discover "the style best suited to yourself" and stick to it, and a childhood reminiscence about a Longfellow poem that taught her to take noble lives as role models.

But Annie's major publications were her memoirs of writers who had been her friends, intimate glimpses of those who had recently died; decorum forbade publishing personal reminiscences of living authors. In the 1880s she produced two essays on Emerson, one on Longfellow, one on Charles Reade, and one on Leigh Hunt. The 1890s were even more productive, partly because so many of her old friends died in that period. She wrote essays about Tennyson, Whittier, Celia Thaxter, Oliver Wendell Holmes, Harriet Beecher Stowe, the Cowden Clarkes, George Eliot, and Thackeray; seven of her ten volumes of memoirs and letters appeared in the same decade: *Whittier: Notes of His Life and Friendships* in 1893, *A Shelf of Old Books* in 1894, the *Letters of Celia Thaxter* in 1895, *Authors and Friends* in 1896, the *Life and Letters of Harriet Beecher Stowe* in 1897, and *Nathaniel Hawthorne* in 1899. Except for the small Hawthorne book and the Thaxter and Stowe letters, most of the material had previously appeared in periodicals, but the number of volumes is nonetheless remarkable. Only two more such books lay ahead, a memoir of Charles Dudley Warner, published in 1904, and seven years later, the *Letters of Sarah Orne Jewett*.

Throughout the years of widowhood, however, and despite her abiding affection for Sarah Orne Jewett and the ongoing excitement of new friendships and new enterprises, she never stopped thinking of herself as the *Boston Evening Transcript* obituary defined her—"Widow of Former Boston Publisher." Cultural historians have made little of her importance to that publisher beyond saying that she was a splendid hostess, making the point that Fields was already a major publisher when they married. But for her active roles in the life they shared, which she continued after his death, Annie Fields deserves recognition as an extraordinary partner.

She observed, she participated, and she left copious records. She had been welcomed into the social circles of the great American and English authors on the Ticknor and Fields list. Her friends included major women writers—Harriet Beecher Stowe, Lydia Maria Child, Julia Ward Howe, Catharine Sedgwick, Rebecca Harding Davis, Harriet Prescott Spofford, Lucy Larcom, Gail Hamilton, Elizabeth Stuart Phelps, Celia Thaxter, Rose Terry Cooke, Louise Guiney, Willa Cather, and (most important) Sarah Orne Jewett—and she welcomed such "new" men as Howells, James, Twain, and Bret Harte. She befriended artists, musicians, and actors, men and women alike (including Anne Whitney, William Morris Hunt, Ole Bull, Christine Nilsson, Adelaide Phillips, Helena Modjeska, Adelaide Ristori, Edwin Booth, and Charlotte Cushman), and a broad range of public figures including Booker T. Washington, Helen Keller, and Alexander Graham Bell. All these relationships, like her public and private efforts on behalf of women and her better known charity work, belong to the same nexus of identity and commitment: she was a charming upper-class Boston woman devoted to family, friends, and high culture. But she was also a self-examining Emersonian committed to self-fulfillment, and an articulate and conscientious woman committed to civic action in support of wider opportunities for everyone—including women, blacks, the poor, the imprisoned, and the deaf.

She also helped determine the course of the *Atlantic Monthly* and the lists of Ticknor and Fields. If her friendships, interests, and standards were essentially the same as her husband's, she nonetheless tilted him, as when she advised him to publish a poem by Louisa May Alcott, a story by Henry James, or a novel by Elizabeth Stuart Phelps. She also directly influenced the writers themselves. By inviting Phelps or Rebecca Harding or Lucy Larcom to share the intimacies of Charles Street and by introducing them to such celebrities as Hawthorne and Emerson, she tacitly encouraged them to prepare new manuscripts for Mr. Fields. In her status as admiring friend, she also swayed seasoned writers, as when she persuaded Stowe to compile *Oldtown Folks* or encouraged Emerson to prepare a new series of lectures. Convincing Sophia Hawthorne to edit her husband's notebooks was yet another way of advancing the cause of literature while helping a friend and doing good business for her husband. As dozens of other examples might be adduced to prove, Annie Fields exerted an important and virtually ignored influence on American literature and thought.

From her own conservative and genteel point of view, however, she was above all a beloved wife. She never wanted or expected fame, though she did require and receive appreciation. She was content with her reputation as a witness rather than a wielder of literary power. Like most women of her class and her time, she would never risk seeming unwomanly. Yet as a gifted woman in a position of power, she managed to develop her talents and exert her influence without violating propriety. In assessing the partnership that was her marriage, one of the greatest paradoxes that emerges is that as her husband's wife and as his widow, always subordinating her identity to his, Annie Fields managed to attain both self-extension and self-fulfillment. As an advocate of the examined life, a woman who valued literature and those who wrote it as guides to self-fulfillment, she had to deal with herself as herself. But as Mrs. James T. Fields, she found herself. We might fault her for not being bolder, but her achievements are more than she would lead us to believe.

Notes

1. *Atlantic Monthly*, July 1915, 21–31; *Century*, May 1899, 122–131. Research for this essay is part of a larger project, a biography of Annie Fields.

2. Most of the information for this paper comes from the correspondence of Annie and James T. Fields at the Boston Public Library; the Henry E. Huntington Library, San Marino, Calif.; the Houghton Library, Harvard University, Cambridge, Mass.; the Massachusetts Historical Society, Boston; and the Henry W. and Albert A. Berg Collection, Astor, Lenox, and Tilden Foundations of the New York Public Library; and from the diaries of Annie Fields at the Massachusetts Historical Society. I am grateful to these libraries for permission to quote. Any unidentified quotations are from the diaries. The two major studies of James T. Fields—William S. Tryon, *Parnassus Corner: A Life of James T. Fields, Publisher to the Victorians* (Boston: Houghton Mifflin, 1963), and James C. Austin, *Fields of the "Atlantic Monthly"; Letters to an Editor, 1861–1870* (San Marino, Calif.: Huntington Library Press, 1953)—provide useful background information.

3. J.T. Fields to Mary Russell Mitford, 27 October 1854, Huntington Library.

4. J.T. Fields to Henry Wadsworth Longfellow, 10 November 1854, Huntington Library.

5. Rufus Griswold and other New York literati were eager to meet the "elect lady" when the Fieldses arrived on their wedding trip, and Washington Irving regretted that "the bad weather has deprived me of the promised visit of yourself and Mrs Fields but hope you may find some more propitious time to make it" (Griswold to J.T. Fields, n.d., but before 15 November 1854, Huntington Library; Irving to Fields, 25 November 1854, Huntington Library).

6. Presumably the wedding was attended by Annie's parents, her three sisters, her brother, and perhaps by Fields's brother George, a partner in a well-known Boston bookbinding firm used by Ticknor and Fields, Benjamin Bradley (Tryon, *Parnassus Corner*, 7). Ann West Adams, born on 6 June 1834, was the sixth of seven children and the fifth of six daughters, including two who had previously died in infancy. The wedding ceremony was performed by the Reverend Dr. Gannett, minister of the Federal Street Church, which Annie had attended as a child.

7. Andrew N. Adams, *A Genealogical History of Henry Adams of Braintree, Massachusetts, and His Descendants* (Rutland, Vt.: Tuttle, 1898), 460; Charles Newton Peabody, *ZAB: Brevet Major Zabdiel Boylston Adams, 1829–1902, Physician of Boston and Framingham* (Boston: Francis A. Countway Library of Medicine, 1984), 1–7. Dr. Adams had been active in the Bunker Hill Association and the Saturday Evening Club as well as the Boston Medical Society and the Massachusetts Medical Society, and had been an instructor at the Harvard Medical School.

8. Mrs. Adams's father was a sea captain who became a merchant on Boston's Long Wharf, and she was a cousin of Louisa May Alcott.

9. What Emerson had to say about his educational goals and methods in his *Reminiscences of an Old Teacher* suggests what a strong force he exerted on her character and the direction of her life, down to her specific commitments to study, diary keeping, and charity work. See Thomas Woody, *A History of Women's Education in the United States*, 2 vols. (New York: Science Press, 1929), 1:348; and George B. Emerson, *Reminiscences of an Old Teacher* (Boston: Alfred Mudger, 1878). Emerson had opened his influential School for Young Ladies in Boston in 1823, eleven years before Annie was born, following two years as principal of Boston's all-male English Classical School. He had become convinced that it was important to educate girls who would in turn be responsible for the education of their children. Friends encouraged him; he was guaranteed a good salary; and thirty-two students were immediately enrolled, as many as he could handle. He wanted them to have "a complete knowledge of our rich and beautiful English language," and to that end, he also taught them Latin, French, and Italian. He had a more practical reason for teaching the girls "Colburn's Mental Arithmetic" (which he had also taught to the boys): it enabled them to add sums faster than shopkeepers. Instruction in other subjects also combined the traditional and the innovative: the girls studied history the "old way," through intense study of excellent writers, but also by using maps to follow events; they studied natural history by experiment as well as by reading, and were instructed to pay close attention to the beauty of nature while thinking deeply about the love of God. He retired in 1855, the year after Annie's marriage.

10. [Annie Adams Fields,] *James T. Fields: Biographical Notes and Personal Sketches* (Boston: Houghton Mifflin, 1881), 52.

11. *Atlantic Monthly*, October 1861, 440. Henry James's comment comes from *The American Scene* (New York: Harper's, 1907), 236.

12. Willa Cather, "148 Charles Street," in *Not under Forty* (New York: Knopf, 1936), 59.

13. Letter of 22 December 1867 to his sister-in-law, Georgina Hogarth, quoted by Edward F. Payne, *Dickens Days in Boston: A Record of Daily Events* (Boston: Houghton Mifflin, 1927), 205.

14. Annie Fields, Diary, 4 December 1863.

15. A typical diary entry in January 1866 reports hours of "Harrieting," talk ranging from gossip about Frederick Law Olmsted's frustrated love affair to Stowe's dreams about her dead son.

16. Annie Fields, Diary, 22 March 1872.

17. J. T. Fields to Zabdiel Boylston Adams, 4 December 1863, Massachusetts Historical Society.

18. H. B. Stowe to A. A. Fields, May 1860, Huntington Library. Stowe was returning with her two daughters, Hawthorne with his wife and three children.

19. Fields's letter of 17 November 1863 is in the Berg Collection, New York Public Library; Annie made her journal entry that same day. The anonymous review by Howe (who probably had not yet learned who the poet was) had appeared on the front page of the *Commonwealth* on 13 November 1863. It must have been particularly galling to the Fieldses that Howe was among those invited to Charles Street for supper following the reading.

20. Annie Fields, Diary, 22 October 1868.

21. J. T. Fields to H. W. Longfellow, 28 August 1872, Houghton Library.

22. Laura Johnson to A. A. Fields, 10 June 1866, New York Public Library.

23. Sophia Hawthorne to A. A. Fields, 1 October 1866, Boston Public Library. The poem "In the Palace" inscribed "To S.H." is in the Berg Collection, New York Public Library.

24. *Asphodel* (Boston: Ticknor and Fields, 1866), 26. Alice is partly a wish-fulfilling self-portrait of the author as a mother; the grieving widower Russell and his beloved daughter are modeled on Robert Russell Lowell and his daughter Mabel.

25. A. A. Fields to Laura Johnson, 26 February 1877, Huntington Library.

26. Thomas Starr King to A. A. Fields, 26 January 1862, Huntington Library.

27. Rebecca Harding Davis to the Fieldses, 21 August 1862, Huntington Library.

28. Elizabeth Peabody to A. A. Fields, 24 December 1863, Boston Public Library.

29. Anna Waterston to A. A. Fields, 29 October 1862, Huntington Library.

30. Abby Morton Diaz to the Fieldses, ca. 1869, Huntington Library.

31. See *The Letters of John Greenleaf Whittier*, ed. John B. Pickard, 3 vols. (Cambridge: Harvard University Press, 1975), 3:55, 99.

32. H. B. Stowe to J. T. Fields, 3 June 1864, Huntington Library.

33. H. B. Stowe to A. A. Fields, 26 July 1864, Huntington Library.

34. H. B. Stowe to J. T. Fields, 19 December 1865, Huntington Library.

35. H. B. Stowe to J. T. Fields, December 1866, Huntington Library.

36. Anna Waterston to J. T. Fields, 3? January 1863?, Huntington Library.

37. L. M. Alcott to A. A. Fields, 24 June 1863, Huntington Library.

38. Annie Fields, Diary, 7 July 1870.

39. Phelps, *Chapters from a Life* (Boston: Houghton Mifflin, 1896), 108.

40. A. A. Fields to Laura Johnson, [24 May 1864], Huntington Library.

41. Sophia Hawthorne to A. A. Fields, 2 August 1864, Boston Public Library.

42. Annie Fields, Diary, 13 May 1872.

43. Ibid., 25 May 1872.

44. Copies of the prospectus are preserved in the Fields collection of the Huntington Library.

45. J. T. Fields to A. A. Fields, 25 January 1875, Huntington Library.

46. J. T. Fields to A. A. Fields, "Thursday" [1875], Huntington Library.

47. Mark De Wolfe Howe, *Memories of a Hostess* (Boston: Atlantic Monthly Press, 1919), 3.

48. For example, see Austin, *Fields of the "Atlantic Monthly,"* 439.

CHERYL B. TORSNEY

The Traditions of Gender: Constance Fenimore Woolson and Henry James

COUCHED IN THE DICTION of other women's writing of the day, Margaret E. Sangster's obituary for Constance Fenimore Woolson, which appeared in *Harper's Bazar* a week after her death in Venice on 24 January, 1894, uses conventional imagery: "Now that the pen has fallen from the nerveless hand, that the busy brain is quiet in the last sleep, that on the roll-call of our women of genius another name must hereafter be printed with the star that signifies decease, we are sorry, *sorry*. We have lost more than we can tell in cold type. But her beautiful books remain, and in their pages, she lives and breathes."[1] Or at least they did, and she did.

As the *Harper's Bazar* notice suggests, Woolson was not always dismissed as a minor writer of local-color fiction. Henry James wrote in 1884 that Woolson (whom he called Fenimore, though her family called her Connie) was the only English-language novelist he read besides William Dean Howells,[2] and he included a sketch of her along with those of de Maupassant, Turgenev, Emerson, George Eliot, Trollope, Daudet, and Stevenson in *Partial Portraits* (1888). Woolson's writing continued to be admired and anthologized through the 1920s. Fred Lewis Pattee declared that "during the seventies undoubtedly she was the most 'unconventional' feminine writer that had yet appeared in America."[3] He offers, however, an unusual assessment of her limitations: "Not in many ways was she significant: in some important details she was actually a retrogressive force. She never wholly outgrew, for instance, the earlier lessons she learned from her first enthusiasm, Charlotte Brontë."[4] In 1936 Arthur Hobson Quinn suggested that "James' judgment [of Woolson's writing] was sounder than that which had apparently forgotten her" and that when she died, she was known as "one of the most consummate artists in that great epoch of the novel."⁵ By 1948, although Woolson's achievement was still reviewed favorably, her reputation had diminished. Alexander Cowie called her a "superior minor writer who is periodically 'rediscovered' by a sensitive critic or a zealous historian."⁶ Two critical biographies of Woolson attempt to reclaim her, but she is normally treated only in passing in studies of regional fiction.⁷ No work to date has effectively resuscitated her reputation.

One reason that Woolson and her work have been consigned to oblivion has been the decidedly male critical bias we see in the scholarship as early as Pattee, who attributes Woolson's insignificance to her unbridled love for Charlotte Brontë. Lyon Richardson apologizes for Woolson in a similar way:

> Her memories of girlhood were sensitive, but only from girlhood's point of view, and one is left with the distinct impression that the daughter-father relationship was more adequately realized in her fiction than that of the daughter-mother. She was careful to choose heroines who were not beautiful, but who possessed some distinction of personality. There is sorrow and abnegation on occasion, but her wives are frequently self-centered and purposeless, whom the men would have done well to avoid. Briefly, nobility is lacking in a number of her characters for the very reason that the basic ambitions, interest, functions, and fruitions of life are lacking.⁸

Richardson faults Woolson, it appears, for her gender and her characters because they are not men with plenty of ambition that gets rewarded in the course of the fiction. It comes as no surprise that Woolson disappears from the anthologies of American short stories just about the time that the canon of American literature comes into being.

Although one expects these sorts of evaluations of Woolson from those unsympathetic with one feminist critical assumption—that women's fiction derives from gender-specific experience—we find Evelyn Thomas Helmick's recent judgment of Woolson harder to swallow, especially since it appears in a collection entitled *Feminist Criticism: Essays on Theory, Poetry, and Prose*: "Such unattractive, if not improbable, martyrs are perhaps part of the reason Miss Woolson's work is seldom read today. . . . Her characters, in exercising a restraint admirable to the Victorian mind, seem wooden and unreal; the endless feminine analysis of emotions and motivations becomes too circumstantial to bear."[9]

Thus it appears that Richardson dislikes Woolson's prose because, to his mind, she writes like a woman, and Helmick's distaste results from the same flavor spicing Woolson's work: "the endless feminine analysis." While Helmick finds redeeming qualities in Woolson, however, she nonetheless rejects the fiction for the same reasons the male establishment does: Woolson's traditional, passive woman's response to experience.

Although a male- (or male-identified) critical bias is one possible explanation for the disappearance of Woolson's works from our literary histories, most likely her name has disappeared because she was born into a lost generation of American women writers. No longer at home in their mothers' domestic spheres but not ready for suffrage, Woolson and others like her, labeled regionalists or local colorists, suffered an identity crisis that manifested itself in diminished fictional forms, like the short story and the domestic sketch. Their work has been perceived as a short, secret passage between the great, echoing halls of romance and realism. And because the passage is secret and few use it, no one else misses it.

Alice Hall Petry offers still another theory to explain the strange disappearance of the once-famous Constance Fenimore Woolson from literary consciousness. "Part of Woolson's decline is due," she reasons, "to the simple fact that she 'existed,' as it were, only in her writings rather than as a distinct personality. She did not explore her inner life, as did Adams in his education; nor has she been granted an exhaustive psychobiography, as has James in Leon Edel's multi-volume analysis."[10] Thus, the reasoning goes, she remains forgotten either because she did nothing to memorialize herself or because no critics devoted their lives to retelling hers.

Edel's biography of James provides, in fact, the most accessible of the available Woolson biographies, and most readers who recognize her name do so because of Edel's valuable research. His recognition of Woolson's role in Henry James's life is, however, a mixed blessing. For although he is to be commended for raising the issue of the writers' relationship, he is primarily responsible for perpetuating the legend of the lonely spinster who carries a torch for the icy James all over Europe. Despondent over her rejected attentions—James paid her visits only out of kindness, so the story goes—Woolson threw herself out of her second-story window on that winter morning in Venice. A guilty James resurrected her in the character of May Bartram in "The Beast in the Jungle."

Such is the fiction penned by Edel, who asks point-blank, "Had her act been a partial consequence of frustration—of frustrated love for Henry?"[11] Edel writes that in the four extant letters from Woolson to James "she plays the woman scorned and the woman pleading; full of self-pity at her footloose state. . . . Their tone, above all else, however, is one of despair and of a touching loneliness—a middle-aged woman reaching out to a man younger than herself."[12] (Edel leads his reader here: Woolson was, in fact, only three years older than James.) Throughout their correspondence, Edel claims, Woolson casts herself in the role of the "rejected woman."[13] The picture he draws is of a desperate, lovesick writer, no longer a cub, nipping at the heels and thereby embarrassing the exalted lion. In relying on the stock figure of the rejected woman, Edel betrays his bias.[14]

James and his contemporaries would not have assented to Edel's portrait of Woolson as "on the whole rather prosy and banal, a journeywoman of letters. Without style, and with an extreme literalness. . . . Her work is minute and cluttered."[15] Edel wrongly assumes that James's praise of Woolson's writing in his *Partial Portraits* is disingenuous, motivated by "loyalty and friendship" rather than by sincere and simple admiration for her achievement: "The final impression can only be that he is honoring Fenimore's dedication to letters less than her devotion to himself."[16] Given James's opinion of the high responsibility of the critic, however, it is unlikely that he would praise Woolson unless he meant it. As he declares in his review of Rebecca Harding Davis's novel *Dallas Galbraith*, the critic "must be before all things clear and empathic. If he has properly mastered his profession, he will care only in a minor degree whether his relation to a particular work is one of praise or censure."[17] Moreover, if James's purpose were to feign for the public, why would the private man write to William Dean Howells that Woolson was the only American novelist he read besides his friend? Why would James, in a letter to his brother William three years after his correspondence with Howells, call Woolson "the gifted authoress?"[18] For James, Woolson exemplifies woman writing in the late nineteenth century, and in her portrait he speaks of her in the same breath as he speaks of Sévigné, de Staël, and Sand. She is to be admired.[19]

Not only James himself but also his sister Alice valued Woolson's fiction. In fact, Katherine Loring, Alice's close friend, was reading

Woolson's story "Dorothy" to Alice as James's sister died. James's sister and Woolson were longtime friends, Woolson visiting frequently and corresponding "about everything from recipes for baked beans to Ruskin" to medical school education for women.[20] Alice offers the negative of Edel's snapshot of the James-Woolson relationship, presenting her brother as an attached admirer. To her brother William she writes that "Henry is somewhere on the continent flirting with Constance," and later to her Aunt Kate that "Henry has been galavanting on the continent with a she-novelist; when I remonstrated he told me that he thought it a 'mild excess.'"[21]

James's frequent references to Woolson in letters to friends contradict Edel's assertion that James rarely mentioned his "virtuous attachment" to others.[22] In a note to John Hay at Christmas 1886, James reports that their "amiable and distinguished friend Miss Woolson . . . dwells at five minutes' distance" and that they meet every few days, frequently dining together.[23] A few months later he describes Woolson to Grace Norton as "an excellent woman of whom I am very fond, though she is impractically deaf."[24] Woolson and James also shared their friendship with fellow expatriate Francis Boott and his daughter Lizzie, their neighbors in Florence. In nearly every letter to Boott, whose song Woolson quotes in "Dorothy," James mentions their mutual friend. In fact, just before Woolson died, James wrote to Boott that he was preparing to "pay a visit to our excellent friend Fenimore." He continues to say that she is exhausted by her revision of her last novel: "She is to have, I trust, a winter of bookless peace."[25] Upon her death, James, horrified and despondent, wrote of the tragedy to at least six different people: Dr. W. W. Baldwin, Rhoda Broughton, John Hay, Francis Boott, Katherine De Kay Bronson, and William James. This is not the response of a man hounded by a woman, but rather of a friend who has lost a companion with whom he shared both professional and personal interests.

The legend of the spinster chasing the lion over a continent is further dismantled by an examination of Woolson's other correspondence, for the tone Edel catches in Woolson's letters to James—paradoxically assertive and simultaneously self-effacing but always effusive concerning her correspondent's latest work—is the same tone she employs in her letters to others whose work she admires: E. C. Stedman, John Hay, and Paul Hamilton Hayne.

To clear things up, or at least to bring them into better focus, given the distorting glasses of history and literary criticism, much of what Edel reports is verifiable. Constance Fenimore Woolson, holding a letter of introduction from Minny Temple's sister, Henrietta Pell-Clark, met Henry James in April 1880. (Edel embellishes the truth when he writes that she came to Europe "half in love with James.")[26] The two writers got along swimmingly, corresponded religiously (Woolson tells James that she writes him mostly to entertain herself), and visited each other frequently. During these visits they walked, toured galleries, and dined. In 1887, in fact, James and Woolson inhabited neighboring apartments of the Villa Brichieri in Florence. As his letters detail, they met in several European capitals in the year following, once discreetly lodged in hotels on opposite banks of Lake Geneva. Certainly James must have admired Constance Woolson and enjoyed her intelligent humor enough to have been distraught over her death.

The documented details of her probable suicide are few. Early in the morning of 24 January, 1894, Woolson rang for one of her servants at the Casa Semitecolo to fetch her some warm milk. Upon returning, the servant found Woolson in a crumpled heap on the pavement below her second-story window. Her favorite gondolier carried her unconscious body back to her bedroom, where she soon died. John Hay handled the funeral arrangements, and Woolson, like Daisy Miller, was buried in the Protestant cemetery in Rome. Reasoning the death a suicide, James, Edel presumes, refused to attend the funeral of his companion. Several months later, however, James volunteered to accompany Woolson's niece to the writer's sealed rooms to wrap up her aunt's affairs, and, Edel says, to see that Woolson had kept her vow to burn his letters upon reading them. Once granted access to her things, James could also destroy any other papers that could be interpreted as incriminating.

Edel's text of James's reading of Woolson's death is a convention-laden male fantasy. In that patriarchal romance the dependent woman prefers not to live at all if she cannot possess the man completely. While there is reason to believe that Woolson threw herself rather than fell to her death in an influenza-induced delirium as others have speculated, it seems unlikely that she was prompted by unrequited love for Henry James.[27] Rather, evidence of a philosophical consideration of suicide, coupled with hereditary and perhaps postpartumlike depression (she had just finished her novel *Horace Chase*) and financial worries, suggests that issues more immediate than Henry James may have driven her to take her own life.

Woolson's books and letters suggest why she may have committed suicide. First, in her personal copy of *The Teaching of Epictetus* she has both bent down page corners and marked with pencil lines the sections justifying suicide.[28] A particularly significant paragraph in the chapter, "On Solitude," is marked in the inside as well as the outside margin with a double line. It reads: "And when, it may be, that the necessary things are no longer supplied, that is the signal for retreat: the door is opened, and God saith to thee, *Depart*."[29]

The chapter note to this passage is also marked with a double line and is especially pertinent since it condones self-annihilation in the face of one's being unable to await "God's time": "But the Stoics taught that the arrival of this time might be indicated by some disaster or affliction which rendered a natural and wholesome life impossible. Self-destruction was in such cases permissible, and is recorded to have been adopted by several leaders of the Stoics, generally when old age had begun to render them a burden to their friends."[30]

Woolson's letters to all of her regular correspondents—E. C. Stedman, her nephew Samuel Mather, and John Hay—are shot through with references to illnesses and attending depression, their onslaughts and retreats. She is ill for months, even entire seasons at a time, with influenza, inner-ear problems (which her doctor diagnoses as neurotic), and "a succession of ailments and difficulties."[31] In one letter, dated 10 December, 1888, she considers her health at that time of year newsworthy for its stability: "I am quite scandalously well this winter. Haven't had an ill moment; and am as stout as can be. I am so much better—my health so much *firmer* than it used to be that it is really quite remarkable. (I was ill last winter; but that was owing to mental depression.)"[32]

Depression, characterized by her as a male monster, is Woolson's nemesis. In a letter to her girlhood friend Arabella Carter Washburn, she acknowledges that she suffers the same fits of depression her father had: "Don't fancy I am sad all the time. . . . But at times, in spite of all I do, this deadly enemy of mine creeps in, and once in, he is master. I think it is inconstitutional, and I know it is inherited."[33] Her recurring malaise becomes even more pronounced whenever she finishes a project, resembling postpartum depression. In a letter to her niece Katherine Mather she writes that the effort of writing a novel "takes such entire possession of me that when, at last, a book is done, I am pretty nearly done myself."[34] When we now read the letter James wrote to Boott only weeks before Woolson's death, in which he wishes her a quiet winter recuperating from the completion of her last novel, we can only smile at the irony.

In tracing the fluctuation of Woolson's moods and health, I have found her depressions to be most severe in midwinter, when daylight hours are short. This pattern suggests that the writer was suffering from Seasonal Affective Disorder, what Jack Fincher describes as "a baffling depression whose cyclic onset appeared to be curiously governed by the changing length of the day."³⁵ In fact, Woolson's references to illness and depression increase considerably during the autumn and winter months. January seems to be the cruelest month for her, while May brings relief. In the last months of 1893 this strange disease may have convinced her that her life was nearing its end, and her thoughts of suicide may have been a self-fulfilling prophecy. In letters preceding her death, we see her dwelling more and more on what she considers her advanced age. Just a month before her death she writes to her nephew Samuel: "But one must do, from day to day, the best one can. And my infirmities are upon me now: they will not grow worse. (This last sentence means that your aunt is already pretty old!) I hope you will not be shocked if I add that for a long time my daily prayer has been that I may not live to be old; I mean really old."³⁶ Three days later, in a short note, she admits that she feels "old, & tired, & indifferent."³⁷

Woolson's sense of helplessness and hopelessness had been accelerated, undoubtedly, by her feeling that she was running out of both time and money. Throughout her years in Europe, Samuel Mather had her power of attorney in America and oversaw his aunt's finances; thus, many of her letters to him concerned the drawing of bank drafts and the sale of property. During the last three years of her life, however, her worry about money grew, and her letters reflect increasing desperation as she felt her lifetime dream of retiring to a quiet Florida cottage slip away. In a letter posted from Cairo and dated 17 April 1890, Woolson writes that although she is enamored of the Holy Land, she cannot allow herself to stay the summer: "No; if I am to get my finances into shape, I *must* give myself to steady work, in the most quiet & unexciting place I can find."³⁸ Two years later, on 8 February 1892, she composes another letter in the same key. I quote from it extensively, as much to make available that "distinctive personality," which Alice Hall Petry thinks missing from our literary histories, as to demonstrate Woolson's growing nervousness over the constraints of time:

> To have done with the blue part first, let me say that I am still suffering from the pain which attacked me a month ago. But it is now much less severe, so that I bear it better. (I have not much fortitude about pain, you know!) The English doctor here, a clever young man, thought the whole affair was neuralgia. "Neurotic" was his word; that is, a malady of the nerves of the head. I did not, in my heart, agree with him. And I think it *now* pretty well decided that it has been a slow gathering in the inner ear, first on the right side; & now on the left. I say "inner," because there

has been so sign of anything *visible* any where. . . . The loss of time preys upon me most of all. I try not to think of it. I read & read. And when I can no longer do that, I even play solitaire! If you & Flora could have peeped in half an hour ago, and seen me seated on the rug, with the kettle on a trivet attached to the grate behind me, & all the materials for the linseed poultices assembled on a tray at one side, while I, with tear-stained face, was drearily playing solitaire on an atlas propped on my knees, you would have laughed, I am sure. I never play games you know; so when I play solitaire, it is desperation indeed.

Later in the letter Woolson responds to her nephew's request that she spend the summer with him and his family at Newport:

I can't come this summer simply because every well moment *must* be given to finishing the novel which begins in a serial in Harper's Magazine next December. I have already postponed it a whole year, owing to the tiresome condition of my health; never really ill, I may say, sadly enough with truth, that for a year I have not been really well. Unless I wish to make Harper's lose all patience with me, I must keep my engagement fully & promptly this time.[39]

Finally, on 20 November, 1893, she asks Sam to sell one of her bonds and send her a thousand dollars to cover the expenses of setting up housekeeping at the Casa Semitecolo. "I have made the necessary first purchases; and now having settled myself for a while, I find I am beginning to be haunted by the fear that my reserve fund at the Bank here is not large enough to leave me free from immediate care."[40]

Personal philosophy, depression, illness, age, and financial worries all probably combined to lead Constance Fenimore Woolson to commit suicide. Early in her career, in a letter of 23 July 1876, she had written to E. C. Stedman asking, "Why do literary women break down so. . . . It almost seems as though only the unhappy women took to writing. The happiest women I have known belonged to two classes; the devoted wives and mothers, and the successful flirts, whether married or single; such women never write."[41] Elaine Showalter has cited "an increase in psychosomatic illnesses and stress diseases" in women writers of Woolson's era resulting from tension over their identities. This generation, Showalter observes, is the first in which female suicide becomes a trend.[42] Woolson's depression and probable suicide, then, suggests that she is an American sister of the British writers Showalter studies in *A Literature of Their Own*. Like them, Woolson is a woman for whom stress and illness became a way of life and drastic means the way of death. Although her death was devastating for Henry James, Edel's suggestion that this sorrow was actually guilt probably resulted from Edel's own fantasy of the literary lion and the spinster.

The standard reading of Woolson's death, now unraveled, begins to suggest how her life and her writing have always been marginalized, have always been read as ancillary to James's. Her life, for example, has been seen as the inspiration for much of James's fiction after her death, following the traditional master-disciple pattern. Edel, for instance, cites Woolson as the real-life May Bartram and suggests that James's sense that Woolson had betrayed him inspired "The Altar of the Dead."[43] Although she aspired to "the style, the manner, the mastery of Henry James," she could only pretend to the Jamesian literary laurel, he asserts.[44]

Woolson's works have been read, even by her champions, as the ash from which the Jamesian phoenix rises.[45] My purpose here is not to create more anxiety by arguing influence, however. Rather, it is more important to recognize how James's and Woolson's differing genders led the two writers to experience the world according to variant patterns as well as to suffer such different historical fates. James, the male, has gone down in history as the master, the patron, with all of the authority those titles imply. Woolson, however, has been remembered as the journeywoman, the protégée, who relied on James for guidance. An examination of *The Portrait of a Lady* and *Anne* demonstrates that literary history has simplified not only the personal relationship but the literary relationship as well.

Both Henry James's and Constance Fenimore Woolson's first important novels were published serially, his in the *Atlantic* (from November 1880 to December 1881) and hers in *Harper's Monthly* (from December 1880 to May 1882). Both are novels of love and marriage, a theme as old as the genre itself. Both *The Portrait of a Lady* and *Anne* present female protagonists akin to the prototypical women's heroine whose characteristics, "intelligence, will, resourcefulness, and courage," have been outlined by Nina Baym.[46] Isabel Archer and Anne Douglas are provincial orphans who are adopted by eccentric aunts following the deaths of parents with whom the aunts had argued. Both young women make a successful entry into society after being taken in by their relations, and both marry men of questionable virtue. In each character's case another man, Ralph Touchett and Gregory Dexter respectively, at some point provides for the heroine's material well-being. Although the novels share structural similarities and a relation to the Ur-plot of trial and triumph as elucidated by Baym, they are based on different gender assumptions, traditions, and development.

Carren Kaston has defended James against the charges of some hostile feminist criticism by noting that "James wrote regularly with a profound sensitivity to what it was and very often still is like to be a woman."[47] Although, as Alfred Habegger asserts, James was "in sympathy with the best feminine value," he was nonetheless male, still on the outside.[48] Still, his effort to understand is genuine, his understanding as certain as possible. From his own hegemonic position, he presents a woman of imagination who, because of the constraints of the male world in which she lives, cannot realize the triumph of that imagination. As Kaston puts it, "such independence to which Isabel at first aspires is unattainable not only because of the existence of others, who constitute society and exert pressure on her, but because of conditions within Isabel herself."[49] It is Isabel's tragedy that she cannot really act independently. She can only be managed. As James writes, "Madame Merle had married her."[50] Even grammatically Isabel is an object, not a subject. She is passive, not active, as a woman in her place was expected to be by a male culture.

Keys to Isabel's failure lie in her own habits of mind, habits born of her reading two classes of literature: romances by and about women and texts from the transcendentalist tradition. These two sources of Isabel's ideas suggest what Kaston calls her "conflicting attitudes toward power: her desire for self-origination on the one hand and, on the other, her attraction to dependency."[51] Isabel (and James, of course) is not at fault; rather, as Kaston puts it, "given the powerlessness women frequently feel, the challenge of self-origination could not easily be met by any woman, even one as generously conceived as Isabel is by James."[52]

From the beginning Isabel understands her world in textual terms. Upon her arrival at Gardencourt, she is thrilled to meet Lord Warburton: "Oh, I hoped there would be a lord; it's just like a novel!" she gushes (27). Indeed, in the following flashback to Lydia Touchett's visit to Albany to fetch her niece, Isabel is ensconced in the library, where she reads indiscriminately, "guided in the selection chiefly by the frontispiece" (33). Her reading includes "the London *Spectator*" and "the latest publications" (41–42), both of which would have treated women's issues. Other evidence demonstrates, however, that Isabel has been reading romantic women's novels as well. These unnamed novels help to set up her expectations only to have reality decimate the tenderly held images.

Mr. Touchett, sensing Isabel's impending disaster, raises the issue of the discrepancy between fantasy and reality in women's fiction, but Isabel either does not hear or does not heed the warning. Their discussion begins with Isabel's wondering whether English character confirms what she has read in books. Her uncle replies that he is unfamiliar with what appears in novels, that he believes only what he has learned from firsthand experience. But Isabel continues to push the question of novelistic representations of reality by asking how she will be treated in society. "I don't believe they're [the English] very nice to girls; they're not nice to them in novels" (58). Daniel Touchett's response might have served to warn Isabel, but finding herself in a situation usually reserved for novels, her ears are deaf to her uncle's warnings.

> "I didn't know about the novels," said Mr. Touchett. "I believe the novels have a great deal of ability, but I don't suppose they're very accurate. We once had a lady who wrote novels staying here; she was a friend of Ralph's and he asked her down. She was very positive, quite up to everything; but she was not the sort of person you could depend on for evidence. Too free a fancy—I suppose that was it. She afterwards published a work of fiction in which she was understood to have given a representation . . . of my unworthy self. . . . Well, it was not at all accurate; she couldn't have listened very attentively. . . . I don't talk like the old gentleman in that lady's novel. . . . I just mention that fact to show you that they're not always accurate." (58–59)

Isabel might have taken to heart James's ironic joke about people who think that novels faithfully record experience, but she does not. Throughout the early sections of the novel, she reads real-life situations according to women's writing conventions: she sees Warburton "as a hero of romance" rather than as a troubled man caught in a changing political order, and his home as "a castle in a legend"; she has read that the English are "at bottom the most romantic of races"; she identifies herself as a young woman being made love to by a nobleman in a "deeply romantic" situation (66, 75, 77, 96). When Henrietta Stackpole tries to penetrate Isabel's novelistically clouded vision by asking her, "Don't you know where you're drifting?" Isabel replies, "No, I haven't the least idea, and I find it very pleasant not to know. A swift carriage, of a dark night, rattling with four horses over roads that one can't see— that's my idea of happiness." Henrietta responds that her language sounds like that of "the heroine of an immoral novel" (146).

That Isabel uses such language should come as no surprise since she understands her world in part through the filter of the romance tradition of women's novels. As William Veeder observes, Isabel talks a conventional line, using the extravagant language of women's fiction. Like women's heroines, she relies on "pretty set-speeches conventional with pretty heroines."[53] Her own naive reading deceives her and tricks her into marriage with a man whose name, Gilbert, suggests the heroes of romances written both by Sir Walter Scott and by Susan Dudley Warner.[54] Following the literary convention of her romance novels, at the end Isabel is left with only one way out—self-sacrifice. Ironically, it has been another women's fiction convention, the sickly, feminized Ralph Touchett, himself a writer (and reader) of the genre, who prepared Isabel for her downfall when he convinced his father to provide for the requirements of his cousin's imagination, thus authoring the pretext of her disaster.

But the romance tradition is not the only literary tradition that fails Isabel. When Mrs. Touchett first meets Isabel in the family library in Albany, the girl has been "trudging over the sandy plains of a history of German Thought" (34). She takes to heart the superiority of the male virtues of logic, reason, and mind over the female ones of emotion, sensitivity, and heart. Had she been conscious enough to note that her reading was indicting her own character, she might have become a resisting reader, recognizing that the texts she was reading made her own gender into the enemy.[55] Isabel's transcendentalist reading tricks her into believing in the possibilities of her own independence, possibilities reserved, according to the American tradition of idealism, for men. Emerson, one of Isabel's heroes, for instance, as Joyce Warren notes, was "unable to see women as individuals like himself. . . . It is clear that his philosophy [of self-reliance and insistence upon high goals] was not intended to apply to women."[56] In the beginning of the novel Isabel is the embodiment of the Emersonian idealist: she believes in the world "as a place of brightness, of free expansion, of irresistible action" (54); she believes in "the continuity between the movements of her own soul and the agitations of the world (41). But Isabel is a woman, as James well knows (as Kaston comments, "Isabel Archer is more than incidentally female").[57] Her reading of a male intellectual philosophy does not serve her; "she had desired a large acquaintance with human life, and in spite of her having flattered herself that she cultivated it with some success this elementary privilege had been denied her" (431). The "privilege" is denied her because of her sex and of her goodness, and both the reader and James mourn her lost opportunity.

Thus, Isabel's naiveté fails her on two levels. First, she thinks the world of the romance novel real, allowing it to dictate experience to her, revealing her dependency; second, she thinks male transcendentalism and idealism written for her, thus revealing her paradoxical desire to write her own text of self. James does not condemn the romance vision itself; however, he thinks that the tradition of German–Concord transcendentalism was responsible for Isabel's naive perception of reality and for her failure to allow her imagination free rein. But finally, Isabel, as a woman in a man's world, a woman written by a man (sympathetic though he be), can only respond as she does: as a mostly passive participant whose glorious imagination will never experience free reign though it may triumph over some of the obstacles it confronts.

Nearly three-quarters of a very long letter from Woolson to James, dated 12 February, 1882, is taken up with her criticism of *Portrait*. By far the most telling of Woolson's responses to the novel is the whole of her last paragraph:

> How did you ever dare write a portrait of a lady: Fancy any woman's attempting a portrait of a gentleman! Wouldn't there be a storm of ridicule! . . . For my own part, in my small writings, I never dare put down what men are thinking, but confine myself simply to what they do and say. For, long experience has taught me that whatever I suppose them to be thinking at any special time, that is sure to be exactly what they are *not* thinking.[58]

Woolson, of course, is making a mild joke, and, in fact, she does attempt several portraits of gentlemen, both in her last novel, *Horace Chase*, and in "Miss Grief," a narrative told from a male first-person perspective. Yet, just as James's *Portrait*, though about a woman, presents a heroine from a male tradition where women, even admirable, imaginative ones, are in a sense forcedly passive, Woolson's narratives featuring male characters evolve from the women's writing tradition described in Nina Baym's *Women's Fiction* and Mary Kelley's *Private Woman, Public Stage*, among others.[59] In this tradition the female character is active, not passive; the protagonist, the writer's alter ego rather than a female character for whom he has a large degree of sympathy. In a letter dated 30 August, 1882, Woolson compares her work to James's:

> All the money that I have received, and shall receive, from my long novel, does not equal probably the half of the sum you received for your first, or shortest. It is quite right that it should be

so. And, even if a story of mine should have a large "popular" sale (which I do not expect), that could not alter the fact that the utmost best of my work cannot touch the hem of your first or poorest. My work is coarse beside yours. Of entirely another grade. The two should not be mentioned on the same day. Do pray believe how acutely I know this. If I feel anything in the world with earnestness it is the beauty of your writings, and any little thing I may say about my own comes from entirely another stratum; and is said because I live so alone, as regards my writing, that sometimes when writing to you, or speaking to you—out it comes before I know it. You see,—I like so few people! Though I pass for a constantly smiling, ever-pleased person! My smile is the basest hypocrisy.[60]

That her writing "comes from entirely another stratum" is undeniable: hers is the writing of a woman, as the passage abundantly demonstrates. It is cautious, modest, self-effacing, yet the turn at the end, the suggestion of wearing a mask, is reminiscent of a familiar strategy used in American women's writing since the time of Woolson's sister New Englander, Anne Bradstreet. Like her letter to James, Woolson's writing employs women's writing traditions, such as the writer's identification with her heroine and the widespread use of feminine archetypal patterns and images; like the domestic writings from the earlier part of the century, Woolson's works empower women in many ways rather than lament their powerlessness in the outer world while compensating them with an imaginative inner life.[61]

Anne, the novel about which Woolson wrote to James, is the first of her strong-women narratives. It was printed in several editions during her life, again following her death, and just recently with a new introduction.[62] Although past critics have praised *Anne* primarily for its local-color descriptions of Mackinac Island, Michigan, many agree that because the novel is replete with issues of self-identity, it deserves renewed attention. The issue of identity is the same one James treats in *Portrait*, yet since male and female definitions of *identity* and *power* differ, the thread is spun out with differing tension by male and female writers.

One of the ways that male and female texts differ is in the identification of the writer with the protagonist. Isabel is not James, nor was she meant to be, and Woolson teases James about his attempt to paint the portrait of a woman. Anne, however, is in many ways Woolson herself, substantiating Judith Kegan Gardiner's hypothesis that a woman writer "uses her text, particularly one centering on a female hero, as part of a confirming process involving her own self-definition and her empathetic identification with her character. Thus, the text and its female hero begin as narcissistic extentions of the author."[63]

Anne Douglas and Constance Fenimore Woolson share interests and background, not the least of which is the name Anne, which Woolson adopted as a pseudonym for her first publication, *The Old Stone House* (1873), a children's book. Both Anne and Woolson were New Hampshire natives, and as children lived for periods on the Upper Peninsula of Michigan, where a memorial to Woolson with the name "Anne" at the head of the tablet was erected in 1916. Both young women, though accomplished in the liberal and fine arts, protest that they are ugly. Woolson's portraits and her descriptions of Anne, however, belie such evaluation. Perhaps as a reaction against her sense that she falls short of the American ideal of beauty, Woolson develops a love of letter writing, the art of communicating without being seen. Anne shares that love. Just as Woolson tells James that she writes to him for her own amusement, Anne, in writing to her fiancé, Rast Pronando, finds that through the use of language she may assert a control over her life. (It is, on the other hand, the workings of language in literature that stand for Isabel's inability to control her life.)

Both Woolson and her textual daughter also assert power and identity in physical activity and exertion. Throughout her life Woolson rowed to release energy as well as to pass a pleasant Saturday afternoon. Near the end of *Anne*, the heroine uses rowing as a release and as a means of coming to terms with her identity. In addition to rowing, Woolson loved any sort of physical activity, especially walking, and her letters are filled with references to hour-long morning walks and afternoon treks of six to eight miles. The place of physical exercise in Anne's and Woolson's lives is reflected in Ellen Moers's reading of walking as a recurring pattern in women's writing, signaling feminist independence and drive.[64]

Woolson's use of archetypal patterns and images in women's writing further identifies her (and *Anne*) with the women's writing tradition, gaining for Woolson depth and power. Among the archetypes Woolson's novel uses in some fashion are those of the green world epiphany (the coming to self in nature) and the greenworld lover (the coming to passion in nature), both elements of the archetypal feminine *Bildungsroman* as discussed by Annis Pratt. As she explains, nature, the stage for growth, activity, and confirmation of self-identity, is where women find "solace, companionship, and independence."[65] An important distinction is to be made here: for the transcendentalists (and for Isabel) nature is intellectualized, as evidenced by the analytic presentation of the subject in Emerson's famous "Nature" essay. Nature is a representative force rather than a fundamentally real part of our lives. In women's writing, however, nature is a personified friend. In the female *Bildungsroman* the girl takes possession of herself in taking possession of nature. Anne loves the trees so much that she talks to them. Like her heroine, Woolson feels most independent and powerful—most herself— out in nature.[66]

The green world is the most important setting in Woolson's novel. In a culminating scene, Anne recognizes her friend's killer and is thus empowered to exonerate her lover through knowledge gained while rowing on a lake. In another of her green world epiphanies "among the arbor vitae, where there was an opening like a green window overlooking the harbor," Anne agrees to marry young Rast Pronando after believing he has been drowned.[67] But Rast is not Anne's green world lover. That figure, associated with the mythic dying god, appears in the person of Ward Heathcote, whose surname is Woolson's adaptation of another famous woman's green world lover. She retailors a rather wild, uncivilized Heathcliff into a more civilized, well-bred Heathcote. A Union captain in the Civil War, he is wounded in West Virginia, and, nearly dead, is restored to life by Anne.

In the archetype, the restorer is a goddess: Aphrodite, Ishtar, or Isis. Anne, in fact, is endowed with similar mythic resonance tying her to the power of the archetypes. From the second page of the narrative, Anne is described as "a young Diana," an allusion that reverberates throughout the novel. Both James and Woolson play on the allusion with their respective heroines; however, James's use is disguised in Isabel's last name while Woolson's use is overt, appealing directly to the women's literary tradition of using goddess archetypes. James uses it from a male perspective to suggest Isabel Archer's female virtue, an abstract idea, while Woolson uses it to suggest Anne's physical "vigor" and "elasticity," a concrete description. Their use of the references to Diana echoes their differing versions of transcendental nature: for James and Isabel it is intellectual; for Woolson and Anne it is sensate.

Anne, posed braiding her hair, is also called Ariadne, a figure as familiar as Diana in the women's literary tradition. Indeed, she is both: in her guise as Diana, she is the huntress who dwells alone in the woods and mountains; as Ariadne, she is abandoned by Rast Pronando. But Anne (Woolson) is also Ariadne, a weaver, a domestic maker of fictions, who grows in that capacity over the course of the novel. Early in her recognition that she enjoys writing, we are told that "she never put down any of her own thoughts, opinions, or feelings: her letters were curious examples of purely impersonal objective writing":

> Egotism, the under-current of most long letters as of most long conversations also, the telling of how this or that was due to us, affected us, was regarded by us, was prophesied, was commended, was objected to, was feared, was thoroughly understood, was held in restraint, was despised or scorned by us, and all our opinions on the subject, which, however, important in itself, we present always surrounded by a large indefinite aureola of our personality—this was entirely wanting in Anne Douglas's letters and conversation.[68]

Throughout the course of *Anne* the heroine's narrative talents grow until, at the climax of the novel, Anne demonstrates her new mastery of narrative form by weaving on the witness stand the fabric of truth, designed to acquit her lover. When the jury cannot arrive at a verdict, Anne rereads the text of the murder herself, discovering the killer. Finally, in the last pages of the novel, the passive voice of her early reflection of writing is rewritten in the active, identifying herself as the star of the show: "I, Anne, take thee, Ward, to my wedded husband, to have and to hold, from this day forward."[69] Unlike Isabel, Anne can assert her identity in the real world as suggested by her new command of language. To the end, Isabel, given her circumstances, cannot vigorously and independently pursue her dream. She remains, in the last words she utters in the novel, an object, as she begs Casper Goodwood, "As you love me, as you pity me, leave me alone!" (489).

Writing her own text of self and arriving at her own identity has not been easy for Anne. At every turn in the novel someone is looking to appropriate her by stripping her of her linguistic being. Rast calls her Diana; Mrs. Vanhorn calls her Phyllis; Helen calls her Crystal (a particularly suggestive nickname since it implies a reflective relationship between Anne and Helen, as a singularly complex inner composition and transparency); and Miss Lois calls her Ruth Young. Her egotistical assertion at the end, "I, Anne," both defines her powerful new statement of identity and marks an assertion of Woolson's fictional power. Tied into archetypal patterns, that power strengthens the weave.

Woolson's power, in *Anne* as well as in other fictions, derives from traditions of women's writing as well as from her own unique talent. The tradition is the most important element that differentiates her from

Henry James, a man who chose (aside from George Eliot, a curious case given her choice of pseudonym) mostly male writers as his models. We realize that Emerson spoke to him, not women like Woolson, when he wrote: "The Poet is representative. He stands among partial men for the complete man." One of Isabel Archer's mistakes is in thinking that Emerson wrote to her. Women, as Ellen Moers suggests by her rewriting of Emerson in her headnote to chapter one of *Literary Women*, are themselves forced tò rewrite Emerson because they belong to a variant tradition.[70] Constance Fenimore Woolson found her representative poets in that tradition, in the works of Elizabeth Barrett Browning, George Sand, George Eliot, and the Brontës. Her individual talent is remarkable, too, not simply for her vivid local-color descriptions of Michigan, Ohio, North Carolina, Florida, and Europe (those landscapes which form the boundaries of her career) but also for her energetic struggle with issues of identity, language, and art. Her relationship with Henry James was not that of a love-starved stereotypical spinster to one of the greatest literary talents of that or any age. It was one of personal, private friendship.

In her fine article, "Archimedes and the Paradox of Feminist Criticism," Myra Jehlen proposes a method of radical comparison to demonstrate "the contingency of the dominant male tradition."[71] Using this method we can project a border between Woolson and James and explore the frontier. Such a technique, akin to Woolson's "way of looking at photographs (likenesses) upside down, [to bring] out undiscovered characteristics,"[72] reveals the inaccuracy of the myth of the lonely spinster who falls first in love with the suave lion and then to her death. To view their relationship upside down—to see James and Woolson as compatriots sharing the literary life of the age rather than as ill-fated lovers—encourages a rereading of *The Portrait of a Lady* and *Anne*, their contemporaneous novels about a woman's struggle for independence and identity. To see James in terms of Woolson and Woolson in terms of James is not to assert the strength of one and the shortcomings of the other, thus organizing their relationship into a hierarchy; rather it is to recognize the divergent gender-inflicted qualities, which work to create variously tinted literary artifacts, artifacts colored, after their first meeting in 1880, by the strong friendship between these two writers.

Notes

I would like to thank the Western Reserve Historical Society (WRHS), Cleveland, Ohio, for permission to quote from Woolson's letters collected in the Mather Family Papers; and the Butler Library, Columbia University, New York, for permission to quote from Woolson's letters in the Stedman Manuscript Collection. I am also grateful to Rollins College, Winter Park, Florida, for allowing me access to the Woolson Collection of memorabilia.

1. Margaret E. Sangster, "Constance Fenimore Woolson," *Harper's Bazar* 27 (3 February, 1894):93–94.

2. Henry James, *Henry James Letters*, ed. Leon Edel, 4 vols. (Cambridge: Harvard University Press, Belknap Press, 1980), 3:29 (hereafter cited as *Letters*).

3. Fred Lewis Pattee, *The Development of the American Short Story: An Historical Survey* (New York: Harper and Brothers, 1923), 250.

4. Ibid., 254.

5. Arthur Hobson Quinn, *American Fiction: An Historical and Critical Survey* (New York: D. Appleton-Century, 1936), 342.

6. Alexander Cowie, *The Rise of the American Novel* (New York: American Book, 1948), 568.

7. See John Dwight Kern, *Constance Fenimore Woolson: Literary Pioneer* (Philadelphia: University of Pennsylvania Press, 1934); and Rayburn S. Moore, *Constance Fenimore Woolson* (New York: Twayne, 1963).

8. Lyon N. Richardson, "Constance Fenimore Woolson: 'Novelist Laureate' of America," *South Atlantic Quarterly* 39 (1940):34.

9. Evelyn Thomas Helmick, "Constance Fenimore Woolson: First Novelist of Florida," in *Feminist Criticism: Essays on Theory, Poetry, and Prose*, ed. Cheryl L. Brown and Karen Olson (Metuchen, N.J.: Scarecrow, 1978), 238.

10. Alice Hall Petry, "'Always, Your Attached Friend': The Unpublished Letters of Constance Fenimore Woolson to John and Clara Hay," *Books at Brown* 29–30 (1982–1983):12.

11. Leon Edel, *Henry James*, 5 vols. (1962; reprint, New York: Avon Books, 1978), vol. 3, *The Middle Years, 1882–1895*, 363.

12. Ibid., 87.

13. Ibid., 88.

14. Edel further reveals his patriarchal perspective in his choice of names for his subjects. Although he will occasionally pair their first names, Henry and Constance, his other pairings, "James and Miss Woolson" and "James and Fenimore," are conspicuous from a feminist standpoint. I am indebted to Susan Allen Ford for bringing this to my attention.

15. Edel, *Middle Years*, 203.

16. Ibid., 204.

17. Henry James, *Literary Criticism: Essays on Literature, American Writers, English Writers* (New York: Library of America, 1984), 223.

18. *Letters*, 3:150.

19. James, *Essays*, 639.

20. Jean Strouse, *Alice James: A Biography* (New York: Houghton Mifflin, 1980), 260.

21. Strouse, *Alice James*, 259.

22. Edel, *Middle Years*, 215.

23. *Letters*, 3:153.

24. *Letters*, 3:176. After the mid-1870s Woolson became increasingly deaf and was finally forced to rely on an ear trumpet.

25. *Letters*, 3:436–437.

26. Ibid., 3:xvi.

27. Woolson's few critics have hesitated to believe, as James apparently did, that her death was a suicide. Most think the circumstances surrounding her death too vague to be certain about.

28. I found Woolson's personal copy of this text in the Woolson House on the Rollins College campus in Winter Park, Florida.

29. Epictetus, *The Teaching of Epictetus*, trans. T. W. Rolleston (London: Walter Scott; New York: Thomas Whittaker; Toronto: W. J. Gage, 1888), 135.

30. Ibid., 200.

31. Woolson to Samuel Mather, 16 January 1884, WRHS. In quoting from Woolson's letters I have retained her idiosyncratic spellings and punctuation.

32. Woolson to Samuel Mather, 10 December 1888, WRHS.

33. Constance Benedict, ed., *Five Generations (1785–1923)* (London: Ellis, 1930), vol. 1, *Voices Out of the Past*, 224 n.

34. Benedict, *Five Generations*, vol. 2, *Constance Fenimore Woolson*, 52.

35. Jack Fincher, "Notice: Sunlight May Be Necessary for Your Health," *Smithsonian* 16 (1985): 72.

36. Woolson to Samuel Mather, 20 November 1893, WRHS.

37. Woolson to Samuel Mather, 23 November 1893, WRHS.

38. Woolson to Samuel Mather, 17 April 1890, WRHS.

39. Woolson to Samuel Mather, 8 February 1892, WRHS.

40. Woolson to Samuel Mather, 20 November 1893, WRHS.

41. Woolson to E. C. Stedman, 23 July 1876, Butler Library.

42. Elaine Showalter, *A Literature of Their Own: British Women Novelists from Brontë to Lessing* (Princeton: Princeton University Press, 1977), 194.

43. Edel, *Middle Years*, 377, 385.

44. Leon Edel, *Henry James*, 5 vols. (1962; reprint, New York: Avon Books, 1978), vol. 2, *The Conquest of London, 1870–1881*, 417.

45. See especially Sharon Dean, "Constance Fenimore Woolson and Henry James: The Literary Relationship," *Massachusetts Studies in English* 7 (1980):1–9. She astutely notes that "The Beast in the Jungle" springs from an entry in Woolson's notebook; "Old Gardiston," a Woolson story, which pre-dates by twenty-one years *The Spoils of Poynton* (written close on the heels of Woolson's death), features a climactic conflagration; "The Figure in the Carpet," the title of the James story, is a phrase from Woolson's notebooks; Woolson's "Transplanted Boy" tells of a child's rejection by adults, much like James's "Pupil"; and Tita, the sister of Anne in Woolson's first successful novel, is the original name of Tina in "The Aspern Papers."

46. Nina Baym, *Woman's Fiction: A Guide to Novels by and about Women in America, 1820–1870* (Ithaca: Cornell University Press, 1978), 22.

47. Carren Kaston, *Imagination and Desire in the Novels of Henry James* (New Brunswick, N.J.: Rutgers University Press, 1984), 40.

48. Alfred Habegger, *Gender, Fantasy, and Realism in American Literature* (New York: Columbia University Press, 1982), 56.

49. Kaston, *Imagination and Desire*, 41.

50. Henry James, *The Portrait of a Lady*, ed. Robert D. Bamberg (New York: W. W. Norton, 1975), 430 (hereafter page numbers are cited parenthetically within the text). For the purpose of this essay I have chosen to use the Norton Critical Edition since it offers a list of textual variants from the first edition of 1881 in addition to the text of the New York edition. Because the 1908 edition differs from the original, written while Woolson was at work on *Anne*, the reader should consult the 1881 first edition variants, as I have done.

51. Kaston, *Imagination and Desire*, 41.

52. Ibid.

53. William Veeder, *Henry James—The Lessons of the Master: Popular Fiction and Personal Style in the Nineteenth Century* (Chicago: University of Chicago Press, 1975), 71.

54. Ibid., 120.

55. For the idea of the resisting reader, I am indebted to Judith Fetterley, *The Resisting Reader: A Feminist Approach to American Fiction* (Bloomington: Indiana University Press, 1978).

56. Joyce Warren, *The American Narcissus: Individualism and Women in Nineteenth-Century Fiction* (New Brunswick, N.J.: Rutgers University Press, 1984), 43, 49.

57. Kaston, *Imagination and Desire*, 40.

58. *Letters*, 3:535.

59. See Baym, *Woman's Fiction*; and Mary Kelley, *Private Woman, Public Stage* (New York: Oxford University Press, 1984).

60. *Letters*, 3:544–545.

61. For extensive discussions of how women's writing empowers its female readers, see for example, Baym, *Women's Fiction*, and Kelley, *Private Woman, Public Stage*.

62. *Anne* was published by Harper and Brothers in 1882, 1903, and 1910, and by Sampson and Low (London) in 1883. The Arno Press has reprinted the Harper's text with a new introduction by Elizabeth Hardwick.

63. Judith Kegan Gardiner, "On Female Identity and Writing by Women," in *Writing and Sexual Difference*, ed. Elizabeth Abel (Chicago: University of Chicago Press, 1982), 187.

64. Ellen Moers, *Literary Women* (1976; reprint, New York: Oxford University Press, 1985), 130.

65. Annis Pratt, *Archetypal Patterns in Women's Fiction* (Bloomington: Indiana University Press, 1981), 21.

66. I located a list of wildflowers Woolson had seen, written in the back cover of a wildflower text in the holdings of the Olin Library at Rollins College,

where I also found two unpublished Woolson poems, "Ferns" and "Fern Fragments," tucked in the back of a book.

67. Constance Fenimore Woolson, *Anne* (1882; reprint, New York: Harper and Brothers, 1903), 132.

68. Ibid., 98.

69. Ibid., 539.

70. Moers, *Literary Women*, 1.

71. Myra Jehlen, "Archimedes and the Paradox of Feminist Criticism," in *The Signs Reader: Women, Gender, and Scholarship*, ed. Elizabeth Abel and Emily K. Abel (Chicago: University of Chicago Press, 1983), 79.

72. Benedict, *Five Generations*, vol. 2, *Constance Fenimore Woolson*, 117.

LISA PATER FARANDA

A Social Necessity: The Friendship of Sherwood Bonner and Henry Wadsworth Longfellow

KATHARINE SHERWOOD BONNER McDOWELL (1849–1883), certainly not a well-known literary figure, has nonetheless earned a place among nineteenth-century American writers for several reasons.[1] As the author of a great many short stories, a substantial sectional romance, innumerable newspaper columns and articles, and many children's stories and poems, Sherwood Bonner (as she finally chose to be known) is considered an early local colorist for her realistic depiction of Southern life and her pioneering use of dialects in her fiction. Upon her death, *Harper's Weekly* estimated her contribution to contemporary literature: "A true child of her epoch, she was a simple naturalist in art, with a strong hand and a delicate touch. Life as she had seen it and lived it in the Southern States of the Union was the object of her attention, and she sketched it in the spirit and the method of a master."[2] Twentieth-century appraisals have been less effusive, but many critics are convinced that she has not received sufficient attention nor been truly understood: "She has not received her due measure. Her critics should acknowledge the merit of *Like unto Like* and place the novel accurately in her career, and literary historians should recognize that twenty years before Kate Chopin wrote so powerfully of a woman's search for self, Sherwood Bonner had explored another Southern woman's awakening."[3]

As amanuensis to Henry Wadsworth Longfellow, Bonner has had the misfortune to be cast as Vivien to his Merlin. Bonner's relationship to Longfellow was crucial to her brief literary career, but "there is no solid evidence to support a Merlin and Vivien relationship and there is noth-

184

ing to indicate, as Edward Wagenknecht points out . . . 'that Longfellow was anything more to Sherwood Bonner than a kindly, affectionate, elderly patron and friend.'"[4] No evidence to prove otherwise has turned up in either Bonner or Longfellow scholarship, but the coincidence of Bonner's literary ambitions and accomplishments with her relationship to Longfellow make the most compelling reason for her weak but tenacious hold on a place in the annals of American literature.

Bonner's two claims to a literary reputation are not accidental. Her letters, available only in an unpublished master's thesis, suggest that despite an obvious naiveté and personal emotional conflicts, Bonner knew what she was after: "It is imperative that I learn how to work and to deny myself—and heaven knows I am doing it now."[5] In light of recent feminist scholarship, the portrait of Sherwood Bonner for which her friendship with Longfellow provides the contours is emblematic of the young female writer during the period of greatest development of our national literature. From Bonner's example, we can learn what it was like to be a female in a male-dominated arena and to work against the constraints of what Barbara Welter has named "purity, piety, domesticity and submissiveness," and we can understand what it meant to be a neophyte in a world of sophisticates and a Southerner in a self-satisfied North.[6]

Bonner's death at thirty-four ended a brief career in which an unlikely friendship with one of literature's eminent figures brought together the quintessential elements of the literary life of nineteenth-century women. Her biography corroborates Nina Baym's statement that "we have tended to let writing by a group of New England born, Protestant and middle class white women stand for all women, and so did women of the nineteenth century!"[7] Katharine Sherwood Bonner McDowell, Southern belle, certainly did, for she sacrificed nearly all to go to Boston and be a writer. She wanted to join the New England ranks, and thanks to Henry Wadsworth Longfellow, that bastion of New England culture, she nearly did.

Katharine Sherwood Bonner was born 26 February 1849, giving her just about thirteen years to learn and come to cherish the life and culture of the antebellum South. She lived for only thirty-four years, and while her first years were nearly idyllic, her final twenty were marked by tragedy, loss, and great stress. The Civil War interrupted Bonner's education, and throughout her life she was to suffer from the lack of formal training. Further, the conflict between the impulse to assume the conventional role of the Southern woman and her desire—actually need—to support herself and pursue an intellectual life plagued her, creating

an existence troubled by instability and the disapprobation of most of
the people who mattered to her.

Bonner was the daughter of Dr. Charles and Mary Wilson Bonner,
gentry of prosperous Holly Springs, Mississippi. They were prominent
in the community and provided for their children a world delineated by
social convention and gentility. "By all accounts both beautiful and
charming, Mary Wilson was a careful product of her southern upper-
class nurturing—graceful, accomplished in the feminine arts, domestic. . . . Dr. Bonner, like the Hamiltons and Bonners before him, was
intellectual and literary. Even more than his wife, however, the doctor
was a highly conventional person."[8]

Bonner's intimate circle included the slave "Gran'mammy," who had
raised her mother, and Gran'mammy's grandchildren, who were as important to Bonner as her own brother and sister. They people her stories, and their depictions are some of her most accomplished work. She
wrote in "Gran'mammy" that "it was Gran'mammy to whom we ran to
tell our triumphs and sorrows; she whose sympathy, ash-cakes, and
turnover pies never failed us! It was she who told us stories more beautiful than we read in any books."[9]

Bonner was reared to believe that women should not have ideas, and
should certainly never express them openly if they did. Her upbringing
typified what Welter describes as the anti-intellectualism of the social
conventions defining a woman's place in nineteenth-century America.[10] Her education was closely confined to those subjects fitting a
woman for the home and the hearth. On the one hand, she seems not
only to have accepted the conditions of such a social reality, but to have
mastered them with great style; on the other is a nagging, and finally undeniable, need to develop her intellect and to write.

Bonner was a precocious child, and her father, whose library was a
haven to her, oversaw her education. One biographer says that after
Gran'mammy, "the second most important influence on the young
Sherwood Bonner was the accessibility and impressiveness of her
father's library. The books were not only abundant but carefully chosen."[11] She tells us in her autobiographical novel, *Like unto Like*, about
the reading habits of the young girls of families like her own:

> They were brought up, as it were, on Walter Scott, they read
> Richardson, and Fielding, and Smollet, though you may be sure
> that the last two were not allowed to girls until they were married.
> They liked Thackeray pretty well, Bulwer very well and Dickens
> they read under protest—they thought him low.[12]

When she reached school age, Bonner was sent to the Holly Springs Female Seminary, whose "object, as set forth by an early president, was to impart a sound, substantial, liberal education, not masculine, but approximating as near to it as the peculiarities of the female intelligence will permit. The curriculum included ancient languages, higher mathematics, natural science, vocal and instrumental music, German, French, chemistry, Christian evidences, English literature and poetry, philosophy and hygiene."[13] Within the limits set by a culture that believed in the "peculiarities of the female intelligence" her early years provided glimpses of an intellectual life, but her world offered little hope of any opportunities to pursue one.

To distance her, at least temporarily, from the war, her parents sent her to a girl's school in Montgomery, Alabama. But by her first summer vacation, she returned to find the war's damage to her hometown extensive:

In the summer, at the end of her term, Kate left Montgomery, itself no longer the citadel it had been six months earlier, to travel through a ruined countryside back to Holly Springs. The last part of the journey she made on the only vehicle left on the Mississippi Central Railroad, a handcar run by a blind man, a cripple, and two former slaves. The Van Dorn raid was only the first of sixty separate raids made on Holly Springs during the course of the war, as the town found itself in the line of one army or another, or, worse, stragglers from both armies. Consequently, even the six months that Kate had been away had wrought devastating change. "I should never have recognized in the dreary village the once prosperous, comfortable little town," she once wrote.[14]

The devastation of her town was to be the first of many tragedies Bonner had to face. She spent some time with an older aunt during the war and there displayed courage and ingenuity when dealing with the soldiers passing by.[15] She did not return to school except for a year during which she attended the Select School For Young Ladies, held at the home of a prominent local family and conducted by their thirty-year-old daughter. The Bonners had managed to keep their home in Holly Springs and many of the black retainers, though freed, remained. Perhaps because the war brought enormous social changes, the townspeople desperately clung to their cultural pretensions. In fact, conventions seemed to have become all the more important and "in their insistence on preserving an intellectual and cultural life amid a land in ruins, they probably succeeded in creating a far more stimulating environment than the one that had existed before the war."[16] Unfortunately, this environment did not yield any more possibilities for a young girl than had been available before the war. Dependency was nearly inevitable — either as a wife or a spinster who, having no husband to depend upon, remained at home.

By the time Bonner was twenty she had mastered the social arts. In fact, while she was often thought daring or somewhat brazen, she was nonetheless something of a socialite, and well suited for the life. She was, by all accounts, a stunning beauty and charming conversationalist. The *Harper's Weekly* memorial essay says that "to the charms of a ripe loveliness of person she added the attractiveness of a happy disposition, bright conversational gifts, and a truly feminine soul.[17]

Bonner's diary for 1869 reveals a young woman participating with great pleasure in the social life of her community and one who, at the same time, was unable to shake her impatience with what often appeared to her a frivolous existence.[18] In her entry dated "September 1 through September" she spoke quite joyfully about her conquests at "the party of the season":

> Soph and I went with Messrs. Watson and Falconer. We didn't finish our toilets in time for the wedding but the party made amends for all. The music from Memphis was glorious and the whole evening was one of unalloyed enjoyment! The gentlemen admired my dress enthusiastically, tho' I did hear of a few proper females hoping, that the next time I wear hoops and not have my dress short enough to show my feet so plainly! But I never received so many compliments in my life and one I never can forget — As I turned him in the dance he bent forward and whispered as if he meant it — "Miss Kate, you look perfectly charming in that dress!" Now allowing a goodly share from my emerald robes and white tulle drapery, the tone at least is left to me — & when did Jimmie Watson ever speak so to me before? —— Flirted with several of my weaknesses — married men![19]

Clearly Bonner enjoyed "sociables"; however, only a month earlier she had recorded her despair over the shallowness and emptiness of the life she was leading:

> Day of misery unutterable! I am a weary, weary, Would God that I were dead! Why is it, why why that I am so hopelessly unhappy

—I feel sometimes that I shall go mad! There is no help for me
—none—all I long for is death and annihilation—, but oh! The
long long years to come—How can I fill them—How can I crush
out these needs of my hungry soul! Oh! God! There is no word I
can find to express what I feel—And from this I turn to the
parlour with a smile and entertain Jimmie & Mr. Wellford like
one who had never learned to sigh or weep—.[20]

Bonner vacillated between the social world and the "needs of [her]
soul," sometimes throwing herself wholeheartedly into fashionable coquetry, sometimes resolving to "renounce society and devote [herself]
to French, German and music."[21]

The frequent swings between the two worlds and the repeated admission of love then contempt for a series of different "beaux" caution
against taking any one statement seriously. We are struck, on the
whole, by an obvious immaturity of this twenty-year-old socialite who
was also quite "literary." Despite numerous avowals of love for Edward
McDowell, Bonner was interested in a number of others. She called off
her engagement to McDowell as frequently as she admitted, "how my
heart turned to him as my all upon earth."[22] The diary reveals a young
woman still overwhelmingly dependent upon the authority of others.
She got a "lecture from auntie for taking part in politics!" and when
to visit poor families in the community she "went on a poor circuit,"
though she "enjoyed it amazingly," her father, she wrote, "stopped my
proceedings in a most summary manner and I am given over to my own
agonizing reflections—."[23] And she was still only planning her future,
choosing a career:

I have thought much of my future and am determined unless I
marry to carve out my own fortune. I have decided to be an actress—after hesitating for a long time in favor of a literary life.[24]

This is the musing of a dreaming youth; she had absolutely no conception of the profession she had selected, nor training, nor any real
chance of putting her plan into action. However, what is clear from the
syntax of the statement alone is a distinct, though perhaps unconscious,
notion of the mutually exclusive worlds of which she dreams, and while
we may not easily credit the individual protestations of love or the
claims for her future, underlying the year's entries are some very clear,
persistent tensions that characterize her life.

What rings true, first of all, are her strong doubts about the nature of marriage. One entry demonstrates Bonner's conception of the drudgery of the lives of most wives but at the same time makes a vow to avoid that possibility. "Marriage is not to sink me into a drudge or nonentity, whatever it may do for weaker sisters," she wrote.[25] Although she finally married Edward McDowell—on Saint Valentine's Day, 1871 —and with great hopes that her marriage would prove an example against those marriages which destroyed women—Bonner was consistently aware of how far from her ideal man Edward really was. In a single entry she wrote, "I received a letter today—the dearest yet,— and I do feel that I love him very truly indeed—I suppose one never meets his ideal."[26] Almost from the depths of her unconscious, her vision of her lover was dual, and at twenty she was at a juncture in her life where her next step would land her, she thought, in heaven or hell:

> I had floated in a region above the earth. A starry realm of love and beauty—The eyes of my soul were closed and I moved on in a strange enchantment—Suddenly light poured upon me—I saw that I stood upon the bank of a flower-wreathed precipice—My affrighted eyes looked down down down down into an abyss of shame and despair—Yet—by my side there stood a radiant form—whether demon or angel my fevered brain knew not and tempted me with words and tones that bewildered my senses, to take the fatal leap—[27]

On her twentieth birthday she was unhappy not because she had failed to find a hero but perhaps because she had failed to become one:

> My birthday! having known some nineteen others, such things have become common, and I can't say that I very heartily echo the kind wishes for "Many Returns" of the same. Twenty years! "nor peace within nor calm around!" To express myself I should sketch a rudderless ship upon a stormy ocean.[28]

However, she succeeded in writing and publishing three short stories during this otherwise frivolous year. These stories, unpolished in many ways, indicate her ability to write marketable fiction; surprisingly, mention of her writing and notices of acceptance are brief and infrequent. Clearly she was proud of her achievement, but quite unable to devote her attention to her work. Frequent self-recriminations about her inability to discipline herself and her insecurities speak for an underlying dilemma throughout her life; she was torn between what she had been taught to expect from life and what she felt she needed to be: "—Rain in the afternoon and great depression of the mental atmosphere—I shall become a maniac unless I can be separated from myself."[29]

Bonner's situation was not unusual for many nineteenth-century women whose options for shaping their lives were severely limited. She envied the freedom of men to pursue the life of the mind. On 9 April she, "by special invitation went to the St. James' Club—what a grand privilege it is to be a man!"[30] Her only real hope must have been in finding a spouse whose thoughts might be congenial to her own and who might support her efforts toward self-definition. Perhaps she believed that if she could find her "hero," as Blythe Herndon thinks she does in *Like unto Like*, the opposition between fulfilling social convention and heeding one's inner voice might be reconciled by a lover's promise: "Whatever sign of affection you have bestowed on me shall always be regarded as a *gift*—something to be grateful for; not as a claim on which to found dominion over you."[31]

Unfortunately, like her heroine, only not in time to prevent her own marriage, Bonner discovered her hopes for such a relationship were unfounded. The man she had admired for being "literary" and intelligent turned out to be an irresponsible dreamer whose series of get-rich-quick schemes failed one after the other. She slowly—but most definitely—felt her life "sink to drudgery and nonentity." A year after her marriage, 14 February 1871, she bore a daughter, named Lilian. Chasing one dream of creating a mercantile empire in Texas, her husband left his wife and child in the care of his family for a short time. In an effort to revitalize their marriage, she and her daughter joined him in May 1873. Says one biographer, "It was this period in Texas that brought matters to a head. Holly Springs, where the society of family and friends diverted Kate from her own dilemma, was quite different from Dallas, where she knew no one, where the full duties of running a household oppressed her, and where she found even the landscape depressing."[32]

In Texas, with a child to care for alone and a husband who succeeded only in failing, Bonner resolved to redirect her life. She determined to leave her husband, take her daughter to her family in Holly Springs, and go east to get an education and become a writer. She planned to attend Vassar, the first women's college offering the same curriculum as that offered in colleges for men. To muster support for such a plan, Bonner wrote Nahum Capen, the publisher of the *Massachusetts Ploughman*, where she had placed her first three short stories. Capen did not, at first, offer encouragement for her plan; he cautioned against leaving her child in the hands of others and warned her about the disapproval with which such action might be met.

Bonner wrote Capen a passionate, defensive response, self-righteously proclaiming,

> I do not belong to that class whose exponents consider that the accidental circumstance of birth renders the parent the only possible guide or instructor of the child. I am conscious enough of my own deficiencies to know that, as I am, I am unfitted for such a responsibility, and unselfish enough to sacrifice my affections for what would certainly eventuate in the child's good.[33]

In all fairness to Bonner, while we may question how prepared she was to care for her child, we must remember that she was herself reared by other than her own mother. Although her mother did not die until she was sixteen, in Bonner's family, as in many Southern homes, the figure of Gran'mammy was the prominent nurturing one. Whether from self-interest (though I think not selfishly) or a sincere wish to support her family, as she said in a letter to her sister, she left Texas with her daughter on 20 August 1873.[34] Perhaps realizing the financial impracticality of her original plan, because she had no support from a bankrupt husband and could have had no hopes of support from a father who could be counted on to denounce her actions, she resolved to go directly to Boston.

Despite objections from her husband's family and her own, Bonner left her daughter with the child's maternal aunt and grandfather and went to Boston in September 1873. It could not have been easy for her to leave Holly Springs, where all her world lay, or to face Boston, still the formidable center of American literary life. As William Dean Howells recalled,

> At Boston chiefly, if not at Boston alone, was there a vigorous intellectual life among such authors as I have named [Lowell, Longfellow, Emerson, Hawthorne, Holmes, Stowe, Thoreau, Prescott]. Every young writer was ambitious to join his name with theirs in the *Atlantic Monthly* and in the lists of Ticknor and Fields.[35]

Boston was a place to which one had to turn to become part of the American literary scene, and though by the end of the century New York and Philadelphia would rival it, outsiders—particularly those from the beaten South and "uncivilized" West—turned to the east—to Boston—with reverence and deference, looking for legitimacy and support. Bret Harte, celebrating his own landscape, came to Boston and even in his ironic comment one can detect the awe: "Why you couldn't fire a revolver from your front porch without bringing down a two-volumer."[36] Bonner shared his regard for Boston and had her own comic sense of its proportion:

> For the native Bostonian there are three paths to glory. If his name be Quincy or Adams, nothing more is expected of him. His blue blood carries him through his life with glory and straight to heaven when he dies, not a question being asked by the fisherman who keeps the golden keys, when his card of introduction is handed in. Failing in the happy accident of birth, the candidate for Beacon Hill honors must write a book. This is easy. The man who can breathe Boston air and not write a book is either a fool or a phenomenon. One course remains to him should he miss fame in both these lines. He must be a reformer. Nothing must be too huge for him to tackle, or wild for him to advocate.[37]

This newspaper essay by a "southern girl turned loose in Boston" appeared very shortly after her arrival there. It is testimony to her savvy as much as to her talent that she recognized the importance of entering Boston's literary community, that she perceived some of its pretensions, and that she so quickly found the people she needed and so quickly and completely won them to her campaign.

As soon as she arrived in Boston, Bonner established a friendship with the Capens, relying on Nahum Capen not for financial support but for many paternalistic considerations she had sacrificed from her own father. In fact, Capen so thoroughly adopted her, he acted as intermediary to her father, sending a letter that demonstrates his care, concern, and understanding of the aspiring young writer:

> From the first I have counseled in a way that all good fathers could approve in fact. I have done what I feel would be right and kind in another extended to my own children.
>
> Your daughter has a very active mind,—more ideas and fancies than her judgement has been able to control. She is doubtless a mystery to herself. She has high aspirations—and she has been unhappy because she could not find or see the means for their development and realization.[38]

In some sense, Bonner's history is typical of many nineteenth-century women because it is a complex blend of contradictory accommodations made to both an inner voice and to social circumstances. Her actions, her abrupt and blatant rejection of the roles she had been expecting to fulfill, brought her to Boston, but to a very great extent her mastery of the social forms and the pose of the weak, dependent female won her the support and affection of those who helped her attain her independence.

> For this clever woman had, to an extraordinary degree, the faculty of enlisting in her behalf the services of those who could help her. . . . She never made the acquaintance of a man of power, intellectual or social, without succeeding in making him feel that to oblige her would give him pleasure.[39]

I am not suggesting that Bonner's Southern-belle style of coquetry was the only tool at her disposal; however, whether she wielded this tool because she could not help it or because she understood the politics of the situation into which she had plunged, she nonetheless used her charms to maneuver herself into a position in the Boston literary scene, under the protection of a series of mentors, each bringing her closer to her goal. First, she became a friend of the Capen family. Capen helped her find a place to live, arranged for her to attend a school for girls, and provided her with part-time employment as his secretary. She was very grateful to him, elevating him to sainthood in one letter to her sister:

> I intend to model my life by a high standard. I think if ever a saint lived upon earth it is Mr. Capen—I could fill page after page telling you of instances of his generosity and unselfishness that have come to my knowledge . . . he is my ideal *philosopher*.[40]

I do not wish to suggest that Bonner was in any way insincere, for her letter rings true. However, notice that her vision of Capen almost automatically placed her in a subordinate position: humble and most grateful.

She soon needed full-time employment and, characteristically, sought the help of an older, successful man. This time she capitalized on her father's friendship with Theodore Dwight, then dean of Columbia Law School in New York. She was desperate for work and tried to interest him in her plight by sending him some of her stories and pictures of her daughter. As one biographer claims, Dwight probably was reluctant to interfere in family matters. He did not respond for two months, and when he did, he suggested that she consider her father her "proper protector."⁴¹ However, in the meantime she had found another protector in Dioclesian Lewis, then gaining a reputation as the father of the temperance movement and prophet of physical culture. She worked as secretary to Lewis, so that by December 1873, just two months after her arrival in Boston, she had found a place to live, begun school, found a job that supported her education and cultural interests, and made friends with some of the most respected members of Boston society. She was ready to begin in earnest the life of the writer. For that she determined to seek help from Henry Wadsworth Longfellow, then at the zenith of his influence. She wrote to Longfellow on 8 December 1873, and openly sought his support, casting herself as the young girl who could, in this unfamiliar place, do with a daddy.

> I am a Southern girl away from home and friends. I have come here for mental discipline and study—and to try to find out the meaning and use of my life. It would be to me a great happiness and help if I might know you. May I come and see you please? and if so will you appoint a day and hour?⁴²

That in this letter she uses her maiden name for the first time since leaving her husband indicates the beginning of a new life independent of him and intensifies her self-portrayal as a young, inexperienced maiden who had to learn all, and who hoped to learn at the foot of a master. The ploy, if it was one, worked, for a meeting was set for the following week. Soon Bonner became a frequent visitor, and their friendship was well established. From their first meeting she earned herself a place in Craigie House.

> As she stood in Longfellow's study, surrounded by the portraits of Sumner, Emerson, and Hawthorne, and examining the inkwell which had belonged to Coleridge, while this other great poet stood by her side, she knew at last she had entered the great world. She intended to remain in it.⁴³

The questions one asks about any mentorial relationship may begin with why it is that a protégée seeks a particular mentor, or why a particular mentor takes on his or her protégée. In this case, why did Sherwood Bonner choose Longfellow from among the host of luminaries living in the vicinity, and why did she choose a man rather than one of the number of women who, like Julia Ward Howe or Mary Clemmer, were successful in the very ways in which she hoped to succeed? We must also ask why Longfellow took Bonner on, and examining the answers we may understand the dynamics of their relationship and their world.

Very little is known about their friendship. The letters from Sherwood Bonner to Longfellow survive, but only one of his letters to her is extant.[44] Early biographers of Longfellow generally ignored their ten-year association; it was not until 1955 in Wagenknecht's biography that she is mentioned at all. And he writes that he gave "her story more space [three and a half pages] than it really deserves in the record of Longfellow's life, partly because she is an interesting figure in American letters and partly to guard against misunderstandings."[45]

Perhaps the neglect was purposeful, raising questions about the social dynamics of American letters. Gossip and insinuation exaggerated the romantic possibilities of their friendship, but an almost conspiratorial agreement among the Boston literary community, at least among what Hubert McAlexander calls "the female literary establishment," has kept Bonner out of literary history. "That group, traditionally a closed shop, had not been kind to Kate in her last years . . . and Kate McDowell was never mentioned in any of their reminiscences of the Boston literary world."[46] A letter from Harriet Waters Preston to Paul Hamilton Hayne occasioned by the publication of *Like unto Like* in 1878, suggests the extent to which rumor had grown among those who resented Bonner. The tone trivializes Bonner's need for separation from her husband and suggests the contempt with which Preston described her situation in Boston:

> I could a "long and very curious tale unfold" about the author [of *Like unto Like*], but fire light, twilight, and unlimited leisure would be needful for its proper amplification, so here are the "heads" only. Kate Sherwood Bonner was the author's maiden name . . . and Miss Bonner married a Mr. McDowell and tired of the monotony of living with him in Texas or some such forlorn region; and came to Boston as a literary adventuress and after a rather severe experience became known to Mr. Longfellow, who admired her (she is a statuesque blonde with cataracts of yellow hair) and employed her as an amanuensis on his perpetual "poems of places." A malign wit once named them "Merlin and Vivien" and the mot became general. . . . All this sounds very badly gossippy, but if you knew how much more is said you would only marvel at my restraint.[47]

The link between the gossip surrounding Bonner's social figure and the literary one she tried to cut is made eminently clear by the fact that it was Preston, not Howells, as Bonner believed, who wrote the rather uncomplimentary review of *Like unto Like* for the *Atlantic*.[48]

The murmurs about Longfellow and "the literary adventuress" no doubt offended Samuel Longfellow and probably account for his virtually erasing all reference to Bonner from his collection of extracts from his brother's journals and correspondence.[49] "So effective were these various protectors of the public good that in the summer of 1978 the staff at Longfellow House had never heard of anyone known as either Kate McDowell or Sherwood Bonner."[50]

After the deaths of both writers and when, therefore, they were unable to refute public opinion, Ellen Kirk's *Story of Margaret Kent* appeared, a thinly veiled story about the friendship between Longfellow and Bonner that amplified suspicion that theirs was a relationship based on romantic love. Unlike the stereotypical pattern of the fawning female protégée, this mentorial relationship (if we are to believe the portrayal of Herbert Bell, aging eminent poet, and Margaret Kent, young Southern woman who, having left her profligate husband, was endeavoring to support herself and her young daughter in Boston by writing) is based on the unconditional devotion of the older man, who regrets not being younger and able to approach the woman on more passionate terms.

That Sherwood Bonner is believed to have written the first half of this novel before her death adds weight to the opinion that Longfellow was infatuated with her.[51] If she did construe the characters and outline their circumstances, it was certainly characteristic of her to use autobiographical material. But she always used it imaginatively, and there is no reason to assume that she did not simply recognize the possibility of Longfellow's affection being romantic and stretch it for effect in the kind of romance she had successfully produced many times before.

Other evidence that their bond may have had at least romantic underpinnings comes from early biographers of Bonner, who discuss Longfellow's relationship to her in broad sweeps, saying such things as, "she seemed to impart new vigor to the white-haired poet."[52] Andrew Hilen, editor of *The Letters of Henry Wadsworth Longfellow*, acknowledges this possibility and points out that there were a number of young women to whom the poet became attached in his last years:

> There were others in whom he took a special interest, motivated by a mixture of unconscious vanity, loneliness, and repressed desire. . . . Longfellow's fondness for Mrs. McDowell is especially intriguing because he wrote fifty-nine letters to her between 1873

and 1881. . . . . As correspondents they seem to have brought pleasure to his final years in a mildly titillating way.[53]

Wagenknecht identifies others. What they have in common is their
youth, their ambition, and their good looks.[54] It is not difficult to accept
such a view of Longfellow; he was in his sixties and essentially living
alone in Craigie House after the tragic death of his second wife.

What is left of their correspondence indicates their mutual respect and
affection. Sometimes Bonner is coy, as in a letter she wrote to him when
she traveled to Europe with Louise Chandler Moulton: "I have just read
your kind and dear letter, which I found awaiting me like a friendly
hand. I am selfish enough to be glad you miss me."[55] And sometimes
Longfellow is sentimental. "Dear Aurora," he writes Bonner on his
sixty-ninth birthday and upon receipt of her letter from Paris, "write me
always in this way, and fear no criticism from me, and write me as often
as you can, nor a moment think it can be too often. I rejoice in your happiness, and am thankful that it has gone so well with you, — I only wish
I could be your cicerone in Rome."[56] They were pleased in each other's
company. Although a close look at the documents surviving may not
settle questions about the nature of their affection, they do suggest interpretations that make the question of romance, finally, beside the point.

First of all, theirs was a business arrangement. Shortly after their
meeting, Longfellow hired Bonner to serve as his amanuensis. She
helped him deal with his "drift of letters" and with his work on the massive *Poems of Places*. In fact, a letter to her sister in which she requested her to locate and copy "a poem about a river the Ducifer the
Neva or the Volga—" because she "told Mr. Longfellow about [it] and
he is very anxious to get it for his poems of places"[57] shows that she
aided him in the compilation of the collection.

Quite likely, the balance of the advantages of their connection tips toward Bonner's side. Longfellow scholars talk vaguely of the pleasure an
old man might find in the company of a young, energetic, bright, and
beautiful woman. His own description of Bonner may well account for
their intimations: "Your joyous nature drinks in the sunshine and repels
the shade."[58] But few have asked whether she had any influence upon
Longfellow's work. It may be, as McAlexander suggests, that Bonner
inspired "The Masque of Pandora," which Longfellow began in January
1875; he did not formally dedicate it to her, but the description of Pandora clearly resembles her. Perhaps insofar as the new realism infused
her work, Longfellow was able to look beyond his own work and hail
Bonner as the master of America's future, a world that, at seventy, he

would never enter. As one might expect in a relationship such as theirs, it was the protégée, the tutee, whose life and work would be more affected by a mentorial relationship, and inasmuch as Bonner actively cultivated one with Longfellow, some of the benefits it brought were concrete. However, they have been, I believe, overestimated and over-blown because they have not been considered in light of the social ne-cessities and constraints female writers faced in the nineteenth century.

One representative estimate of Longfellow's influence on Bonner's work is William Frank's:

> The exact nature of Bonner's relationship with Longfellow consti-tutes one of the few unanswered questions concerning her life, but one has no doubt about the poet's literary influence on the nature, content, and direction of Bonner's work. . . . One has little doubt that the early local-color stories and the later Realistic ones of Sherwood Bonner owe much to Longfellow's suggestions. In this regard, Longfellow was to Sherwood Bonner what William Dean Howells was to Stephen Crane.[59]

Biographers seem to have confused a benefit to her career with a benefit to her art. Unquestionably they are related, though in Bonner's case the difference is important. By giving her the job as his amanuensis, Long-fellow afforded her more than the opportunity to support herself; he gave her the kind of job that left her time to write:

> You can be of the greatest help to me in the Poems of Places. It would occupy two or three hours in the morning only, and you would have the afternoons and evenings entirely free. The work itself would not, I am sure, be distasteful to you, as it deals with poets and poetry.[60]

More important, working for Longfellow brought Bonner to Craigie House, where she met a steady stream of the famous people whom he frequently entertained. Any friend of Longfellow's soon became, at least superficially or until his death, a friend of Boston literati. He intro-duced Bonner to Louise Chandler Moulton, with whom she later trav-eled to Europe; he wangled her an invitation to the Radical Club, an elite literary society, "a galaxy of genius and high talent . . . organized by the Rev. John Sargent and Mrs. Sargent, at whose home the meet-ings took place. Among these were Emerson, Sumner, Dr. and Mrs. Howe, John Weiss, Theodore Parker, Dr. Hedge, Colonel Higginson,

James Freeman Clarke, the Rev. Phillips Brooks, John Fiske, David
Wasson, Mrs. Cheney, the Rev. W. H. Channing, Mr. and Mrs. Edwin
P. Whipple, Mrs. Moulton, Mr. Frothingham, Henry James, Miss
Peabody, Professor Peirce, Professor Calvin E. Stowe, Lydia Maria
Child, John G. Whittier and many other notable people."[61] Bonner par-
layed these introductions and meetings into opportunities as a writer.
By the winter of 1873 and spring of 1874 she was correspondent for the
Memphis Avalanche, sending reports from "The Hub." She published
interviews with such notables as Mary Clemmer, Ralph Waldo Emerson, Julia Ward Howe, Wendell Phillips, and of course, Longfellow.
The introduction most important to Bonner was the one Longfellow arranged with William Dean Howells; Bonner knew that he and the *Atlantic* were the literary powers to reckon with and conquer. That she failed
to make a conquest of Howells even though her fiction began to develop
in the mode of the new realism that he advocated may tell us as much
about the changing dynamics of the literary scene as it does about a
significant reason for Bonner's failure to sustain a large audience. Her
letter to her sister indicates how well she knew whose influence it was
important to cultivate and how effectively she mined her connection to
Longfellow in an attempt to do so:

> Am going Saturday with Mr. Longfellow to call on Mr. Howells,
> the Editor of *Atlantic Monthly* and author of those charming
> books "Their Wedding Journey — & A Chance Acquaintance."
> He is a man I've long wanted to meet, and I'm all a flutter of de-
> lighted anticipation. Have had my b. silk fixed short and will get
> some fawn-colored gloves and new bonnet strings and curl my
> hair — Hope to strike his majesty favorably tho I hear he's a stern
> business man. And hope I may be very much impressed — as it
> takes one nail to drive out another you know![62]

Besides giving her the opportunity to meet the greats and the aspiring
greats who visited Craigie House, Longfellow promoted her work ener-
getically. He sang her praises and predicted her potential as the writer of
"The Great American Novel." He urged his friends to take notice of her
work and to think favorably of it. On 6 October 1878, he wrote to James
T. Fields, saying,

> I hope, also, that you will like "Like Unto Like," Mrs. McDow-
> ell's novel. It is a very clever book, full of humor and dramatic
> power, by which I mean power of delineating character. You will
> be pleased and surprised.[63]

Under his sponsorship she obtained an audience and publisher at Harpers, and opportunities to publish in *Lippincott's, Harper's Weekly, Youth's Companion*, and *Cottage Hearth* were probably more forthcoming than they might have been had she not had Longfellow's endorsement. His support advanced her career by much the same means as patronage still works today; he brought Bonner into the network, giving her the chance to succeed or fail.

On a deeper level Longfellow gave her the kind of encouragement she never received from her father. Dr. Bonner remained aloof, even if he was proud of his daughter's literary accomplishments, and she never fully reconciled with him; her letters show how she sought his approval and never seemed sure she had earned it. After cataloging her recent successes and literary acquaintances she ended one letter to her father: "On the whole Dr. Bonner your children seem to make a favorable impression in all places—tho' in the bosom of the family their virtues are not conspicious."⁶⁴ Her closing reveals how she sought his approval and suffered from his reticence: "Good-bye my dear father. I long for a letter from you and Aunty and am / Your loving Daughter / K."⁶⁵ Longfellow's recognition of her talents must have done much to legitimize her choices as her father had failed to do.

This kind of emotional support suggests a paternalistic view of his relationship to Bonner, a view further borne out by the fact that she more than once petitioned him for financial assistance. In 1878, when she had returned to Holly Springs to nurse her brother and father who were dying from the yellow fever epidemic in the South, she cabled Longfellow, knowing full well she could rely upon his help: "Help for God's sake. Send money father and brother down yellow fever alone to nurse."⁶⁶

In 1881, shortly before his death and some time after she had permanently returned to Holly Springs, Bonner asked Longfellow for money to save her family home from auction. That she turned to him on these occasions is an indication of just how much like a father she felt him to be. When in fact there were many to whom she might have gone for financial help, she sought it from someone she knew would support her as unconditionally as a loving parent. For example, she could easily have obtained the money from Colton Greene, who evidently was so much in love with her that years after her death and upon his own, he settled his sizable fortune upon her daughter.

The basis of the mentorial relationship was a paternalism, natural to Longfellow, particularly apt for Bonner, and I submit, inherent in the very need that women writers had for mentors in the literary world of the time. Bonner, for personal, psychological, and social reasons, was the perfect protégée, and the aging, well-established poet the likely patron. He had a reputation for supporting young writers, a reputation Bonner celebrates in "Longfellow's Home": "The young poet who goes to Longfellow with his verses need not fear a cold reception or an indifferent listener."[67] And it is one for which he has been remembered: "No one who asked decently at his door was denied access to him."[68]

It would be unfair to Longfellow to condemn him for his generosity; indeed he is especially noted for his kindness to young writers of both genders. That he willingly assumed a paternalistic role shows perhaps the social limitations upon his own behavior rather than any desire to belittle or patronize those whom he helped. The public dubbed him our patriarch; that he fulfilled his role with such generosity is to his credit.

A perpetual adolescence to which Bonner seemed condemned, first because of her own psychological necessities and then because of the social realities for female writers, accounts in great part for her efforts to enlist Longfellow's help and then, in the long run, to rebel against the cultural authority that he so perfectly represented. If we look closely at his ultimate effect upon her career and his lack of it upon her work, we can detect ways in which she cherished his approval but either ignored or sabotaged its good effects.

First, we must place their relationship in its social context; mentorial relationships were part of the social reality of the nineteenth-century literary world. There was a network of writers and publishers who not only influenced what was written, but what was published and then what was reviewed. Although the locus of power was shifting from Boston to New York, and from the old gray beards and Brahmins to the young realists like Howells and James, the network held sway. To have ignored this reality would have been foolish; Bonner's sometimes masterful exploitation of it, however, may well have been her biggest mistake.

Understanding of a friendship that in isolation appears intensely affectionate is tempered by what we realize is social necessity — and social form — for both Longfellow and Bonner. For instance, what appears to be a forthright and irresistible request for aid in her first letter to Longfellow became a tool when it appeared almost verbatim in her letter to Emerson.[69] That letter won an interview that she used as the basis for "The Hub's Good Side: Ralph Waldo Emerson Interviewed by a Fair Southron." Longfellow's recommendations pale a little, since he offered much the same for all who asked. His letter of introduction for Bonner to Thomas Bailey Aldrich is strikingly similar to a letter of introduction he wrote for another young writer, Laura A. Brown, to William Dean Howells.[70]

Longfellow's praise for Bonner's work must also be heard over the echo of his unwillingness to criticize the work of others. Howells recalls, "The ill will that seemed nearly always to go with adverse criticism made him distrust criticism, and the discomfort which mistaken or blundering praise gives probably made him shy of all criticism."[71] Perhaps this explains why he never completed a review of Bonner's first novel, *Like unto Like*, although his support would have greatly added to its success. However, the fragment available promises a critically bland though positive appraisal; he speaks of the novel's strengths in general terms and ignores the weaknesses that truly mar the whole: "The style is throughout easy and unaffected; delicate touches of humor enliven its pages, and the various characters are described and developed with great dramatic power."[72]

Bonner took very little instruction from Longfellow for her writing. He supplied a poem for "Lilly's Earrings"[73] and an outline for the plot of "Two Storms," but Bonner's writing both succeeded in meeting popular demands and also matured in ways that, rather than following Longfellow's vision or style, were almost antithetical to them. When she dedicated *Like unto Like* to him (1878) with a poem testifying to her gratitude and affection to this "man whom many love and all revere," she believed that it was to him she "owed all." However, what she owed was the career opportunity of his sponsorship, not her art; she had produced a novel that drew on realities other than those he could have taught her and a world view to which the author of "Evangeline" or even "The Masque of Pandora" could probably not have subscribed.

In fact, Bonner almost completely rejected the advice from Longfellow to write about her current experience. In her letters are occasional references to a book she titled "Prodigal Daughter," which may be what finally became *The Story of Margaret Kent*; however, she evidently abandoned that project in favor of other work, and her first novel, *Like unto Like*, was a sectional romance drawing heavily on her childhood and youth in Holly Springs. For this work, Longfellow could have offered little insight, and she seems to have sought none, although she was anxious to show him the fait accompli and have his support in her search for a publisher.

Like unto Like rises above the other sectional romances of the period because of her realistic treatment of the awakening of a young woman's sense of self and a nascent feminism that explains her failure to reunite North and South neatly through the marriage of the young Southern girl to her Northern hero. Their differences are irreconcilable primarily because the protagonist, Blythe Herndon, discovers that she is unwilling to serve any ideology or relinquish her own voice for the din of that ideology's powerful male spokesman.

Longfellow's mentorship is particularly questionable since *Like unto Like* and much of her work during the late 1870s places Bonner as a transition figure between the tradition he so fully embodied and the fully blown realism of the turn of the century. She could evoke a landscape filled with voices of ordinary, often unsavory folk, and recreate a variety of communities in the South and Midwest with such skill that she has been seen as a pioneer local colorist. Years before Joel Chandler Harris's *Uncle Remus*, her stories of the enslaved South employed various dialects to bring the nuances of the society to life. Shedding any romantic vision, and any remaining traces of her youthful reading of writers like Scott, she grew more and more able to depict an independent, somewhat cynically realistic world view. Her writing matured. When she did go to school to some writers, it was not to Longfellow, but to the new local colorists, for she always felt herself "a sort of rara avis" in Boston and believed she could sell the stories about her own faraway places. She imitated Mary Murfree (Charles Egbert Craddock) and George W. Cable because she needed to write what would sell; after realizing the popular success of Murfree's Tennessee stories, for example, Bonner wrote "Lost and Found" and then spent a month in Tennessee researching the material for some of the stories later collected in *Dialect Tales*.[74] She wrote a number of stories, including her mountain tales, to earn the money that *Harper's, Lippincott's,* or *Youth's Companion* would pay for a "local color" piece. These are not always her best, yet she could produce something so remarkable as "Volcanic Interlude," which while evidently derivative of Cable's work, was so inflammatory it caused many people to cancel their subscriptions to *Lippincott's* because of the story's direct treatment of Southern sexual mores and miscegenation.

Bonner was no feminist, but she came close to being one. Perhaps it is possible to understand her relationship with Longfellow and the society that he represented in terms of the recurring pattern in her life. Her writings and behavior display a genuine discomfort with any establishment, but she particularly suffered the oppression of a thinking female in a world governed by men and restricted for women.

She tried hard "to *conform*," as she wrote Longfellow from Galveston, where she had rejoined her husband to attempt a reconciliation. There she hoped "this lesson in repression would be good for me."

Edward McDowell, Uncle Robert, and Aunt Mary proved too repress-
ive; between Uncle Robert's "object[ing] strenously" to her reading
Rousseau's *Confessions* and "a persistent course of darning socks," she
was drawn back to Holly Springs, then to Boston within six months.[75]

So many times did she win the hearts of and seek the aid of men in the
establishment (be it Southern, Northern, social, or literary) that her relationship with Longfellow may be the most developed version of a
series of attachments that she first sought then jeopardized or relin-
quished. A letter of 12 August 1879, seven months before she left Boston only to return for medical treatment two years later, displays a
mixture of self-confidence with her belief that she needs and wants the
help of an "other." She often spoke boldly to her mentor but was, at the
same time, afraid of losing his affection.

> Do you know I have a very tenacious belief in myself? I cannot
> help believing that I shall succeed. I have moments of horrible
> discouragement; especially between the hours of six and eight in
> the evening when I say to myself a thousand times over that I was
> mad not to take the one chance God gave me—of staying in
> Holly Springs and dying of the fever. Yet always I revive, and
> feel strong enough to move mountains and assured of my future.
> If only I did not have to fight so much single-handed. If only there
> was one on earth who understood me, and had faith in me, and
> would help me, without a brutal statement of my difficulties.
> Sometimes I lose faith in everything; and I have such sad and
> dreadful thoughts that if you could look into my heart you would
> pity me.—But I am continually checked in my confidences to
> you. You once called me your sunshine. I fear so much becoming
> your *cloud*.[76]

Such vacillating is typical of adolescence, and Bonner's approach to
her mentor may be in part like that of the adolescent who chafes a little
under the influence of an authority to which she soon hopes to accede.
There is no evidence to indicate that she actually revolted, though her
letters to Longfellow are sometimes petulant in their demands for his attention or support. Her rebelliousness in this relationship took the form
of her rebellion against the authority of the Boston literary community.
Though she had come to join their ranks, and sought and won a mentor
to help her, she jeopardized his support and certainly minimized its
effect by her "slight taste for bohemianism [he had] sometimes gently
regretted from time to time" and by offending the powerful Boston
literati.[77]

One must wonder, for instance, at the motives that led Bonner to seek entrance to the Radical Club, cultivating the attentions of Mrs. Sargent after Longfellow had arranged an initial meeting, and subsequently to write "The Radical Club: A Poem Respectfully Dedicated to the Infinite by 'An Atom,'" a biting satire of this intimidating group and its intellectual pretensions.[78] To many, her criticism was presumption, and it proved a fatal error. As the anonymous reply to her satire, *The Radical Club: A Poem Respectfully Dedicated to an Atom by a Chip*, told her, she had been unforgivably guilty of "Touching with irreverent fingers / Hoary heads the Hub reveres."[79] With "The Radical Club," Bonner became well known in Boston—the *Boston Times* had such demand for her piece the paper reprinted and then brought it out as a separate pamphlet—but she was never secure.

It is interesting to note that while the Radical Club was not a women's club, it was one of very few intellectual clubs with a powerful and influential membership that included women. In fact, in this club all of the powerful female literati—Julia Ward Howe, Louise Chandler Moulton, Harriet Beecher Stowe, Lydia Maria Child, and Mary Sargent, for example—were members. It was, perhaps, the only club in which serious dialogue occurred among the eminent literati of both genders, and it had widespread admiration among the reading public, for the group published its essays in the *New York Tribune*. One admirer wrote to "the members of Radical Club . . . that for months I read what the great men and women who compose this body have said; and I have learned to love them all."[80] It was foolish to offend them.

Even Longfellow could not smooth the way to all places as time went on. No one openly rejected his protégée, but she was wounded by social slight after social slight. After one literary breakfast to which she was not invited, she wrote him: "And indeed I should have enjoyed seeing and hearing all those lovely people. . . . Do tell me that it would not have been *possible* for you to have procured me an invitation. It is the only thing that can soothe my regret. Horrid Mr. Howells—he *might* have—"[81] Finally, in the face of the enemies she had made, not by her lack of talent but by her "unusual" situation in what she had dubbed "the moral lighthouse" of Boston and her seeming disrespect for the "Hoary heads" of that city, she had limited even the good efforts of a protector such as Longfellow.

And she did so knowing fully how precarious her situation had been:

I do not know whether I have changed or whether it is the thought of having Lilian with me, that influences me. . . . I could even find it in my heart to wish that I had not written the "Radical Club." I want no more enemies; but only friends among those who are strong and good. If Mrs. Julia Ward Howe were not so brilliant and busy a woman I should hope to gain her friendship. She has been very lovely to me; and no one has ever fascinated me more. Do you know if she has returned from Europe?[82]

Bonner, in this letter of 1877, may have been maturing; as she planned to bring her daughter to Boston and establish a home there, she was contemplating a protective friendship with a socially secure woman at a time when she appears to have found a formula for life in Boston that would be above reproach: "In the past perhaps there has been something unusual in my position—something difficult of explanation to a stranger; but as a *mother* living in Boston according to her husband's wish for the education of their child, no gossip could touch me."[83]

Bonner's life in Boston was difficult not simply because of her "unusual" situation. Her experiences, despite the protection of "the great grey patriarch," forged the writer out of the young Southern girl, but by severity rather than any lasting boon from her patron. Her failed marriage left her persistently concerned about money, for after a brief attempt at reconciliation in 1879, she realized she could hope for no support for herself or her daughter. In 1878 she lost her brother and father to yellow fever; she had returned to Holly Springs to nurse them, but was unable to save them. Since her father died intestate, she was forced into dealings with her brother-in-law (her own husband's brother) that brought about a breach with her sister and forced her to depend almost totally upon her writing to support herself, her daughter, and their aunt. By 1880 she left Boston to spend a year in Illinois, where after establishing residency she filed for a divorce. This she obtained in May 1881. In the last two years of her life, she tried frantically to keep writing, to collect her stories into three volumes, and to establish her small family in Holly Springs.[84] After such difficulties, she faced the last one—a breast cancer that caused her great pain for more than a year before it finally killed her on 22 July 1883.

Circumstances had forced Bonner to mature; slowly she had grown less and less able to sustain the habitual demeanor of a young Southern girl in need of a protector. Although she always cherished and respected Longfellow, she finally made little use of his mentorship. Perhaps the saddest irony of her life was, as Robert Pierle suggests, that ultimately her attachment to Longfellow, that "living monument to the romantic movement in America . . . sank her name into near oblivion for the past century." Pierle explains that as Longfellow's protégée, "the name of Sherwood Bonner was tied irrevocably to an unfashionable movement in American literature. . . . It may be that [Longfellow's] own well-intentioned aid was the very thing which has thus far prevented others from thinking of her" as Longfellow did—as "the American writer of the future."[85]

When we examine a friendship such as the one between Longfellow and Bonner, we are faced with the cultural imperatives that created it and, sadly, those that weakened it. Through her energetic attempt to ingratiate herself into the society of the North she discovered her allegiance to the South; through her attempt to enter the literary scene in Boston she discovered a social power that could fashion such formidable enemies that one needed powerful friends; through her attempt to become a writer who could support herself she learned how to write and found her identity. Had she lived at a later time, Bonner might not have felt the need to rely so heavily upon the help of others—ironically, to do what she finally did, single-handed. She might have realized that her strong, though sorely tested, sense of self resisted not only the notion of mentorship but the obligation to acquiesce to established order. Rather than sabotage her own gifts and risk the loss of truly generous friendships, she might have realized what she had been able to accomplish independently. Freed from the adolescent pose she had assumed, perhaps to compensate for her "unusual" situation, she might have challenged the system rather than been beaten by its silence. The largest irony of all, and the one that extends Bonner's story to many women of her time, is that during a time when our culture called so loudly for a new, American identity, for a voice that would speak through the power of self-definition, something, some set of mores, muted the voices of so many women.

Notes

1. My spelling of Katharine Sherwood Bonner McDowell's name is taken from George Polhemus, "The Correct Spelling of Sherwood Bonner's name," *Notes and Queries* 7 (July 1960): 265. Polhemus points out that Bonner's name "is frequently misspelled in standard reference books." He explains the historical reasons for variant spellings and cites primary documents, most importantly the writer's will, for the definitive spelling.

2. *Harper's Weekly*, 11 August 1883, 503.

3. Hubert McAlexander, Jr., "A Reappraisal of Sherwood Bonner's *Like unto Like*," *Southern Literary Journal* 10 (1978):106.

4. Rayburn S. Moore, "'Merlin and Vivien'? Some Notes on Sherwood Bonner and Longfellow," *Mississippi Quarterly* 28 (1975):184.

5. Jean Nosser Biglane, "An Annotated and Indexed Edition of the Letters of Sherwood Bonner" (Master's thesis, Mississippi State University, 1968), 26.

6. Barbara Welter, "The Cult of True Womanhood, 1820–1860," *American Quarterly* 18 (1966):151–174.

7. Nina Baym, "Melodramas of Beset Manhood: How Theories of American Fiction Exclude Women Authors," *American Quarterly* 33 (1981):123–139.

8. Hubert H. McAlexander, *The Prodigal Daughter: A Biography of Sherwood Bonner* (Baton Rouge: Louisiana State University Press, 1981).

9. Sherwood Bonner, *Suwanee River Tales* (Boston: Roberts Brothers, 1884), 8.

10. Barbara Welter, "Anti-Intellectualism and the American Woman," *Mid-America* 48 (1966):258–270.

11. William L. Frank, *Sherwood Bonner* (Boston: Twayne, 1976), 23.

12. Sherwood Bonner, *Like unto Like* (New York: Harper and Brothers, 1878), 17.

13. McAlexander, *Prodigal Daughter*, 9.

14. Ibid., 15.

15. Several biographers discuss Bonner's experiences during the six months that she lived with her aunt while the war was going on. Her own account is "From 60 to 65," *Lippincott's* 18 (October 1876): 500–509, in which she tells a story of outwitting some Yankee soldier who intended "confiscating" her aunt's mules.

16. McAlexander, *Prodigal Daughter*, 19.

17. *Harper's Weekly*, 11 August 1883, 503.

18. William Lake Frank, ed., "Sherwood Bonner's Diary for the Year 1869," *Notes on Mississippi Writers* 3 (Winter 1970):111–130; 4 (Fall 1971):64–83; 4 (Spring 1971):22–40.

19. Frank, "Diary," 4:37.

20. Ibid., 4:33.

21. Ibid., 4:39.

22. Ibid., 4:77.

23. Ibid., 4:31.

24. Ibid., 4:78.

25. Ibid., 4:38.

26. Ibid., 4:34.

27. Ibid., 4:70.

28. Ibid., 3:119.

29. Ibid., 4:39.

30. Ibid., 3:124.

31. Bonner, *Like unto Like*, 139.

32. McAlexander, *Prodigal Daughter*, 49.

33. Ibid., 44.

34. In her letter of 13 November 1873 (Biglane, "Letters," 26), Bonner explained her intentions to her sister: "I have vowed never to cost him another cent, and perhaps if those who blame me in my present course *knew all—which no one that lives will ever—*they would judge me far differently."

35. William Dean Howells, *Literary Friends and Acquaintance: A Personal Retrospect of American Authorship* (New York: Harper and Brothers, 1900), 12–13.

36. Ibid., 181.

37. Sherwood Bonner, "From the 'Hub': A Southern Girl's Experience of Life in New England," *Memphis Avalanche*, 15 March 1874, 2.

38. Frank, *Sherwood Bonner*, 47.

39. *Harper's Weekly*, 11 August 1883, 503.

40. Biglane, "Letters," 26–27.

41. McAlexander, *Prodigal Daughter*, 51.

42. Biglane, "Letters," 29.

43. McAlexander, *Prodigal Daughter*, 57.

44. Longfellow wrote fifty-nine letters to Bonner, many of them in French. In her preface to *Suwanee River Tales*, Sophia Kirk claimed to have them in her possession. Following that, B. M. Drake, in his essay, "Sherwood Bonner," in *Southern Writers: Biographical and Critical Studies*, ed. William M. Baskerville 2 vols. (Nashville: Publishing House of the M. E. Church, South, 1903), quotes from several Longfellow letters to Bonner, having had the letters in his possession. Since then, however, the whereabouts of these letters is unknown.

45. Edward Wagenknecht, *Longfellow: A Full-Length Portrait* (New York: Longmans, Green, 1955), 283.

46. McAlexander, *Prodigal Daughter*, 222.

47. Moore, "'Merlin and Vivien'?" 182.

48. McAlexander, *Prodigal Daughter*, 222.

49. Samuel Longfellow, ed., *Life of Henry Wadsworth Longfellow* (Boston: Houghton Mifflin, 1893). See McAlexander, *Prodigal Daughter*, 221, for some instances in which Longfellow's diary was edited to excise mention of Bonner.

50. McAlexander, *Prodigal Daughter*, 222.

51. All biographers of Bonner discuss *The Story of Margaret Kent*, noting the similarities of the main characters to Bonner and Longfellow. Some mention the possibility that Kirk merely finished the novel begun by Bonner, but only McAlexander in *The Prodigal Daughter* makes a detailed and convincing case for such a claim.

52. Alexander Bondurant, "Sherwood Bonner: Her Life and Place in the Literature of the South," *Publications of the Mississippi Historical Society* 2 (June 1898): 44.

53. Andrew Hilen, ed., *The Letters of Henry Wadsworth Longfellow*, 6 vols. (Cambridge: Harvard University Press, 1982), 5:10.

54. Wagenknecht, *Longfellow*. Wagenknecht "glance[s] at his friendships with women during the twenty-one years of life which remained to him" (278)

after Fanny Appleton Longfellow's death. See pages 278–288 for his discussion of these friendships.

55. Biglane, "Letters," 48.

56. Hilen, *Letters of Longfellow*, 6:109.

57. Biglane, "Letters," 68.

58. Drake, "Sherwood Bonner," 2:85.

59. Frank, *Sherwood Bonner*, 134–135.

60. McAlexander, *Prodigal Daughter*, 83.

61. Lilian Whiting, *Boston Days* (Boston: Little, Brown, 1902), 276–277.

62. Biglane, "Letters," 31–32.

63. Hilen, *Letters of Longfellow*, 6:394.

64. Biglane, "Letters," 64.

65. Ibid.

66. Ibid., 96.

67. Sherwood Bonner, "Sherwood Bonner's Letter: Longfellow's Home —Its History," *Memphis Avalanche*, 26 December 1875, 2.

68. Howells, *Literary Friends*, 197.

69. The text of this letter from the Emerson Collection, Houghton Library, Harvard University, is provided in McAlexander's *Prodigal Daughter*, 60. It does not appear in the Biglane collection of Bonner's letters (see note 4 above).

70. Hilen, *Letters of Longfellow*, 6:204, 347.

71. Howells, *Literary Friends*, 199.

72. George Polhemus, "Longfellow's Uncompleted Review of *Like unto Like*," *Notes and Queries* 6 (February 1959):48–49.

73. George Polhemus, "An Uncollected Longfellow Poem," *Notes and Queries* 9 (March 1962): 96–97.

74. Sherwood Bonner, *Dialect Tales* (New York: Harpers, 1883).

75. Biglane, "Letters," 74.

76. Ibid., 111.

77. Ibid., 83.

78. Sherwood Bonner, "The Radical Club: A Poem Respectfully Dedicated to the Infinite by 'An Atom,'" *Boston Times*, 8 May 1875.

79. *The Radical Club: A Poem Respectfully Dedicated to an Atom by a Chip* (Boston: Boston Times Publishing, 1876).

80. Mary Sargent, *Sketches and Reminiscences of the Radical Club of Chestnut Street, Boston* (Boston: James R. Osgood, 1880), 396.

81. Biglane, "Letters," 115–116.

82. Ibid., 83.

83. Ibid.

84. Bonner published *Dialect Tales* in 1883, and *Suwanee River Tales* was published posthumously in 1884. She had begun to prepare a third collection, which she called *Romances*, but died before it was completed.

85. Robert C. Pierle, "Sherwood Who? A Study in the Vagaries of Literary Evaluation," *Notes on Mississippi Writers* 1 (Spring 1968): 18–22.

JOANNE B. KARPINSKI

When the Marriage of True Minds Admits Impediments: Charlotte Perkins Gilman and William Dean Howells

AT FIRST GLANCE, the intellectual minuet between Charlotte Perkins Gilman and William Dean Howells seems vulnerable to Gertrude Stein's complaint about Gilman's onetime home of Oakland, California: "There isn't any *there*, there." Unlike the Larcom-Whittier relationship, for example, this one lacks an elaborate prior myth to deconstruct.[1] Nor is there a complex text of correspondence to (mis)-read, as in the case of Dickinson and Higginson. But postmodern criticism alerts us to the heuristic value of absence, allowing us to focus on Howells' cautious fulfillment of the mentorial role he had initiated with such rhetorical fervor. Sincere but correct, Howells was not suited by temperament or conviction to become the passionate champion that Gilman had hoped for.

Gilman's first major poem, "Similar Cases," was published in the April 1890 issue of the socialist periodical the *Nationalist*, where it attracted the appreciative attention of William Dean Howells. Gilman recorded his "unforgettable letter" and her reaction to it in her autobiography:

> DEAR MADAM,
> I have been wishing ever since I first read it—and I've read it many times with unfailing joy—to thank you for your poem in the April *Nationalist*. We have had nothing since the Biglow Papers half so good for a good cause as "Similar Cases."

And just now I've read in *The Woman's Journal* your "Women of To-day." It is as good almost as the other, and dreadfully true.

Yours sincerely,

Wm. Dean Howells

That was a joy indeed. . . . There was no man in the country whose good opinion I would rather have had. I felt like a real "author" at last.[2]

Gilman's enthusiastic response to Howells's letter may seem overdone to twentieth-century readers for whom Howells's reputation has been eclipsed, but in 1890 Howells was a name to conjure with. As editor of the prestigious *Atlantic Monthly*, as a contributor of fiction and reviews to such significant periodicals as the *Century* and *Scribner's*, and as writer of "The Editor's Easy Chair" column for *Harper's Monthly*, he was "in a position of greater prestige and authority than any other reformer of his time."[3] Thus, Gilman had good reason to be pleased. As fellow socialist Edward Bellamy wrote to Howells in thanks for his praise of *Dr. Heidenhoff's Process*, notice from such an august quarter was "as refreshing to me as you may suppose a note from Hawthorne in recommendation of one of your earlier efforts would have been to you."[4]

The esteem in which Howells held Gilman's writing receives forceful expression in his 1899 article, "The New Poetry," published in the *North American Review*:

Her civic satire is of a form which she herself invented; it recalls the work of no one else; you can say of it (and I have said this before), that since the Biglow Papers there has been no satire approaching it in the wit flashing from profound conviction . . . but the time has not yet come when we desire to have the Original Socialists for our ancestors, and I am afraid that the acceptance of Mrs. Stetson's [Gilman's first married name] satire is mostly confined to fanatics, philanthropists and other Dangerous Persons. But that need not keep us from owning its brilliancy.[5]

As Gloria Martin points out in her dissertation on women in Howells's criticism and fiction, the irony of Howells's assessment might seem at first to be directed against Gilman, but is in fact directed at his audience, "implying that only when the country has accepted the humane theories of socialism will Stetson's work become as respectable as Lowell's famous satire has now become." Martin characterizes this passage as "a rare acceptance of another author by Howells into the privacy of the editorial tone."[6]

Personal similarities and political sympathies disposed Howells to be appreciative of Gilman and her work. Both writers experienced financially insecure childhoods, with their mothers marshaling the family struggle for economic security. Each fought with recurring depression from adolescence until late in life. Gilman's affiliation with socialism came early and enthusiastically, while Howells embraced the same social philosophy later in life and more gradually. Never the ardent feminist that Gilman was, Howells nevertheless supported the cause of women's equality with a vigor unusual for a man of his times.

With so much in common, it would seem inevitable for the dean of American letters to foster the professional fortunes of the young woman whose work he praised so highly. Instead, Howells temporized, using his influence to get her work brought out by other publishers than those with which he was directly associated. Why did the budding mentorial relationship not flourish? Apparently, it suffered from a residual timorousness on Howells' part about the bitterness of Gilman's social indictment, even at its most humorous. Moreover, Howells' relationship with his oldest daughter and with the female writers whose work he did promote suggest a patriarchal temperament poorly suited both to Gilman's emotional needs and to her style of writing.

Gilman's father, Frederick Beecher Perkins, held a variety of editorial and library jobs while trying unsuccessfully to establish himself as a fiction writer. He left the family when Charlotte was nine, after increasingly lengthy periods of separation during which he left his family (four children, of whom only Charlotte and her older brother, Thomas, survived infancy) in the care of relatives. After his departure from the family scene, Charlotte's mother supported the household by taking in boarders or by acting as companion to invalid relations, since Frederick's contributions were both meager and irregular. Periodically, Gilman would attempt to reestablish contact with her absent father, but found him emotionally as well as physically distant.[7]

Howells's praise of her poetry and political opinions thus satisfied a deep thirst for something like paternal approval. However, Gilman could no more rephrase her polemics to please Howells's sense of decorum than she could retract the impolitic kiss she once offered her father in the Boston Public Library.

Like Gilman, Howells had spent his childhood wandering nomadically on the frontiers of respectable poverty. His father, William Cooper Howells, began married life as an itinerant printer. He moved rapidly into the editorial office, where radical opinions in both religion and politics often irritated his subscribers. His outspoken support of abolition and the Free-Soil party lost him several positions at newspapers run by the Whig party in Ohio, while his ardor for the mystical doctrines of Emanuel Swedenborg outstripped even the New Church loyalists of that state. The senior Howells had "the heroic superiority to mere events and shifts of fortune which was in keeping with his religion and his temperament as an idealist,"[8] but the loss of income and alienation from community life were more difficult for his wife and family to bear.

Staunchly loyal to her husband, Mary Dean Howells undertook the financial management of their affairs to protect the family from the consequences of his principled indifference to money. Like Mary Perkins, she took in boarders. When Howells again found editorial work in a more congenial political climate, she had title to the business and the property placed in her name and that of her oldest son.

These mothers, forced into roles of unusual self-reliance, were deeply influential on Gilman and Howells. Neither woman particularly liked the autonomy that was thrust upon her; Gilman's mother cast herself as the victim of fate, while Howells's steeled herself to endure what she could not cure. The frictions produced between their dislike of their new roles and their competence in pursuing them greatly affected their children.

Gilman alternately blamed her mother's smothering affection for driving her father away, admired her as a tower of strength in adversity, and resented the severity and irritability that her mother's overwhelming responsibilities had engendered. Howells idolized his father's principles, but keenly felt the consequences of his honoring them. As a result, his naturally lively affection for his mother grew into an attachment so fervent and idealized that it became unbearable for him to leave her, even for a brief period. Several times in his adolescence he was humiliated by having to return home from a job because of homesickness.

Ironically, Howells adopted toward his own family the role of Victorian paterfamilias despite the opportunity afforded by his upbringing to evade this stereotype, since his wife and oldest daughter suffered debilitating health conditions. His acquiescence to the prevailing mythology of gender had tragic consequences for the family. Convinced by the doctors he consulted that his daughter Winifred's reluctance to eat was psychological rather than physical in origin, Howells committed her to a variety of therapeutic regimes, and regarded her resistance to these as a contest of wills.[9] When a postmortem examination revealed an organic cause for her pain, Howells was devastated by remorse, although he accepted the doctors' reassurance that the problem could not have been discovered by the diagnostic procedures then available.[10] Even after her death, however, Howells continued to associate Winifred's symptoms with a level of intellectual activity deemed excessive for a woman.[11]

This inability of a loving and compassionate father to comprehend his intellectual daughter's illness seems the more poignant in that Howells himself periodically suffered from bouts of an acute but obscure malaise that left him unable to work or study. He recovered his health by resorting to the type of nature cure imposed on his daughter Winifred, but these breakdowns permanently dimmed the optimism of his earlier character.

Gilman's physical and emotional makeup, so similar to his own, might have disturbed Howells by its likeness to Winifred's as he understood it. Gilman's adult life alternated between periods of exultant productivity and paralyzing depression. Already at age fifteen she wrote to her long-absent father for "a good strong dose of advice" on this issue:

"Unstable as water, thou shalt not excel" said the patriarch to his son. The words often ring in my ears, and I sometimes feel, as if there was not hope, and the irrevocable Word of the Lord had pronounced my doom. That is in my intervals of depression; few and far between you may think, but it is not so. I often feel hopelessly despairing, at my total inability to *work*. [Emphasis in the original][12]

Adolescent hyperbole aside, this preoccupation with the necessity of useful work and the emotional obstacles to accomplishing it satisfactorily reappears in Gilman's letters and journal entries ever after. "Useful work" for Gilman always meant something creative or done for the public good. The traditional work of women exacerbated her depression, particularly after her marriage to Walter Stetson and the birth of their only child, Katherine.

Paradoxically, these depressions spurred her literary career. Her poem "The Answer," an outcry against the "work that brainless slaves might do" that ultimately kills an optimistic bride, won first prize for the year from the *Woman's Journal*; more important, it strengthened her affiliation with the American Woman Suffrage Organization, which sponsored the journal.[13] Also, Gilman's struggle with the misdirected therapy prescribed for her depression formed the anecdote for "The Yellow Wallpaper," the story for which she is best known today.

Unable to endure the tension between growing public success and domestic misery, Gilman sought professional help. Dr. S. Weir Mitchell, who had treated several of Gilman's Beecher relatives for "nervous ailments," prescribed his six-week "rest cure": bed rest, massage, lots of food, and complete avoidance of mental stimulation. Gilman followed the regimen under Mitchell's supervision, but once she returned home, his admonition—"live as domestic a life as possible. Have your child with you all the time. Have but two hours intellectual life a day. And never touch pen, brush or pencil as long as you live"[14]—drove her to the brink of mental collapse. In desperation, Gilman abandoned the regime and her household. The separation from Stetson became permanent; divorce followed soon after.

Curiously, this emancipation from traditional womanliness did not put an end to Gilman's depressive episodes. Any protracted contact with domesticity—her own or others'—tended to bring one on. She visited Jane Addams at Hull House and was so impressed by the "useful work" done there that she intended to stay on, but soon the drudgery and dreary climate overcame her. After an enthusiastic beginning, a trip to England to participate in the socialist experiments of the Fabians came to a similar end.

Gilman wrote in her memoir that "Mr. Howells told me that I was the only optimist reformer he ever met,"[15] but for much of his life this evaluation was true of Howells himself. Brought up in the golden age of American rural egalitarianism, Howells increasingly saw the values of that era sacrificed to the rampant acquisitiveness of the industrial Gilded Age. Two major influences on this altered point of view were the Haymarket bombing and Howells's introduction to the Christian Socialism of Tolstoy.

Howells was one of the few opinion leaders of the era to defend the Haymarket anarchists in print, and he was pilloried in the press for it. Although Howells vacillated for weeks after writing to the anarchists' defense attorney that he believed the defendants to be innocent, he ultimately acted courageously on the attorney's advice that Howells initiate a press campaign in their behalf. Thus it appears that fear of controversy alone cannot account for Howells's holding back in his mentorial relationship with Gilman.

Just at the time that he was forced to confront the accumulated shortcomings of his beloved Republic, Howells "became interested in the creed of Socialism," in which "the greatest influence . . . came to me through Tolstoy."[16] Tolstoy's repudiation of industrial society, based as it was on the Christian tenets Howells had imbibed as a youth, revived Howells' optimism by redirecting it:

Tolstoy gave me heart to hope that the world may yet be made
over in the image of Him who died for it. . . . He gave me new
criterions, new principles.[17]

Howells acted on his new convictions both in his own fiction and in
the editorial support he gave to other writers of similar persuasions. He
gave an enthusiastic review to Edward Bellamy's utopian novel *Looking
Backward*, which reversed the trend of mixed reviews and poor sales
that had initially greeted the book. Hamlin Garland credited Howells's
favorable review of *Main-Travelled Roads* with winning it a place in the
east. Thorstein Veblen's biographer noted that Howells's two laudatory
columns on *The Theory of the Leisure Class* "helped to make the book a
sensation."[18] And, at various times, Howells published his admiration
of Charlotte Perkins Gilman. Late in his career he praised her work as
"witty and courageous," adding that "the best things that have been said
about woman suffrage in our time have been said by Charlotte Perkins
Gilman."[19]

When Gilman received Howells's compliments on "Similar Cases,"
she sent a copy of his letter to her friend Martha Lane, with the following comments:

I'm glad you thought my poem funny. I herein boastfully enclose
a copy of a letter showing it was thought rather more of by some!
. . . Isn't that a delightful letter? I am so pleased too to find the
man thinks well of Nationalism in spite of its "flabby apostle."[20]

The "apostle" was Edward Bellamy, whose novel was helped to prominence by Howells's favorable review.

Gilman was prepared by nature and education to embrace the Nationalist creed, which expounded the necessity of the government's taking
complete control of the means of production in order to eradicate the
panoply of evils generated by laissez-faire economics. Like Howells,
Gilman had grown up in a family atmosphere suffused with belief in
progress. Her maternal relatives, the Nonconformist Beecher preachers,
extended from the spiritual to the social sphere their conviction that the
individual could improve his own life with the help of grace. Reading
lists compiled by her father nurtured this conviction into support for the
theories of the Reform Darwinists, who saw evolutionary progress as
the collective right and duty of the entire enlightened human species.

This linking of social progress to natural law appealed to Gilman's
personal tendency toward rational optimism and preference for provable

over revealed truth. For Gilman, the "will of God" meant "health, intelligence, normal development, beauty, joyous fulfillment of all life's processes," and she believed that "economic measures which promote such things must be in accordance with it."[21] As Howells had also done, Gilman rejected sectarian Christianity in favor of a God-ordered universe in which Christian ethics assisted the laws of evolution to pursue the perfection intended by the Creator. Both authors linked social responsibility to religious tenets rather than political ideology.

The family environment also oriented Gilman toward feminism. Her great-aunts included the novelist Harriet Beecher Stowe, Catharine Beecher (the architect of "domestic feminism"), and suffrage worker Isabella Beecher Hooker. Gilman came to know these women and their convictions during the extended family visits brought about by her father's lapses in financial support. From them she learned that women could have a stimulating intellectual and social life of their own, without standing in the shadow of husband or father, yet without sacrificing womanliness.

She also learned that exposing men's exploitation of women to public criticism would bring a storm of recrimination around a woman's head, but that a strong woman could survive it. Harriet Beecher Stowe provoked a considerable scandal when she insisted on publishing Lady Byron's accusation that her husband had seduced his half sister. Isabella Beecher Hooker caused a major rift in family relations by supporting fellow suffragist Victoria Woodhull's right to publish the story of Henry Ward Beecher's many lapses from the sexual propriety expected of a minister. These role models undoubtedly assisted Gilman in managing the spiteful publicity generated by her divorce as well as reinforcing her outspoken opinions about women's rights. Nationalism and feminism worked together, in Gilman's view; nationalism was "the most practical form of human development," but equality of the sexes was "the most essential condition of that development."[22]

For both Gilman and Howells, the political rights of women were founded on their equality with men. Howells was frequently misunderstood on this topic, because his fiction treats women evenhandedly rather than idealistically: *Dr. Breen's Practice*, for example, deals with the setbacks experienced by a female homeopathic doctor in her encounters with the male-dominant allopathic medical establishment; *A Woman's Reason* looks at the limited economic options open to a woman lacking a male protector; and *A Modern Instance* charts the catastrophic effects of the stigma of divorce on a woman's life. In his "Editor's Easy Chair" column, Howells argued that women had the duties of citizens, and therefore should have citizens' rights as well. Since women lived within the State, they ought to be able to vote on its practices, and since they had to pay taxes, the principle of "no taxation without representation" ought to entitle women to suffrage.[23]

Howells wrote on women's issues as part of a general commitment to social reform. Gilman did the reverse: she committed herself to a general reform of "masculinist" social order as a precondition to the achievement of equality for women. Her monumental study of *Women and Economics* (1898) won her international recognition. It was followed by *Concerning Children* (1900), *The Home: Its Work and Influence* (1903), *Human Work* (1904), *Man Made World; or, Our Androcentric Culture* (1911), and *His Religion and Hers: A Study of the Faith of Our Fathers and the Work of Our Mothers* (1923). For seven years (1909–1916), she published a quarterly journal called the *Forerunner*, writing all the columns, fiction, poetry, and even the advertisements herself. She supported this endeavor by lecturing and contributing to other publications. The *Forerunner* addressed feminist issues great and small: suffrage; dress reform; sexual autonomy and family planning; the efficient management of housework, cooking, and child care by experts; men's oppression of women and women's oppression of themselves.

The quarterly serialized Gilman's utopian novel, *Herland*, which pictures the successful operation of a society entirely without men. Miraculously endowed with the power to reproduce by parthenogenesis when a catastrophe permanently isolates the women at home from the men who have gone off to war, the female citizens of Herland put the stamp of nurture on traditionally male domains. When a trio of male adventurers stumbles upon this sanctuary, their efforts to comprehend its extraordinary environment and to explain the workings of their own society produce a humorous and satirical indictment of sex-specific divisions in human activity. Thus, this utopia avoids the usual pitfall of the genre, namely ponderous didacticism, a fault that mars its sequel, *With Her in Ourland*.

Howells, too, used the utopian genre to envision a society based on gender equality. His Altrurian romances assume that an enlightened proletariat would use the democratic process to ensure that men and women have not only equal opportunities but equal obligations in the economic, political, and domestic spheres. With women freed from the pressure of supporting the entire family unit, both sexes of Altrurians are able to achieve their full human potential. Curiously, the American woman who travels to Altruria and marries there follows a career path not unlike Gilman's: she becomes a traveling lecturer, combining intellectual work and domestic chores through a communal housekeeping arrangement. This heroine's name, Eveleth Strange, brings together the female archetypes of Eve and Lilith without reference to the sanctified, pedestaled archetype of the Virgin.

More important to the cause of gender equality than Howells's fiction, however, was his editorial support of women writers. In "Recollections of an *Atlantic* Editorship," Howells lists nineteen women whose work appeared during his tenure and adds that he does not know whether he published more men or women,

> but if any one were to prove that there were more women than men I should not be surprised. . . . For in our beloved republic of letters the citizenship is not reserved solely to males of twenty-one and over.[24]

As Ann Douglas Wood points out, Howells held up for special praise several representatives of the local-color school, finding that their "directness and simplicity" is of a piece with "the best modern work everywhere."[25] While the high quality of the local colorists' literary achievement and the sincerity of Howells's support for them are incontestable, these women's motives and methods are so different from Gilman's that it is easy to see why Howells, admiring the former, would be disconcerted by the latter.

The qualities of style that Howells praised in the work of the local colorists were on the whole foreign to Gilman's. While the local colorists wrote in the realistic mode, Gilman's fiction and poetry were unabashedly romantic in the intensity and extravagance of her expression. In general, Howells disparaged the romance genre for presenting women with unwholesomely exaggerated role models, and for making it possible for them to take refuge from their real problems in a world of fictional triumphs. Gilman's utopian novels and serial fiction could be seen as vulnerable to such a critique, but oddly enough in this context, the Gilman short story that Howells elected to anthologize belongs to the Gothic tradition. Even when Howells writes about Gilman's poems, which do not exhibit the presumed defects of the romance genre, a consistent motif of his letters to Gilman is enthusiasm for her convictions tempered by genteel consternation over her verbal deportment.

The restraint that differentiated the local colorists' literary style from Gilman's extended to their professional styles as well. Contrasting them to the assertively professional women of the earlier sentimentalist school, Wood notes that the local colorists tended to be reclusive "pure artists," neither subscribing to the cult of domesticity nor competing in the male-dominated marketplace. While the former quality places their writings in the artistic and social vanguard, the latter preserved their personal aura of conventional femininity. That both qualities figured centrally in Howells' esteem of these women can be seen in his correspondence with and about them.

In an 1885 letter to Edmund Gosse, for example, Howells expresses his astonishment that "Charles Egbert Craddock" turns out to be a woman writer in terms that revere her feminine weakness:

> We are just now in an excitement as great as the Gosse boom at its wildest, about Charles Egbert Craddock, the author of the Tennessee mountain stories, who has turned up in Boston, a little *girl-cripple* [emphasis in original], not so big as Pilla. . . . She has a most manful and womanly soul in her poor, twisted little body. Her stories are extraordinary; but I dare say you know them.[26]

A similar emphasis appears in a fulsome but domesticated compliment to Sarah Orne Jewett:

> You have a precious gift, and you must know it, and can be none the worse for your knowledge. We all have a tender pleasure in your work, which there is no name for but love. I think *no* one [emphasis in original] has shown finer art in a way, than you, and that something which is so much better than art, besides. Your voice is like a thrush's in the din of all the literary noises that stun us so.[27]

It is hard to recognize in this rhetorical throwback to the "sweet singer" that stereotyped an earlier generation of literary women the same stylist whom Howells had praised in the *Cosmopolitan Magazine* for "the perfect artistic restraint, the truly Greek temperance" of her prose.[28]

In several respects, Gilman's career differed from those of the local colorists whom Howells deservedly placed on a critical pedestal. Gilman made her living by writing, while of that group "only Freeman and Stuart supported themselves by their pens."[29] In addition, she earned money from public speaking, still a daring occupation for a female at the turn of the century. She wrote and spoke explicitly about the invidious way "in which the sexuo-economic relation has operated in our species,"[30] while the local colorists' frequent focus on female protagonists living independently from men only implicitly addressed the material price paid for this autonomy. Neither in their person nor in their work did the local colorists challenge conventionally imposed standards of feminine virtue, while Gilman did both.

These differences are significant because Howells indulged in the unfortunate habit of impugning the femininity of women writers with whom he disagreed. He once wrote to Henry James about his unpleasant meeting with "a certain celebrated lady novelist, who once turned to criticism long enough to devote me to execration" that "I find I don't take these things Pickwickianly; but she avenged me by the way she dressed and the way she talked. I wish I could present you with the whole scene, but I mustn't."[31]

It should be noted that Howells's admiration for Gilman's writing evidently did not extend to appreciation for her unconventional domestic arrangements: her divorce from Walter Stetson and relinquishment of their daughter's custody to him and his new wife, who happened to be Gilman's best friend and her housemate during her year of separation (Hill asserts that Gilman encouraged Stetson to court her friend).[32] He attached the following acidulous biographical account to an 1898 letter from Gilman recommending some stories written by her "friend and co-mother," Grace Ellery Channing:

> Mrs. Stetson's "co-mother" is married to Mrs. Stetson's divorced husband. Mrs. S. attended the wedding and gave her young daughter to her "co-mother" as a wedding present.[33]

The scandalous "abandonment" of her five-year-old daughter, Katherine, to the child's father and stepmother on the undoubtedly accurate grounds that they were better suited both temperamentally and economically to take care of her haunted Gilman's career as a writer and lecturer for years; however, Howells's privately expressed opinion did not prevent him, or his wife and daughter, from socializing with Gilman. He attended her lectures—indeed, on one occasion she substituted for him on the lecture platform when he was unable to keep a speaking engagement—and she visited Howells's family at home. Gilman regarded this friendship as a "special pleasure."[34]

Howells could offer unqualified enthusiasm for Gilman's "Similar Cases" because it satirized resistance to social change without going into embarrassing particulars. Written in the "thump and swack" meter popular to nineteenth-century oratorical verse, the poem's three "cases" represent stages in evolutionary development: the Eohippus, the Anthropoidal Ape, and the Neolithic Man. Each of these announces to his coeval creatures his vision of his future greatness, but is hooted down by them on the basis of his present unprepossessing status. "You would have to change your nature," argue the soon-to-be evolutionary castoffs against the aspirations of the progressive species.

The best verse of the poem shows the Neolithic Man's unfazed awareness that civilization will have its pitfalls as well as peaks:

> We are going to live in cities!
>   We are going to fight in wars!
> We are going to eat three times a day
>   Without the natural cause! . . .
> We are going to have Diseases!
>   And Accomplishments!! And Sins!!![35]

This irony within an irony is typical of Gilman's satire at its sharpest. The barb seems at first somewhat softened by the fact that the "similar cases" under discussion have come to view from the pre-societal past, but a missing case is clearly implied by the "you would have to change your nature" refrain—that of women, whose efforts to evolve into fully human dignity and competence were regularly condemned as "unnatural" in Gilman's era.

In his letter congratulating Gilman on the appearance of "Similar Cases," Howells also complimented her poem "Women of Today" (that Howells read it in the *Woman's Journal*, sponsored by the American Woman Suffrage Association, testifies to his sympathetic interest in this issue). This short work chastises the "women of today who fear so much / The women of the future," and who proudly cling to the traditional roles of mother, wife, and housekeeper. The poet questions whether the "woman of today" indeed fulfills these roles: as a housekeeper, unlike her ancestors, she only keeps servants, and she cannot even keep them in service for long; as a wife, who in principle holds the key to her husband's heart, she must fear the consequences of the prevailing sexual double standard; and as a mother, she must suffer the grievous knowledge that half of the children born in the nineteenth century were doomed to die in infancy. The jeremiad predicts that the "woman of today" will never improve her blighted lot unless she can recognize her contentment as an unenlightened sham:

And still the wailing babies come and go,
And homes are waste, and husband's hearts fly far,
There is no hope until you dare to know
The thing you are![36]

Howells somewhat overstated the case when he told Gilman that this
poem "is as good almost as the other"—it lacks the lash of wit to give it
energy, and tries to supply the missing verve with exclamation points
—but he was no doubt correct in calling it "dreadfully true." However,
as will be seen more strongly in his response to "The Yellow Wallpaper," the word "dreadfully" and its synonyms apparently cut two ways
in Howells's lexicon: the production of dread in the reader may be a
worthy aesthetic goal, yet not be worthwhile as a publisher's risk.

Six months after his first paean, Howells again wrote to Gilman, this
time on letterhead from the *Cosmopolitan Magazine*'s editorial depart-
ment:

Do you think you could send me for this magazine something as
good and wicked as *Similar Cases*, and of the like destructive tendency? And could you send it "in liking?"[37]

Gilman sent him "The Amoeboid Cell," which recounts a conversation
between an amoeboid cell and a specialized one, in which the latter
urges the advantages of development upon the former.

The amoeba resists the motion, unwilling to lose its personal freedom. The specialized cell retorts that in its present state the amoeba is
just a "speck in the slime at the birthday of time," subject to mass death
at the whim of nature. In contrast, the specialized cell enjoys the fruits
of cooperation, while retaining the pleasures of diversity's "limitless
range."

In the last stanza, the amoeba appears to get its just deserts, but the
smugness of the specialized cell is also undermined by the final line of
the poem:

Just then came a frost and the Amoeboid Cell
Died out by the billion again;
But the Specialized Cell
In the body felt well
And rejoiced in his place in the brain!
The dead level of life with a brain![38]

Howells's letter of response to this offering giveth with one hand and taketh away with the other, as do many of his assessments of Gilman's writing:

> The Amoeboid Cell is so good that I think it deserves working over more carefully, and condensing a good deal. I don't like any part of the joke that's in the spelling, like "individualitee" and "anybodee," and I think your moral is a little too sharply pointed. Couldn't it be incidental, somehow? Perhaps I am over-particular, but then I always think I am worth pleasing, as an admirer of your gifts.[39]

The available correspondence does not indicate whether Gilman made the effort to please the "admirer of her gifts," but "The Amoeboid Cell" never appeared in the *Cosmopolitan Magazine*.

Gilman's and Howells's estimates vary about his role in the publication of "The Yellow Wallpaper." By Gilman's description, Howells was an ineffective advocate for the story:

> This ["The Yellow Wallpaper"] I sent to Mr. Howells, and he tried to have the *Atlantic Monthly* print it, but Mr. Scudder, then the editor, sent it back with this brief card:
>
> Dear Madam:
> Mr. Howells has handed me this story. I could not forgive myself if I made others as miserable as I have made myself![40]

After lamenting Scudder's lapse of perception ("I suppose he would have sent back one of Poe's on the same ground"), Gilman notes that she then put the story in the hands of a commercial agent, who placed it with the *New England Journal*. The agent never transmitted the *Journal*'s stipend to the author.

In "A Reminiscent Introduction" to the anthology in which Howells finally reprinted "The Yellow Wallpaper," however, he credits himself with assuring the story's first appearance in print:

> It wanted at least two generations [after Poe] to freeze our young blood with Mrs. Perkins Gilman's story of *The Yellow Wallpaper*, which Horace Scudder (then of *The Atlantic*) said in refusing it that it was so terribly good that it ought never to be printed. But

terrible and too wholly dire as it was, I could not rest until I had corrupted the editor of *The New England Magazine* into publishing it. Now that I have got it into my collection here, I shiver over it as much as I did when I first read it in manuscript, though I agree with the editor of *The Atlantic* of the time that it was too terribly good to be printed.[41]

While Gilman could scarcely blame Howells for Scudder's refusal to print "The Yellow Wallpaper" in the *Atlantic Monthly*, she either did not know about Howells' efforts to "corrupt" the editor of the *New England Journal* or did not appreciate them sufficiently to take note of them in her memoir, where she records only the activities of the tightfisted commercial agent.

In addition to accounting himself more active in the publication of "The Yellow Wallpaper" than Gilman acknowledged, Howells's introductory assessment of the piece in his anthology suggests—by its repetition of the adjective "terrible"—the grounds for his reluctance to press Scudder more assertively for the story's publication. During his own tenure as editor of the *Atlantic Monthly*, Howells had a taste of the consequences that could attend the publication of material "too wholly dire" for the public taste.

In September 1869, Howells brought out Harriet Beecher Stowe's "True Story of Lady Byron's Life," which included Lady Byron's accusation that her husband had committed incest with his half sister. The content of the charge was moral indignation about the things a married woman must endure with patience, but public indignation with the *Atlantic Monthly* for putting such shocking material in print cost the magazine 15,000 subscribers.[42] Since Stowe was absolutely determined to publish her exposé somewhere, and since Howells wanted to keep her contributing to the *Atlantic Monthly* despite his reservations about any particular article, he could hardly have refused to print it. This episode, however—the third publication scandal to plague the magazine during Howells's association with it, although the only one for which he was accountable—made Howells somewhat more chary of offending the subscribers' sense of decency. This hard-earned editorial caution would have led Howells to respect Scudder's decision not to "make others miserable" by publishing "The Yellow Wallpaper."

Gilman was not unaware of Howells's aesthetically if not politically conservative tastes. Although she valued his praise, his writing was

never a favorite of mine you know. His work is exquisite, painfully exquisite, but save for that Chinese delicacy of workman-
ship it seems to me of small artistic value. And its truth is that of
the elaborate medical chart, the scientific photograph.[43]

On the other hand, she apparently was not aware of the painful personal connection that Howells had had with the rest-cure regimen lam-
basted by "The Yellow Wallpaper."

S. Weir Mitchell, who had supervised Gilman's disastrous rest cure,
was a personal friend and artistic discovery of Howells, who published
some of the doctor's fiction in the *Atlantic Monthly*. Mitchell had also
prescribed this treatment for Winifred Howells, who gained physical
strength but died of "a sudden failure of the heart" while under his care.

It is unclear whether Howells understood that Mitchell's methods
were the particular target of Gilman's wrath in "The Yellow Wallpaper"
at the time that she sent it to him for the *Atlantic Monthly*. Not until her
letter to Howells accepting his invitation to anthologize the story in
1919 does Gilman make this explicit:

> Did you know that that one piece of "literature" of mine was pure
> propaganda? I was under Dr. Weir Mitchell's treatment, at 27.
> . . . I tried it one summer, and went as near lunacy as one can, and
> come back. So I wrote this, and sent him a copy. He made no re-
> sponse, but years after some one told me that he had told a friend
> "I have completely altered my treatment of neurasthenia since
> reading "The Yellow Wallpaper." Triumph![44]

Gilman's failure to credit Howells with facilitating the initial appearance of "The Yellow Wallpaper" in print follows a pattern of denying
the actual contributions of those who, in Gilman's opinion, ought to
have done more. Her correspondence with Lester Ward, the father of
American sociology, shows a similar reaction.[45]

In 1893, the year following the publication of "The Yellow Wallpaper," Gilman brought out a volume of her collected poetry, entitled *In
This Our World*. Again, Howells sent Gilman a letter praising the
poems and their author in the warmest terms:

> I am ashamed not to have said long ago how much pleasure we
> have all taken in your book of poems. They are the wittiest and
> wisest things that have been written this many a long day and
> year. You are not only the prophetess of the new religion (in the

new conception of religion) but you speak with a tongue like a two-edged sword.

Once again, however, Howells's reservations begin to appear even as he praises:

> I rejoice in your gift *fearfully* [emphasis added], and wonder how much more you will do with it. I can see how far and deep you have thought about the things at hand, and I have my bourgeois moments when I could have wished you for success's sake to have been less frank. But of course you know that you stand in your own way![46]

Thus it comes as no surprise that Howells graciously declines the opportunity to escort any more of Gilman's poems into print:

> I like your Immortality, but I can understand why magazines would not. As to the volume of poetry, I suggest your sending it by Ripley Hitchcock, the literary man of Appletons, who have just brought out Bellamy's book. He will give it intelligent attention, and I beg you to quote me as cordially in its favor as your self respect will allow. I will tell him you are going to send it.[47]

The poem that magazines would not like depicts a conscious being in various stages of evolution: as grass, ape, man, and immortal soul. In its earliest avatars, the conscious being passively endured its fate or futilely rebelled against it. As man, it self-consciously gloried in its existence and learned to aspire to immortality. So far so good, in terms of conventional Christian evolution. The penultimate stanza, however, attacks the vision of the afterlife's reward as "hypothetical" as well as egotistical ("In this an endless, boundless bliss I see, — / Eternal me!"), while the final verse contradicts the idea of divine providence with a perspective supremely indifferent to human events:

> When I was a man, no doubt I used to care
> About the little things that happened there,
> And fret to see the years keep going by,
> And nations, families, and persons die.[48]

The bromidic concluding couplet—"I didn't much appreciate life's plan / When I was a man"—can hardly counteract the acid tone of the poem as a whole.

230 JOANNE B. KARPINSKI

Since Gilman published only the one collection of poetry, it is not clear whether Howells' letter refers to a projected second volume or to the 1898 reprint of *In This Our World*. In either case, Gilman's self-respect apparently would not allow her to quote Howells cordially enough to "the literary man at Appletons"; no second volume ever appeared, and the copyright to the 1898 reprint was entered by Small, Maynard and Company of Boston.

Except for including "The Yellow Wallpaper" in *The Great Modern American Stories*, Howells's mentorial efforts for Gilman did not operate on the practical level; however, he never ceased to offer her sweeping moral support on the order of "when the gods really wake up and begin to behave justly you will have no cause to complain."[49] Why did Howells prefer to leave Gilman's career in the lap of the gods when he took other women writers under his own wing? The evidence suggests that while Howells held in high esteem Gilman's passionate defense of principles he, too, held sacred, he could not espouse her rhetorical and personal flamboyance. From childhood on, the ideal of the gracious lady exercised a powerful attraction over him. As Edwin H. Cady notes:

> His recollections of their drawing rooms and conservatories in *Years of My Youth* is almost a hymn to the ladyhood he learned to worship in Columbus. In later life he became disenchanted of almost all his other romanticisms. But he never entirely sloughed off his worship of the lady, though by means of it he gained deep insights into the nature of the civilized woman.[50]

Even on the issue of women's suffrage, about which Howells believed Gilman to have been the best and wisest exponent, his approach is genteel where Gilman's is wryly impatient. Howells believed that suffrage would come to women (in some unspecified, spontaneous manner) when women themselves sufficiently wanted this right. Gilman gleefully satirized this point of view in a poem entitled "Women Do Not Want It":

> What women want has never been a strongly acting cause
> When woman has been wronged by man in churches, customs, laws;
> Why should he find this preference so largely in his way
> When he himself admits the right of what we ask to-day?[51]

Perhaps, too, Gilman sought a mentorial relationship with Howells at a level of emotional intensity to which he was not prepared to respond.

Her letters of compliment to him are couched in no more exaggerated terms than his to her, but women of that period were expected to express themselves to men more circumspectly; apparently even Walter Stetson felt that his wife's demonstrations of emotional need were a little too frank.[52] Their correspondence indicates that Gilman initiated all the meetings that took place between them, with Howells occasionally (though graciously) demurring on the grounds of his own or his family's ill health.

Certainly her need for his assistance was great, since she published almost all of her works at her own expense, but the directness of her appeal may have put off a man accustomed to being the patriarch in such situations—he wrote to Lucy Larcom, for example, "You take rejection so sweetly that I have scarcely the heart to accept anything of yours."[53]

In the letter that thanks Howells for wishing to include "The Yellow Wallpaper" in his anthology, Gilman anxiously seeks his approval of her magazine:

> Please—did you ever receive either one of the bound volumes of the first year of my precious *Forerunner*? . . . I did want you to notice *my baby*, and tried twice, letter and book.[54]

Howells's one-line reply simply regrets that he never received her book, ignoring her plea for reassurance.

Summing up the successes and failures of her efforts to place work in magazines other than the *Forerunner*, Gilman made a list of those who were "good friends among editors." Howells's name is not among them, although she claims to have had so many that she can "by no means remember them all."[55] Recalling Theodore Dreiser's gloomy advice to "consider more what the editors want," Gilman explains the reason she ignored his counsel:

> There are those who write as artists, real ones; they often find it difficult to consider what the editor wants. There are those who write to earn a living, who if they succeed, *must* please his purchasers, the public, so we have this great trade of literary catering. But if one writes to express important truths, needed yet unpopular, the market is necessarily limited.[56]

Taking into account its defensively self-congratulatory tone, this explanation seems essentially valid with respect to Howells's unwillingness to publish Gilman's work himself or to strongly advocate its publication by his powerful friends.

It was undoubtedly easier for Howells to praise Gilman's opinions than to take responsibility for them. Nevertheless, Howells's public votes of confidence in Gilman's writing enhanced its credibility and gave it a broader forum than it had achieved on its own. Despite his reservations, Howells kept faith with Gilman—in his fashion.

Notes

1. The Howells biographies I consulted (see below) simply do not mention the Gilman connection, probably because the major ones were written before interest in her work was revived in the early 1960s. Hill's biography of Gilman (see below) merely refers to Howells's enthusiasm for Gilman's "Similar Cases" and *In This Our World*, and notes his socialist sympathies. Hill only goes up to 1896 in this volume, so perhaps she will have more to say in a subsequent installment. In her introduction to Gilman's *Herland* (New York: Pantheon, 1979), vii, Ann J. Lane says that Howells "did much to sustain her career," but does not go into detail. So far as I know, the present study is the first treatment of the Gilman-Howells relationship.

2. Charlotte Perkins Gilman, *The Living of Charlotte Perkins Gilman: An Autobiography* (New York: Arno Press, 1927), 113.

3. Robert L. Hough, *The Quiet Rebel: William Dean Howells as Social Commentator* (1959; reprint, Hamden, Conn.: Archon Books, 1968), 4.

4. Edwin H. Cady, *The Road to Realism: The Early Years (1837–1885) of William Dean Howells* (Syracuse, N.Y.: Syracuse University Press, 1956), 173. Bellamy probably did not know how close to the mark his compliment came. When Howells first arrived in New England, he achieved an audience with Nathaniel Hawthorne. Upon learning that Howells intended next to visit Ralph Waldo Emerson, Hawthorne gave Howells one of his visiting cards to take to Emerson; the card bore the message, "I find this young man worthy" (Hough, *Quiet Rebel*, 1).

5. William Dean Howells, "The New Poetry," *North American Review* 168 (May 1899):589–590.

6. Gloria M. Martin, "Women in the Criticism and Fiction of William Dean Howells" (Ph.D. diss., University of Wisconsin, 1982), 170.

7. Mary A. Hill, *Charlotte Perkins Gilman: The Making of a Radical Feminist, 1860–1896* (Philadelphia: Temple University Press, 1980), 38–41, and passim.

8. Cady, *Road to Realism*, 28–39.

9. William Dean Howells to his father, 18 November 1888, 30 November 1888, and 6 January 1889, in *Selected Letters of W. D. Howells*, ed. Geroge Arms, Don L. Cook, Christopher K. Lohman, and David J. Nordloh, 6 vols. (Boston: Twayne, 1980), vol. 3, *1882–1891*, ed. Robert C. Leity III, 235, 243.

10. Howells to his father, 17 March 1889, and Howells to S. Weir Mitchell, 7 March 1889, in ibid., 3:249, 247.

11. Ibid., 3:53.

12. Hill, *Gilman*, 39, quoting a letter from Gilman to her father, undated (probably after 1875); quoted by permission of the Arthur and Elizabeth Schlessinger Library, Radcliffe College, Cambridge, Mass.

13. Hill, *Gilman*, 136.

14. Gilman to Howells, 17 October 1919; quoted by permission of the Houghton Library, Harvard University, Cambridge, Mass.

15. Gilman, *Living*, 182.

16. Hough, *Quiet Rebel*, 29, quoting Gilman, "Mr. Howells' Socialism," *American Fabian* 4 (February 1898):2.

17. William Dean Howells, *Criticism and Fiction* (New York: Harper's, 1910), 183–184.

18. Hough, *Quiet Rebel*, 112–113.

19. Joyce Kilmer, "War Stops Literature, Says William Dean Howells," *New York Times*, 16 December 1914.

20. Hill, *Gilman*, 176.

21. Gilman, "A Socialist Prayer," *Forerunner* 2 (May 1911):124.

22. Gilman, unpublished lectures given on 20 and 21 December 1890, quoted by Hill, *Gilman*, 182.

23. Howells, "Editor's Easy Chair," *Harper's Monthly* 111 (October 1905):796; and 118 (May 1909):967.

24. Howells, "Recollections of an *Atlantic* Editorship," quoted by Martin, "Women in Howells," 186.

25. Ann Douglas Wood, "The Literature of Impoverishment: The Women Local Colorists in America, 1865–1914," *Women's Studies* 1 (1972):4, quoting Howells, *Criticism and Fiction* (1910; reprint, New York: Hill and Wang, 1967), 134, 168–169.

26. *Selected Letters*, 3:117.

27. Ibid., 3:305.

28. "Editor's Study" (April 1891), 804–805.

29. Wood, "Literature of Impoverishment," 15.

30. Charlotte Perkins Stetson [Gilman], *Women and Economics* (Boston: Small, Maynard, 1898), 75.

31. *Selected Letters*, 4:305.

32. Hill, *Gilman*, 158.

33. Gilman to Howells, 8 March 1898; quoted by permission of the Houghton Library.

34. Gilman, *Living*, 222.

35. Gilman, "Similar Cases," in *In This Our World*, 3d ed. (Boston: Small, Maynard, 1898), 99–100.

36. Gilman, *Our World*, 128–129.

37. Howells to Gilman, 10 December 1891; quoted by permission of the Schlesinger Library.

38. Gilman, *Our World*, 205–208.

39. Howells to Gilman, *AESL*, 31 January 1892; quoted by permission of the Schlesinger Library.

40. Gilman, *Living*, 119.

41. Howells, "A Reminiscent Introduction," in *The Great Modern American Stories* (New York: Boni and Liveright, 1920), vii.

42. Cady, *Road to Realism*, 136.

43. Gilman to Martha Lane, 27 July 1890, Rhode Island Historical Society, quoted by Hill, *Gilman*, 176.

44. Gilman to Howells, 17 October 1919; quoted by permission of the Houghton Library.

45. Gilman was much impressed with Ward's gynecocentric theory of evolution (which held that in most species the female controlled both selection of the mate and reproduction, making her rather than the male the dominant partner), and did much to popularize it in her own writing. When Ward complained that his theory had not received the attention it deserved, Gilman wrote several letters reminding him of her appreciative efforts in its behalf. When no acknowledgment of her reminders appeared, she sent him a copy of her book *Human Work* and expressed the hope that she would someday have the time to read some more of his writing: "So far—except for the Phylogenic forces in Pure Sociology; and some of the shorter papers— . . . I have not really read you at all." Thus prodded, Ward finally produced the desired tribute:

> I have read your book. I could hear my own voice all the time. But of course, it was not an echo. It is pitched much higher than I can strike and differs also entirely in *timbre*. (See Hill, *Gilman*, 266–267)

46. Howells to Gilman, 11 July 1894; quoted by permission of the Schlesinger Library.

47. Howells to Gilman, 25 June 1897; quoted by permission of the Houghton Library.

48. Gilman, *Our World*, 62–63.

49. Howells to Gilman, 8 May 1911; quoted by permission of the Schlesinger Library.

50. Cady, *Road to Realism*, 74.

51. Gilman, *Our World*, 156–157.

52. Hill, *Gilman*, 123.

53. Cady, *Road to Realism*, 242, quoting Daniel Dulany Addison, *Lucy Larcom: Life, Letters, and Diary* (Boston: Houghton Mifflin, 1894), 189.

54. Gilman to Howells, 17 October 1919 (emphasis added), quoted by permission of the Houghton Library.

55. Gilman, *Living*, 302–303.

56. Ibid., 304.

Brief Biographies

Sherwood Bonner (1849–1883)

Katharine Sherwood Bonner McDowell was a Southern writer best known for her local-color stories and her pioneering use of dialect. She also achieved notoriety as amanuensis to Henry Wadsworth Longfellow. She arrived in Boston from Mississippi in 1873 and spent the next decade writing letters and stories for such periodicals as the *Memphis Avalanche*, *Lippincott's*, *Harper's Weekly*, and *Cottage Hearth*. She published her regional novel, *Like unto Like*, in 1878, and then prepared three collections of stories: *Dialect Tales* (1883), *Suwanee Tales* (1884, published after her death), and a collection entitled *Romances* (which was never published).

Emily Dickinson (1830–1886)

Although virtually unknown in her lifetime, Emily Dickinson has long been recognized as a major poet. She lived all her life in Amherst, Massachusetts, except for a brief period at Mount Holyoke Seminary, a trip to Washington and Philadelphia, and several visits to Boston. Only a few of her poems were published in her lifetime, and the alterations made by editors sometimes annoyed her. In 1890 Mabel Loomis Todd and T. W. Higginson edited the *Poems of Emily Dickinson*; ten subsequent volumes were brought out by Dickinson family members from 1891 to 1945. It was not, however, until Thomas H. Johnson's *Poems of Emily Dickinson* was published in 1955 that readers had an accurate edition of her work.

Fanny Fern (1811–1872)

A journalist for twenty-one years, Fanny Fern (Sara Willis Parton) was the first woman newspaper columnist in the United States and the most highly paid newspaper writer of her time. She began writing for the Boston papers in 1851, and her sharp, satirical articles were immediately pirated by newspapers all over the country and across the Atlantic. In 1853 her collection of articles, *Fern Leaves from Fanny's Portfolio*, became a best-seller and was followed by eight other collections and two novels. *Ruth Hall* (1854), which reflects Fern's belief in economic independence for women, is nearly unique among nineteenth-century American novels in its portrayal of a woman who fulfills the American dream entirely on her own. In 1856 Fern began an exclusive column with the *New York Ledger* that ran continuously until her death in 1872.

Annie Adams Fields (1834–1915)

Annie Adams Fields is remembered today as America's foremost literary hostess and the wife of publisher James T. Fields. For thirty-four years after his death, she augmented her reputation by writing memoirs of the celebrated writers of her time. She sustained friendships with other women of literary and artistic talent (most notably, Sarah Orne Jewett) and produced a novel and several volumes of verse. In addition, she was an effective civic reformer—a founder of the Associated Charities of Boston and author of the best-selling manual, *How to Help the Poor* (1883). She was an example of Boston's best traditions of high culture, public service, and "true womanhood."

Margaret Fuller (1810–1850)

Margaret Fuller, one of the best-educated women or men of her time, was a member of the transcendental group that included Emerson, Thoreau, Alcott, and Channing. She conducted "conversations" for women, edited the influential *Dial*, published translations of Goethe, and became a reporter for the *New York Daily Tribune*. *Summer on the Lakes, Woman in the Nineteenth Century*, and *Papers on Literature and Art* are her most important works. Sent to Italy to cover the revolution of 1848, she married there and had a child; the entire family was drowned on the way to America.

Charlotte Perkins Gilman (1860–1935)

A pioneer writer and speaker in sociology, Gilman achieved an international reputation with six books in the field published between 1898 and 1923, but she refused offers to teach in universities because her own education had been so unsystematic. Her poetry is collected in *In This Our World* (1893); her prose fiction is uncollected, although "The Yellow Wallpaper" is frequently anthologized, and her utopian novel, *Herland* (1912), was reprinted in 1979.

Lucy Larcom (1824–1893)

Famous in her day as an inspirational poet, Lucy Larcom appears in literary history either as an adjunct to Whittier or as a former mill girl. In fact, she was a teacher (both on the western prairies and in prestigious Wheaton Seminary), a magazine editor, a poet, and a free-lance writer and lecturer. Her works include innumerable magazine and newspaper poems, several collected volumes, articles, newsletters, religious books, and her best and best-known work, *A New England Girlhood.*

Frances Sargent Osgood (1811–1850)

Remembered today because of her association with Edgar Allan Poe, Frances Sargent (Locke) Osgood published poems and prose sketches in newspapers and magazines and wrote or edited eleven books of poetry. Married to portrait artist Samuel Stillman Osgood, she was a part of the New York literary circle until her death in 1850.

Constance Fenimore Woolson (1840–1894)

Born in New Hampshire in 1840, Constance Fenimore Woolson began to publish in the early 1870s. She wrote travel features for the *Daily Cleveland Herald*, stories and articles for prestigious national magazines, and a pseudonymously published children's book entitled *The Old Stone House* (1873). *Castle Nowhere: Lake Country Sketches*, her first short-story collection, was published in 1875, followed by *Rodman the Keeper: Southern Sketches* in 1880. Her best-known work is the novel *Anne*, published in 1883.

Index